Foucault and Politics

THINKING POLITICS

Series Editors: Matthew Sharpe and Geoff Boucher

Politics in the twenty-first century is immensely complex and multi-faceted, and alternative theorisations of debates that radically renew older ideas have grown from a trickle to a flood in the past twenty years. The most interesting and relevant contemporary thinkers have responded to new political challenges – such as liberal multiculturalism, new directions in feminist thinking, theories of global empire and biopolitical power, and challenges to secularism – by widening the scope of their intellectual engagements and responding to the new politics. The thinkers selected for inclusion in the series have all responded to the urgency and complexity of thinking about politics today in fresh ways.

Books in the series will provide clear and accessible introductions to the major ideas in contemporary thinking about politics, through a focus in each volume on a key political thinker. Rather than a roll-call of the 'usual suspects', it will focus on new thinkers who offer provocative new directions and some neglected older thinkers whose relevance is becoming clear as a result of the changing situation.

www.euppublishing.com/series/thpo

FOUCAULT AND POLITICS
A CRITICAL INTRODUCTION

Mark G. E. Kelly

EDINBURGH
University Press

Edinburgh University Press Ltd
The Tun – Holyrood Road
12 (2f) Jackson's Entry
Edinburgh EH8 8PJ
www.euppublishing.com

Typeset in Sabon by
Servis Filmsetting Ltd, Stockport, Cheshire,
and printed and bound in Great Britain by
CPI Group (UK) Ltd, Croydon CR0 4YY

A CIP record for this book is available from the British Library

ISBN 978 0 7486 7685 9 (hardback)
ISBN 978 0 7486 7686 6 (paperback)
ISBN 978 0 7486 7687 3 (webready PDF)
ISBN 978 0 7486 7689 7 (epub)

Contents

Abbreviations of Foucault's Works

AB   *Abnormal.* Translated by Graham Burchell. (London: Verso, 2003).

AK   *Archaeology of Knowledge.* Translated by A. M. Sheridan Smith. (London: Tavistock, 1972).

BB   *Birth of Biopolitics.* Translated by Graham Burchell. (Basingstoke: Palgrave Macmillan, 2008).

BC   *Birth of the Clinic.* Translated by A. M. Sheridan. (London: Routledge, 1989).

DE(vol.) *Dits et écrits.* 4 vols. (Paris: Gallimard, 1994).

DL   *Death and the Labyrinth: The World of Raymond Roussel.* Translated by Charles Ruas. (New York: Doubleday, 1986).

DP   *Discipline and Punish.* Translated by Alan Sheridan. (London: Allen Lane, 1977).

EW(vol.) *Essential Works.* 3 vols. (New York: The New Press, 1997, 1998, 2000).

FIR   Appendices to Janet Afary and Kevin B. Anderson (2005). *Foucault and the Iranian Revolution: Gender and the Seductions of Islam.* (Chicago: University of Chicago Press).

GSO   *The Government of Self and Others.* Translated by Graham Burchell. (Basingstoke: Palgrave Macmillan, 2010).

HM   *History of Madness.* Translated by Jonathan Murphy and Jean Khalfa. (London: Routledge, 2006).

HS   *Hermeneutics of the Subject.* Translated by Graham Burchell. (Basingstoke: Palgrave Macmillan, 2004).

HS(vol.) *History of Sexuality.* 3 vols. Translated by Robert Hurley. (London: Penguin, 1978, 1985, 1985).

OD   'Orders of Discourse', *Social Science Information*, 10:2 (1971), 7–30.

OT   *The Order of Things* (London: Routledge, 2002).

PK   *Power/Knowledge*. Edited by Colin Gordon. (Brighton: Harvester, 1980).

PP   *Psychiatric Power*. Translated by Graham Burchell. (New York: Palgrave Macmillan, 2006).

PPC   *Politics, Philosophy, Culture*. Edited by Lawrence D. Kitzman. (New York: Routledge, 1988).

RM   *Remarks on Marx*. Translated by R. James Goldstein and James Cascaito. (New York: Semiotext(e), 1991).

SD   *Society Must Be Defended*. Translated by David Macey. (New York: Picador, 2003).

STP   *Security, Territory, Population*. Translated by Graham Burchell. (Basingstoke: Palgrave Macmillan, 2007).

Acknowledgements

During the time this book was written, I have accumulated many debts to a plethora of intellectual confrères, companions and colleagues, particularly at the University of Western Sydney and Monash University. I will, however, constrain myself here to thanking those who have aided in some direct way with the production of this book.

Thanks are due to Adam Jasper Smith and the Faculty of Design, Architecture and Building of the University of Technology, Sydney, for arranging an honorary fellowship for me there, which provided me with library services vital to the production of this book during an early phase of research.

Thanks also to my former students Lenin Gatus and Tracy Sealey for their proofreading.

On the publishing side, I'd like to acknowledge Carol Macdonald for initially suggesting the idea of writing a more introductory book on Foucault's political thought, and for bringing me on to Edinburgh University Press's list; I would like to thank Geoff Boucher and Matt Sharpe for welcoming my contribution to their series, and the staff at Edinburgh's politics division for their patience.

This book incorporates some brief phrases, shorter than a sentence in length, from my *Internet Encyclopedia of Philosophy* article, 'Michel Foucault's Political Thought'.

Introduction

Foucault Now

This is a book about Michel Foucault and politics. Its remit encompasses Foucault's own politics, his political thought and the political impact of that thought.

Foucault's name has become ubiquitous in the humanities and social sciences in recent decades, more commonly mentioned than that of any other thinker in history (Times Higher Education 2007), but its meaning remains ambiguous for all that. Politically, it has been turned to a variety of contradictory purposes, from updating Marxism to defending liberalism. The possibilities for diversity in the use of Foucault's name are in no small part due to the diversity of positions he himself took during his twenty-five-year career.

While Foucault has been invoked by a range of causes, people want to invoke him not because he was clearly a member of their ideological tendency but because he was an original thinker who defied categorisation. In the words of his sometime friend Gilles Deleuze (1988, 30), with Foucault's work it was 'as if finally, something new were emerging in the wake of Marx'. That is, to unpack the hyperbolic implications of this characterisation, Foucault's work is the most important contribution to political thought since that of Karl Marx a century before. I'm sure most experts on political thought would think this an exaggeration. I, however, do not. While I can hardly claim to know a century of political ideas in its entirety, it seems to me that Foucault is the most significant political thinker of the twentieth century. I do not expect you to agree with me, but perhaps you will take the fact that it is possible for me sincerely to make such a statement as indicative that Foucault's thought at least holds some import. His radical reconception of power in particular seems to me to be a watershed moment in the history of political thought, albeit one that has still yet to be fully thought through. In the profusion of usages of his concepts, Foucault's users almost

1

all backslide towards more conventional, and in a few cases more nihilistic, positions than he himself took.

Despite the political importance of Foucault's thought, and perhaps to some extent because of its radicalness, the study of politics is an area in which Foucault was until recently relatively neglected by comparison with other social sciences and the literary humanities. His reception in political studies is mainly oriented towards the decade of his output, the 1970s, during which his work was at its most overtly political, and during which a single, crucial shift occurred. Two concepts of Foucault's from this time, 'biopolitics' and 'governmentality', have been particularly influential in this area. The appropriation of these concepts has gone in widely diverging directions, which was to an extent Foucault's own intention, inasmuch as he presented his thought during its more political phase after 1970 as being a conceptual 'toolbox' from which one might take what one needs (DE2 523).

Without diminishing the shifts in Foucault's position over time, I will argue that he was consistently radical and, in a certain sense, progressive. There are several problems for this account, however, which must be considered fully. One is that, during a major part in his career, political concerns were superficially almost absent from his work. This could be said to be another reason for his relatively late take-up in politics compared to other academic disciplines. Foucault published eleven books during his lifetime. The immediate picture that emerges from these is not one of a primarily political thinker. Only three of these books are overtly political – and one of those, 'The Order of Discourse', is largely apolitical and so short that when it was translated into English it appeared as a journal article rather than a book. These three political books form a series, written between 1970 and 1976, under the rubric of 'genealogy'. If one looks only at Foucault's books, this phase might seem a relatively minor one. During the second half of his career, between 1970 and 1984, he published only five books, compared to six between 1954 and 1969. However, if one looks at the material by Foucault that is now, posthumously available in print, the quantity from the later period dwarfs that from the first. There are twelve Collège de France lecture series (of which nine have been published at the time of writing), each book length, from this second period, as well as a number of other lecture series of Foucault's from other venues, whereas there is nothing comparable from the earlier period. If we count each of these series as a book of Foucault's, which is how they are now being published, they in effect together outnumber the books he actually had published during his life. Moreover, we have a wealth of short pieces and interviews from these years after 1970. In the original four volumes of his collected shorter works, *Dits et écrits*, one volume collects all the work up to 1969, compared to three volumes of work from 1970 onwards. That is, 75 per cent of his shorter writings and interviews are from 1970 and after. Overall, almost 75 per cent of the total material we have by Foucault is from the period after 1970, when he went through what I will refer to as his political turn. If 'Foucault' is the name of the body of work we have extant that bears his name, then Foucault has become a predominantly political figure in the time since his biological death, starting decisively with the publication of the *Dits et écrits* in 1994, and accelerating with the publication of the Collège courses from 2000 onwards. This politicisation of Foucault is still not over, as lecture series continue to appear in print.

That said, there will be an opposite tendency at work in this book of mine, namely to go back to Foucault's books. In the light of all this material of Foucault's that now swirls around us, I think there is some necessity to insist on the privileged status of the material that he actually saw fit to publish, namely Foucault's canonical books and substantial essays published during his lifetime. The reason I speak of *canonical* books is that Foucault sought to have his first single-authored book, *Mental Illness and Psychology*, suppressed later in his life, which puts it in a dubious category of its own. We could include in the canonical category those talks of his that he allowed to have published during his lifetime, and those interviews of his which he authorised for publication. He insisted on editorial approval for interviews, hence they represent somewhat considered opinions of his, although the questions he addresses are dictated by others. Then we have the lectures series that have appeared only posthumously, which Foucault was confident in enough to deliver publicly, and which were based on written scripts, hence were considered, but which he did not deign to publish. We have peculiar reason in Foucault's case to be wary of any posthumously published material, because he explicitly requested that there be *no* posthumous publication of his work. There are some lectures from these series that he did allow to be published during his lifetime (these are, namely, the first two lectures of *Society Must Be Defended*, published first in an Italian collection in 1977, the fourth lecture of *Security, Territory, Population*, published as 'Governmentality', and an excerpt from the 1983 lecture series), but the fact that these are relatively few can be taken to underline that he did not generally think of the lectures as publishable material.

He, indeed, tried even to limit the audiences that came to hear these, though this is presumably for functional reasons. There are also interviews that Foucault himself did not allow to be published, which have the most dubious status of all, since Foucault deliberately decided not to allow any audience beyond the interviewers to see them. Roger-Pol Droit's *Entretiens* are perhaps the most blatant example of this, interesting though they are. There are at least two interviews in a liminal category of having his approval for publication, but which he did not seek to edit as was his usual practice. One is the very last interview of his life; another interview in this category is the one that is addended to the English version of *Death and the Labyrinth*.

Works in all of these categories should be understood in their concrete contexts. They were all interventions in a discursive field, and must be understood as such. None of Foucault's output was attempting to articulate a transcendental system. Foucault quite explicitly had no such systematic intention. They may be understood as interventions of different types and finality aimed at achieving different effects. The requirement here is the reference not to Foucault's intention but to a concrete context of articulation, to a discursive and epistemic field of production. This is not to imply that this is Foucault's way of reading texts, though it has a somewhat Foucauldian flavour. It is in any case the methodology I will adopt.

This book is doing at least three things. It is supposed to serve as a general introduction to Foucault, presupposing no particular knowledge of his thought. It is also supposed to deal with the specifically political aspect of his life and thought comprehensively. It is lastly trying to take a distinctive and unique approach to Foucault, making original claims, based on original scholarship. This last purpose takes it beyond being a mere introduction.

This book is laid out in chronological order. I do this mainly because it would be misleading at best to try to group together Foucault's thought from across his career all together at once. Although I do believe, and have argued elsewhere (Kelly 2009), that Foucault's thought can be seen as a single perspective, this is a contentious view to take. Given that this book is supposed to be critical, I choose instead the more objective treatment of taking Foucault one book and one phase of his career at a time. A problem this presents for readers is that many readers will be interested primarily in the more political phase of Foucault's career, broadly the 1970s in particular, and thus will want not want to wade through multiple chapters of background just to get to that point. If you do have such specific interests, and lack time, you should of course skip ahead to the relevant chapter.

Foucault Then

Michel Foucault (1926–84) was a French intellectual. Though he came from a privileged background, and can be counted as a member of France's educational elite, he was also in many ways an outsider, particularly because of his homosexuality.

Foucault was born in Poitiers, a provincial French town, to a well-to-do family. He came of age during the wartime occupation of the town by German forces. After the war, Foucault went to Paris, in order to seek entry to the most prestigious French institution for the study of the humanities, the École normale supérieure (ENS). He was successful and, once at the school, he came under the influence of the Marxist philosopher Louis Althusser, himself then a student, and joined the French Communist Party, though Foucault would soon break with Marxism. His studies focused on philosophy, a subject of peculiar prestige in the French education system. He went on to study the then rather novel discipline of psychology. After some years of teaching and research in France, Foucault spent several years abroad, first in an academic post in Sweden, then diplomatic cultural posts in Poland and Germany. During this wandering, he wrote his first major book, the lengthy *History of Madness*, which he published in France as his main doctoral thesis in 1961. He then returned to France to take up his first full-time university appointment, at the provincial University of Clermont-Ferrand. He lectured there until 1966, when he again left the country, to take up a post teaching philosophy at the University of Tunis. He returned to France again in 1969, to head a new philosophy department in Paris, before the following year being elected to a chair at France's most prestigious academic institution, the Collège de France, a post that he held for the rest of his life. He gave the annual lectures at that institution that were the requirement of the post from then on every year but one until his death in 1984. This death resulted from a sudden illness, generally recognised now to have been caused by AIDS.

These are the skeleton facts of Foucault's life. In what follows, we will flesh them out with detail, in order to tell the story of the relationship between Foucault's thought and politics. It will be the story of the interactions that his thought had with politics, the political uses to which it has been put. While he was alive, there was an active relationship of feedback, with Foucault engaging in debates which he affected and which affected his thought in turn. Since his death, there is a continuing story, one in which Foucault has in any literal sense ceased to be an active participant, a story of appropriations and contestations of his thought.

Our concern here of course is more with Foucault's thought than with his life. It is tricky to characterise his thought in disciplinary terms. The most obvious disciplinary classification to give it would be as 'history', perhaps specifically the 'history of thought'. Foucault invented for himself in the later phase of his career the title of 'Professor of the History of Systems of Thought'. The 'systems' part of this title is important, however. Foucault did not do the history of thought as it was ordinarily done. His methodology varied throughout his life, but it was never something that was accepted unproblematically by historians as an instance of their art. Late in life, Foucault also took to describing himself as a philosopher, and he was trained as one, but he was perhaps even further from what is ordinarily described as philosophy than he is from what is ordinarily defined as history. He has also been retrospectively interpreted as a sociologist, and his work of the 1970s in particular is certainly close to being sociology, though he never thought of himself this way. He occasionally wrote works of literary criticism too, though this was relatively normal practice for French philosophers, as was writing about politics.

Regardless of how it is labelled (and I think what Foucault gives us in the end is a lesson in the limitations of these disciplinary divisions), I think there are four features that all Foucault's mature, canonical, post-1961 work has:

1. It is historical, dealing either with the past, in the sense of a period which is divided by some span of time from the present, or with the question of how to interpret the past;
2. It deals primarily with the analysis of discourse, in the sense of an attention not only to historical 'facts' but rather primarily to what was *said* in the past, and indeed the way that what was said was constituted in what may be called discursive formations;
3. It offers explanations that may be characterised as objective, rather than subjective. That is, Foucault starts from an analysis of systems rather than experience, even if he is, particularly in his earliest and last work, concerned to explicate experience and even subjectivity itself through this mode of approach. I take it

that Foucault's explanation of the subject is profoundly anti-subjectivist. Others I think read Foucault as effectively restoring sovereignty to the subject in his late work. Some do this in a critical way, as a way of discrediting Foucault's earlier positions. Others do it naively, confusing Foucault's position with more standard positions on subjectivity.

4. It is iconoclastic, even contrarian, seeking to demonstrate how our key concepts, or our understandings of key concepts, are inventions of a recent date, thus undermining their appearance of transcendent universality. This is not to say that Foucault does not himself posit things that seem to be transhistorical in scope: subjectivity, power, knowledge, pleasure, and bodies serve as transhistorical concepts in Foucault. However, these things are held to take radically different forms in different historical periods.

The big question for this book is of course what Foucault's politics is. Of course, the answer to this question depends on how one defines politics. Foucault himself works with at least two, quite different, definitions of politics. I think these broadly correspond to the two possible definitions of politics. 'Politics' is of course derived from the Greek *polis*, the city or city-state. Clearly, politics does not refer to the city itself, which we in English refer to using words derived from the Latin *urbs*, most obviously 'urban'. Rather, we use 'politics' to refer to the *governance* of the Greek city-state. But this may be understood in two directions. On the one hand, it may be understood to refer to the state itself. Politics thus comes to mean the struggle for the control of the state. On the other hand, it may be understood to apply to a much wider field of social contestation, not so much about the state but about society. Foucault uses it in both senses. Our task is to understand what his orientation is in both these directions. It can be summarised by saying that he, at least in his later work, explicitly opposed the politics of the state, and counterposes to this the politics of society. The lesson of Foucault's later work is that power is to be found throughout society, literally everywhere and in everything, not merely the pursuits and organisations we normally classify as 'political'. He uses the word 'political' thereafter as the adjective that corresponds to the noun 'power'. This is not a self-serving redefinition so much as a recognition that politics in our narrower senses is really the result of much broader social processes.

I will characterise Foucault's politics as left-wing and progressive, primarily a matter of engaging in criticism and lauding resistance, and to this extent describable as broadly 'libertarian', though Foucault is not classically libertarian inasmuch as the notion of freedom does not play a foundational role in his politics. He is anarchist and socialist inasmuch as he urges us to fight against existing power structures, but neither anarchist nor socialist in so far as he does not have an a priori commitment to abolishing the state or capitalism, nor an alternative vision of how society ought to operate.

This Book

There is a book on Foucault with an introductory section entitled 'Not Another Book on Foucault!' Not only is this present book yet another book on Foucault but it is yet another book on Foucault by an author who has already written two books on Foucault (Kelly 2009; Kelly 2013b), one of which already deals with Foucault's work from a political angle. I therefore want to explain here what this book does that others do not, and in particular what distinguishes it from other books I have written.

The thing that differentiates this book from most others on Foucault is its focus on Foucault's relation to *politics*. As we outlined above, Foucault's work is largely political, but, in ways we indicate, other aspects of his thought have received much more treatment. There are perhaps only three books out of the dozens on Foucault that have focused squarely on interpreting his political thought, leaving aside some works which deal with specific political elements of his thought. One such book on Foucault and politics is my own *The Political Philosophy of Michel Foucault*. Overall, my aim has been to minimise the overlap between this book and the earlier one as much as is possible. Major differences between this current book and that earlier one of mine are that:

1. This book is slightly shorter and aims to accommodate a more novice reader.
2. This book is more recent. This is important for at least two reasons. Firstly, my own thinking has inevitably changed somewhat. Secondly, additional primary and secondary literature has appeared in the interim, changing the state of scholarship on Foucault.
3. The earlier book is specifically a book of philosophy, whereas this one is about politics. I was concerned there mainly with the philosophical aspect of Foucault's thought, whereas here I'm

concerned with his politics. This present book thus deals with his specific political positions and concepts, whereas in the other book I was concerned only with the philosophical generalities. In particular, specific concepts like governmentality and biopolitics were hardly dealt with in the earlier book, whereas here they receive full treatment. Concrete implications were also generally not explored. There is still quite a lot of philosophy in this book too, unavoidably, since we are dealing with the thought of a philosopher. In particular, there remain questions about the philosophy of history: what is history for Foucault, and what is its aetiology? The political import of this question is that the way we answer it affects our understanding of the significance of historical events and their interrelation. This question leads me to consider for the first time the relationship of Foucault to perhaps the greatest philosopher of history, G. W. F. Hegel. The political importance of Foucault's relationship to Hegel can be attributed primarily to the extent to which Hegel's philosophy is the major single philosophical influence on the most prominent political thinker of the last two centuries, Marx.

4. This book is critical; the other book was deliberately sympathetic, an attempt to defend everything Foucault said. I argue in the earlier book that Foucault does produce a coherent philosophical and political perspective, despite many twists and turns in its elaboration. Of course, to criticise Foucault does not imply alleging that he is incoherent. Indeed, literally, to be 'critical' does not imply saying anything pejorative at all. Although criticism, and its various cognates such as 'criticise', 'critic' and 'critique', have clear negative connotations to most minds, literally they can be understood simply to imply analysis. The point is to probe Foucault's position, to examine it, not to be particularly excoriatory but also not to be particularly sympathetic either. This nevertheless in itself differentiates this book from my first one. Of course, to criticise Foucault in the sense of conducting a thorough and penetrating but non-polemical analysis is entirely Foucauldian in spirit – indeed, it is arguably more truly Foucauldian than the more loyal interpretation, since Foucault had no desire to propound a dogma or found a school.

5. This book is more comprehensive. My first book began by deliberately skipping over Foucault's first several books. This one will not. The overlooking of *The History of Madness* is partly due to the fact that it appeared in full in English translation only in

2006, forty-five years after its original publication in French, by which time I had to all intents and purposes already written my first book, though it did not actually appear in print for more than two years after that. I would maintain that to elide it did make sense from the point of view I had at that time, which was to give an account of the nuances of Foucault's position in its most developed form. Indeed, in my first book I engage relatively little with any of Foucault's books, even those of the greatest political relevance. This is because I was mainly interested at getting at the philosophical framework behind the books, which meant dispro-portionately leaning on his comments in interviews. By contrast, here, my method is more straightforward, with an essentially biographical approach that deals with Foucault's thought as it appeared. Since I am trying to be critical, I also pay more atten-tion to possible biographical motivations of Foucault's ideas.

STRUCTURE OF THE BOOK

The structure of this book follows the chronology of Foucault's life, while also being ordered by themes. This is possible because Foucault tends to deal with different themes at different points in his career.

The book begins with a short chapter dealing with Foucault's early engagement with Marxism. This is crucial because Foucault's politics can, in my opinion, only be understood as an ongoing reac-tion to Marxism that never entirely escapes the broad shadow cast by Marxism across the twentieth century.

The second chapter deals with madness and psychology, primarily in Foucault's early work of the 1950s and early 1960s, but it is also necessary here to refer to his work on the same topic in the 1970s, particularly in order to establish the political stakes of this theme.

The third chapter deals with Foucault's 1960s output, a period where his reflection came to rest almost entirely on language and 'discourses', dealing with the political significance of this thought.

The fourth, fifth, sixth and seventh chapters comprise the core of this book, dealing with the most intensely and explicitly political period in Foucault's thought. The fourth chapter deals with his polit-icisation from 1968 onwards, his development of a new methodol-ogy, 'genealogy', and his activism around and writing about prisons. The fifth chapter deals with his reconception of the notion of power in the mid-1970s. The sixth chapter deals with his work on sexual-ity and, more importantly perhaps, his articulation of a concept of biopolitics at the same time. The seventh chapter deals with the turn in his political thought at the end of the 1970s, towards the concept of 'government'.

The eighth and final chapter deals with the political dimensions of the last years of his life, the 1980s up to his death in 1984. This chapter deals with his writings on Iran, and his articulation of notions of ethics, spirituality and subjectivity.

In the Wake of Marx

Foucault's thought bears the marks of many significant influences. A particularly prominent influence is the thought of Friedrich Nietzsche, and of French Nietzscheans such as Georges Bataille and Pierre Klossowski; Foucault (PPC 251 / DE4 704) once described himself as 'simply Nietzschean'. Foucault was also influenced by Martin Heidegger, an influence unavoidable for French students of his generation; he was taught by Maurice Merleau-Ponty, one of France's greatest interpreters of Heidegger, and he later engaged with and was influenced by the Heideggerian psychoanalysis of Ludwig Binswanger and the Heideggerian literary theory of Maurice Blanchot. He on a couple of occasions towards the end of his life expressed a deep fidelity to Heidegger's thought (HS 189, PPC 250). Foucault was furthermore greatly influenced by the tradition of French philosophy of science represented proximally by Georges Canguilhem, who was an important patron of Foucault's career.

When it comes to politics, however, I will suggest that the decisive influence on Foucault is that of Marxism, even if all his other influences also come to bear on the political aspect of his thought. In

Marxism

Marxism is the political ideology descended from the thought of the nineteenth-century German philosopher and revolutionary Karl Marx. It centres on the conviction that the work class or 'proletariat' have a historic mission to liberate themselves by abolishing capitalism, the rule of the 'bourgeoisie'. Marx referred to his convictions not as 'Marxist', however, but as 'communist'. In the twentieth century, the word 'Communist' came to be peculiarly associated with the form of Marxism emanating from Lenin, the leader of the Russian Bolsheviks who seized power in the Russian Revolution of 1917 to form the world's first Marxist state, the Soviet Union.

terms of actual thinkers, Marxism refers primarily, of course, Karl Marx himself, dead for forty-three years before Foucault's birth.

We must here understand the political environment in which Foucault found himself. As we have mentioned, Foucault's teenage years were spent in a provincial French city, Poitiers, which was in the northern part of France that found itself occupied by German forces following the Fall of France in 1940.

Foucault moved to Paris in 1945, just after the end of the War, to take classes in pursuit of entry to France's most prestigious venue for higher education in the humanities, the École normale supérieure. He entered the ENS in 1946. There he met Louis Althusser, who was only slightly ahead of him at the school despite being eight years older, having had his start date at the school delayed by war years spent in a German prison camp. Althusser was to become a major Marxist philosopher, perhaps the most influential French Marxist thinker of the twentieth century, committed to an unorthodox but supposedly faithful interpretation of Marx's thought. Before that, however, he was an early mentor of Foucault's.

This time represented a high-point for the popularity of Marxism in France. After initial vacillation, the Marxists of the French Communist Party (Parti Communiste Français – hereafter 'PCF') had formed the most effective component of the armed resistance to the German occupation. The decisive role played by the Soviet Union, of which the PCF was the French representative, in defeating Hitler buoyed the popularity of communism in much of the world. The French establishment by contrast was tainted in no small part by its involvement in collaboration with the Germans. The PCF participated in a national unity government, headed by the conservative anti-fascist leader Charles de Gaulle, in the dying stages of the war, and by 1946 was briefly the largest party in France, in terms both of members and elected representatives, participating in an elective government, a three-party left coalition. Students of Foucault's generation, himself included, looked to the PCF as the party of the future. Althusser joined the PCF in 1948, and Foucault followed in 1950. Unlike Althusser, whose commitment to the Party would be lifelong, Foucault left soon thereafter. He was never properly active in the Party, and seems to have always had his reservations about it.

The details of Foucault's departure from the PCF are obscure, with conflicting accounts. If, as Macey (1993, 41) suggests, Foucault did not actually actively leave the PCF but rather simply allowed his membership to lapse by not renewing it, it would be impossible to gauge the date that he decided to quit with certainty, but it was in either 1952 or 1953. The importance of the date of Foucault's departure from the PCF, and the difficulty in determining it, both lie in the question of his motivations for leaving. Foucault himself tells us in 1978 that 'When I left it was after the famous "doctors' plot" against Stalin, in the winter of 1952' (RM 52). The affair in question was the culmination of a series of persecutions of Jews, falling now in this case on Jewish doctors, by Soviet authorities. The proximal cause of this was the newly created state of Israel's siding decisively with the West in the Cold War. Like many French, Foucault felt a certain guilt about the Holocaust in which many of his countrymen had been complicit, and was a lifelong philo-Semite and supporter of Israel (Macey 1993, 40). However, Foucault's statement about the date of the plot is not strictly accurate – it in fact occurred in January 1953, though of course that was still in the same winter. Foucault goes on to imply however that he left not because of the plot but because of the revelation that the plot they'd all been told about in the PCF was revealed, after Stalin's death a few months later, to have been a complete fabrication (RM 53). This then implies that Foucault left in 1953. However, the chronology provided by Foucault's partner Daniel Defert in *Dits et écrits* clearly indicates that Foucault departed the PCF in October 1952 – while confusingly seeming to indicate that this is the month of the doctors' plot (the 'blouses blanches' affair, as it is called in French; DE1 20). It would seem that either Defert is wrong about the date or Foucault did not leave the PCF because of anti-Semitism in the Soviet Union, or because of lies about this; although there was a wave of anti-Semitic purges in the Soviet sphere of influence from late 1952, Foucault could not have been aware of any of them in October. There are certainly other reasons Foucault might have had for leaving. One which Foucault himself talks about was the PCF's homophobia (Friedrich 1981, 148). He accuses the PCF of marginalising him because he was homosexual.

Marxism continued to enjoy a certain degree of hegemony in French intellectual life in the postwar decades, a fact emblematised by the status of the existentialist philosopher Jean-Paul Sartre, an explicit partisan of precisely the 'Marxist humanism' that both Althusser and Foucault in their different ways opposed, as the dominant intellectual figure of the age. Sartre remained outside the PCF, though he sympathised with its cause.

The Communist Party failed to dominate postwar politics, however. Inevitably, given the role of the Western allies in liberating France, it was their agent, Charles de Gaulle, who dominated postwar French politics. Yet De Gaulle was determined to restore France's status as a great power. This entailed maintaining a certain distance from America and its satellite Britain. This was compatible with allowing the Communists to take a significant, but subordinate, role in French society. The Soviet Union, to which the French Party maintained a tight loyalty until the 1960s, was relatively content with this state of affairs (Wilson 1981). On the one hand, it was happy to see De Gaulle take an independent stance to the USA and had no interest in undermining him. On the other, the Soviets had agreed that France would be in the Western sphere of influence, and had little interest in trammelling this arrangement, since they wanted the West to stay out of their sphere of influence in Eastern Europe in turn. So, France was capitalist and, while the French Communist Party explicitly opposed capitalism, it in practice never made any attempt to overthrow it. Rather, it contented itself with a certain internal opposition to French government policy, with a leading role in the trade union movement, and with dominating certain sections of intellectual life. Thus, Foucault encountered Communism initially as offering the great alternative to the France he'd grown up in, but quickly experienced it as part of a new establishment, an essentially conservative force in French society in relation to culture and even politics.

While Foucault had rejected the Communist Party by 1953, this did not yet imply a theoretical rejection of Marxism. It was in 1953 that he wrote his first book, *Maladie mentale et personalité* (Mental illness and personality), published in 1954. The book concludes with a Marxist analysis of mental illness as something produced by capitalism, which alienates us from the world around us, reducing it to commodities and exchange values. It also notably acknowledges the theories of psychology then favoured in Moscow (Macey 1993, 66).

This is an odd book in Foucault's corpus, and he treated it fundamentally differently from his others. Firstly, it is the only book of his he ever revised: he replaced the Marxist material in it for a 1962 second edition, with a revised title, the word 'psychology' now replacing 'personality'. He later, after a reprint in 1966, prevented it being reissued altogether. When a translation of the 1962 edition was later produced in English as *Mental Illness and Psychology*, he tried unsuccessfully to stop its publication (Macey 1993, 64). Foucault thus effectively disowned this book, unlike any other he wrote, and indeed not only the Marxist component but ultimately the entire text. This can be said to be because the book was a hotchpotch of different perspectives, all of which Foucault was later to reject, Marxism with psychoanalysis and phenomenology (Kelly 2010). It is instructive, however, that his juvenile Marxism was the first thing that he excised.

Foucault was to later claim that he had 'never been a Freudian [or] a Marxist' (EW2 437). This claim is hard to reconcile with the clear sympathies for psychoanalysis and Marxism that one encounters in *Maladie mentale et personalité*. One could say that Foucault is in denial about his past. More generously, Foucault is saying not that he has not been influenced by psychoanalysis and Marxism but that he never had a thoroughgoing allegiance to either perspective, or, perhaps, that though he had thought he did, as in the case of his membership of the PCF, what he thought Marxism was at the time and what it really was were two different things.

Be this as it may, between 1954 and 1962 he conclusively departed from Marxism. No new political position took its place, however: he became basically apolitical, in the sense of having no strong orientation or involvement in politics, though he certainly continued to be an interested observer of politics, and to do work that had political stakes. He explains this himself by saying that 'The experience of politics had left a rather bad taste in my mouth. I had closed myself up in a kind of speculative scepticism' (RM 134).

Though his path from disillusionment with the PCF to the disillusionment with politics is clear, it is not so clear *why* he took this trajectory. Many who were disillusioned with the PCF continued to be active in politics outside it, often to the left of the PCF, notably in this period Trotskyists, and most interestingly the Socialisme ou barbarie group of post-Trotskyist intellectuals. Why did Foucault not gravitate towards such left-wing Marxism? Or alternatively, why did he not gravitate towards the centre or right, towards the political mainstream? Any explanation we give will be speculative, but, as far as speculation goes, I think there are a number of reasons that can be proffered. Firstly, there is no indication that Foucault ever had any sympathies for any ideological position to the right of Marxism, be it centre-left, centre-right, fascist, liberal or conservative. Foucault has been accused of sympathies with all of these positions, and we will deal with such allegations in due course. These allegations mostly pertain to his overtly political work after 1970, in any case. The point at present is to deal with the period in which he was relatively apolitical, which is to say the late 1950s and the 1960s.

Foucault tells us, for example, that during the French colonial war in Algeria, which occurred during his relatively apolitical period, he opposed the war (RM 74) – something that could not be said without qualification of many on the French left, and which would hence tend to position Foucault on the far left (RM 110; Wall 1977). However, in the 1960s he co-operated with French government policy, served on a commission on educational reform and considered becoming a career bureaucrat, and he had friends in mainstream politics from his days at the ENS. However, I would argue that none of this equates with actual sympathy for the politics of the government, so much as simply working within the structures that already existed. Since Foucault's actions in such roles were never notably reactionary, I tend to see this simply as an example of non-political activity, rather than right-wing political activity, simply working within existing structures.

If, however, he was in effect on the far left as I argue, why did Foucault not align himself with the forces to the left of the PCF? Was he so disillusioned with Marxism by his contact with it in the PCF that he eschewed all Marxist groups, even those that were hostile to the PCF? This is one possible explanation, and certainly Foucault would later exhibit intermittent overt hostility towards Marxism per se, and indeed explicitly reject the main non-Marxist ideology of the far left, anarchism. Yet, it is not clear that there was any disillusionment with Marxism implied in his decision to leave the PCF: he apparently continued to adhere to its theoretical framework, and his reasons for leaving are surely to do with the appalling behaviour of a Soviet state and French Party that could easily be dissociated from Marxism qua ideology, especially from the relatively non-Leninist variety represented by a group like Socialisme ou barbarie. Foucault's hostility to Marxism per se we will date to later experiences.

A prosaic reason why Foucault might not have gone over to some kind of oppositional Marxism is that he might not have had any contact with them to speak of. Whereas the PCF was a massive institution that a student in the 1940s could not avoid coming into contact with, the other groups were smaller and easier to miss. It is perhaps not plausible to suggest that Foucault literally never heard of Socialisme ou barbarie, but he never makes any direct or overt reference to it in any of his published work, nor does he ever mention in any of his writings or interview its founders and leading lights, Cornelius Castoriadis or Claude Lefort, despite their position as relatively prominent intellectuals in France in later years. Many of its other members Foucault does mention, but these are figures, such as Guy Debord, Jean Laplanche and Jean-François Lyotard, who went on to be well known for intellectual work after that movement. Foucault was not known for his gregariousness during his student years – indeed, he was relatively solitary – and though he might have known that various far-left groups existed, he might not have had the direct contact with them which is an important precursor to becoming involved with them. A related possible reason for not joining another group is simply the relative marginality of such groups: the PCF was actually threatening to usher in a revolution in the 1940s, in a way that other groups were not. Hence, belonging to the PCF meant having illusions about changing society that other groups could not match. Another, related, possibility is that he had imbibed a prejudice against other left groups while in the PCF, which he retained afterwards.

One might ask also why he never gravitated towards anarchism. He is reported to have described himself as an anarchist to a friend once off-handedly during the 1960s (Eribon 1991, 131). Later, in the 1970s, he comes across anarchism as a historical curiosity during his researches for *Discipline and Punish*, wherein nineteenth-century anarchism is the closest thing Foucault discovers to his own insights about the prison (DP 292). There has been an attempt to recuperate Foucault for anarchism, most notably represented perhaps by Todd May's (1994) work incorporating Foucault into a 'poststructuralist anarchism'. One wonders why Foucault was once drawn to Marxism but never to anarchism. One imagines that it can be explained dually by Marxism's greater prominence in France and its greater theoretical sophistication. But in the end final answers elude us in the absence of direct answers by Foucault to this question. Still, as we will see there are several points on which Foucault diverges from both Marxism and anarchism, which we will note as they arise.

Foucault's own explanation for his political inactivity after the PCF, that he just felt sick with political activity after his (rather limited) experience with that organisation, and for quite a long time simply ceased to be interested in political activity in the strict sense, is perhaps the simplest explanation of all. It was not long before Foucault left France entirely. He thus turned his back on both politics and his country, but I will argue that neither thing really left his mind. Indeed, we can say that such an active reaction can only betoken a certain preoccupation. Moreover, while he was not politically active, and out of France for most of the period until the late

1960s, his work shows considerable underlying orientation towards France and political problems.

The political aspect of Foucault's work, in rejecting the restricted field of the political as it is ordinarily construed, I will understand in relation to Foucault's ongoing abreaction against Marxism and the PCF. Foucault continually engaged with Marxism not only because of his own early, renounced Marxism but also because Marxism continued, in changing ways, to exercise a hegemonic influence on radical French thought and politics. Marx had a greater political influence on the history of the twentieth century than any other thinker, and it was the world Communist movement that was the primary conduit for this influence. While the PCF never ruled France, it carried an unparalleled intellectual weight: no other party had such a clear philosophy, had the name of a philosopher associated with it. No other party commanded the same allegiance among academics. A dividing line was drawn in French academia for decades after the War between Marxists and non-Marxists, and a somewhat different line between Communists and non-Communists. The difference between these two distinctions, between intellectual adherence to Marx and adherence to the Party which claimed to represent him, created a substantial blurred area in which many of the most influential intellectual figures of the day, most notably perhaps Jean-Paul Sartre, existed. While Foucault seemed to be rather clearly in the non-Marxist camp, certainly from the perspective of committed Marxists like Sartre, Foucault's relationship to Marx is never simple. He by turns criticises and utilises him, though these moves are not always made explicitly.

It is worth noting that neither Foucault's departure from the PCF nor his divergence for Marxism prevented him and Althusser from remaining friends (their friendship did suffer a breach, but later). There is a certain irony that, despite his unconcealed disdain for the PCF, Foucault remained closer to the Party member Althusser than he did to any extra-Party Marxists or leftists. There is an element of accident here, no doubt, that he and Althusser happened to have been friends from the ENS. But there was also a deeper intellectual affiliation between the two, which put them both at odds with the mainstream of French Marxist thought. Despite Foucault's repudiation of Marxism, the two can be seen as pursuing the same project in essential respects. For one thing, both were trying to challenge the doctrine of 'humanism' which dominated French thought, including Marxism, at that time. Althusser did this using the language of

Marxism, within the Party, whereas Foucault did it from outside using a more heterodox perspective. Foucault never engaged in direct polemics against the Party, or indeed against anyone else: he maintained in later years that he was opposed to polemics on principle, though it would perhaps have been professionally incautious to tilt directly at such powerful institutions as the PCF or Marxism in any case. His strategy was rather to produce an alternative theoretical position, to challenge Marxism by offering an alternative. Indeed, it is debatable to what extent Foucault's position was ever really necessarily hostile to Marxism. As we will see, there is some hostility, but it is far from total. He tells us that what most offended Marxists were his attacks on humanism and the so-called 'philosophy of the subject' – a line of criticism that Althusser took up even more pointedly, while maintaining (albeit with some theoretical contortions) that the anti-humanist position was the truly Marxist one. Althusser himself thus always took a relatively sympathetic view of Foucault's researches, as did those close to the older man. This led by 1970 to the publication of a positive review of Foucault's then-recent *Archaeology of Knowledge* in a party organ, written by an Althusserian, Dominique Lecourt, who interpreted Foucault's position as being essentially Marxist (Macey 1993, 216).

Both Foucault and Althusser thus belonged to the same general theoretical tendency, what is often called 'French structuralism', a name Foucault objected to, preferring rather to define the movement in terms of 'the calling into question of the theory of the subject' (RM 58). That is to say, where most French philosophy of the time started with the conscious subject of experience and asked how things seemed to that subject and how things could be made better for that subject, Foucault and Althusser wanted to mine beneath the subject and ask how that subject was produced in the first place. Foucault was quite explicit about his filiation to this movement in so far as he consistently made common cause with its leading lights during the 1960s.

There is another commonality between Foucault and Althusser that seems surprising in light of their later theoretical orientations, namely that they both wrote pre-doctoral dissertations on the thought of the nineteenth-century German philosopher G. W. F. Hegel (Macey 1993, 32). This is particularly surprising in Althusser's case because Althusser's main explicit theoretical project involved cleansing Marxism of its Hegelian elements. In Foucault's case, it is surprising simply in so far as he almost never mentions

Hegel in his work. It is less surprising when one considers the intellectual terrain the two of them would have encountered as young Marxists in the postwar period, however. French philosophy had only really discovered Hegel, the most prominent German philosopher of the nineteenth century, during the mid-twentieth century, and then only through the introduction of Marxism to France after the Russian Revolution. Hegel's magnum opus, *The Phenomenology of Spirit*, published originally in 1807, did not appear in a full French edition until 1941. Its translator, Jean Hyppolite, taught the *Phenomenology* to Foucault when he arrived in Paris to study immediately after the War (Macey 1993, 32). Hegel during this period was effectively a new, fashionable thinker, the prevailing interpretation of whose work made him seem radical and aligned to Marxism. Marx himself was indeed considerably influenced by Hegel. Nevertheless, I think it is accurate to say that for Foucault, as for Althusser more explicitly, much of his later project was oriented towards getting away from Hegel. For Althusser this meant trying to excise Hegel from Marxism, an effort which Althusser (2006) ultimately admitted was impossible. For Foucault, the more obvious effort was to distance himself from Marxism, but elements of the residual Hegelian influence on Marx are precisely a source of positions from which Foucault sought to distance himself. That is, while Althusser tried to rid Marxism of Hegel, Foucault sought to get away from Hegel by leaving Marxism behind altogether. The commonality of Hegel and Marxism against which Foucault would react is an attempt to give a predictive overview of history, understanding historical change as 'dialectically' progressive, and allowing us to predict its future unfolding, or at least have an overall understanding of its past dynamics. For Foucault, no such overall understanding of history is possible. Not coincidentally, perhaps, French readings of Hegel such as Hyppolite's (1969, vi) tended to ignore this philosophy of history in favour of other aspects of Hegel's thought. Hyppolite (1969, VIII), moreover, despite devoting much of his life to studying Hegel, was in the event quite sympathetic to Althusser's anti-Hegelian position.

We should note the political importance of this anti-Hegelianism; it is not merely a question of a scholastic debate. The political stakes of claiming to understand history are very real, particularly in the practical context of twentieth-century Marxism. If we understand history, then we can know what will happen next, and plan accordingly. In particular, it gives believers great confidence in the rightness of their actions, such that anyone who opposes them is castigated with standing in the way of an objectively necessary and inevitable historical progression. It is this arrogance that Foucault objects to.

Foucault's anti-Communism thus cannot be equated with conservatism. If anything, it was a radicalism, though of course Marxists did not see it that way. Rather, from *The History of Madness* onwards, they tended to accuse him of being a reactionary.

2

Madness and Psychology

In this chapter, I deal with Foucault's earliest work and its main theme, madness, within his thought more generally, in relation to politics. It has four sections, the first dealing with Foucault's life and work during the 1950s, the second with his *History of Madness*, the third with its political dimension and the fourth with criticism of Foucault's views on madness.

Psychology, Exile and Disillusion

By the end of his time at the ENS and in the PCF, Foucault's primary interest was increasingly the study of psychology. This was a practical and an academic interest, rather than an overtly political one, at least initially. It was also, we will conclude, a personal one. It continued, however, to have a political dimension and the research it led to was highly political in its implications.

The main subject of Foucault's undergraduate study was philosophy. Little can be read into this, given the level of prestige that subject enjoys in France, and the absence of an equivalent qualification (the all-important *aggrégation*) in alternative subjects conforming to Foucault's interests, such as sociology and psychology. He did, however, study psychology avidly and went on to take a degree in it in 1949 after having completed his philosophy degree (Macey 1993, 36). At the time, psychology was a new, cutting-edge discipline in France. Via these studies, Foucault came to observe patients in psychiatric hospitals, specifically the Sainte-Anne hospital in Paris (Macey 1993, 36). His association with this institution would last many years, encompassing attendance at lectures by the pre-eminent French psychoanalysts of the day, Daniel Lagache and Jacques Lacan, close contact with patients and involvement in their treatment in an unofficial capacity (Macey 1993, 56–7). Foucault was also, from 1950, involved in a similar capacity in the treatment of mental patients at a hospital for prisoners (Macey 1993, 58).

Psych-

The uninitiated are often confused by the distinction between the three terms 'psychology', 'psychiatry' and 'psychoanalysis'. All three share the same root word, *psyche*, the mind. Psychology is the academic study of the mind. Psychiatry, on the other hand, is the medical discipline connected with the treatment of mental disorders. Psychiatrists are thus doctors specialising in mental illness. Some psychologists, people with an academic background in psychology, are 'clinical' psychologists, which is to say they practise in a medical setting but are not medical doctors. Psychoanalysis, by contrast, is a specific approach to treatment of mental problems, with its own peculiar psychological theory, founded by Sigmund Freud (1856–1939). Psychoanalysis has in certain times and places been the dominant theory and practice in both psychology and psychiatry. This is to a large extent the case in France today, as it was for much of Foucault's life. It was also the case in America in the middle of the last century. That is, most psychiatrists and psychologists in France, and formerly in America, were psychoanalysts, and indeed vice versa, that is, most psychoanalysts were active in the professions of psychiatry and psychology. This has ceased to be the case in English-speaking countries in recent decades, where psychoanalysis has been marginalised. Foucault is critical in his work of all three things, psychiatry, psychology and psychoanalysis, though in subtly different ways.

This was not the whole extent of Foucault's encounter during these years with the psychiatric establishment, however. He also encountered it as a patient. The details of his private life at this time are somewhat tenebrous, but it is clear that he suffered from depression – suicide attempts are rumoured – and was sent by his father to see a psychiatrist (Macey 1993, 28). I would suggest that this is important to understanding his intellectual trajectory: Foucault experienced medical psychology and psychiatry not merely as an observer but as one who was classified by it, or at least who felt himself to be so classified. This goes some way to explaining both his interest in and his ultimate hostility to the psychiatric establishment, though of course one should not attempt to reduce his analysis to a sublimated grievance. In an unpublished interview, Foucault tells, in answer to a question about why he wrote his *History of Madness*, that

In my personal life, from the moment of my sexual awakening, I felt excluded, not so much rejected, but belonging to society's shadow. It's all the more a problem when you discover it for yourself. All of this was very quickly transformed into a kind of psychiatric threat: if you're not like everyone else, it's because you're abnormal, if you're abnormal, it's because you're sick.[1]

He thus links his psychiatrisation back to his homosexuality. That he should be treated as sick because of his homosexuality is unexceptional, given that homosexuality was classified as a psychological disorder in much of the world for much of the twentieth century.

Foucault went on to complete a further diploma in psychology in 1952, before obtaining his first academic appointment teaching psychology within a philosophy department, at Lille, in the same year (Macey 1993, 47). He would later be employed for some years in this capacity on a permanent basis at Clermont-Ferrand. This should not be taken, however, to imply any enthusiasm for or fidelity to the discipline of psychology. Indeed, he would seem to have held it in disdain (Macey 1993, 47).

It was nevertheless the subject of Foucault's first published works. One of these was *Mental Illness and Personality*, already mentioned above. This was, in its first edition (which is not the one translated into English), a pointedly political work, with Marxism as its concluding moment, seeing mental illness as essentially produced by our social form, capitalism, with revolutionary political change as the ultimate solution to such maladies.

This work appeared in 1954. In the same year a second book appeared, a translation by Foucault of Ludwig Binswanger's *Dream and Existence*, a relatively brief essay accompanied by an introduction by Foucault that was much longer than Binswanger's text. Binswanger had developed a form of psychoanalysis based on Martin Heidegger's thought. Foucault's introduction situates this work as an invaluable supplement to conventional, Freudian psychoanalysis. Politics is entirely absent here: whereas in *Mental Illness and Personality* Foucault drew from three perspectives, Marxism, psychoanalysis and Heideggerian phenomenology, to produce a hybrid account, he deals here only with the last two, without Marxism, and thus without politics. It is not entirely clear which text of Foucault's was written first. Macey (1993, 63) infers from the absence of reference to his own work on Binswanger in *Mental Illness* that the latter must have been written previously. I am not convinced, however, that one can infer anything from the difference between the two texts since they deal with different things, one the history of mental illness, the other strictly with a recent development in psychology.

After these texts, Foucault in effect entered a long theoretical gestation, during which he wrote his doctoral thesis, towards which he was already making his first tentative steps in 1952. It would not see the light of day until 1961 as *Folie et déraison: Histoire de la folie à l'âge classique* (Madness and unreason: history of madness in the classical age, lately published in English as *The History of Madness*).[2] During the intervening period, Foucault's teaching of psychology and contact with psychiatric institutions ceased, and he left France, writing the thesis in some dislocation from the context in which his interest in the topic had been aroused.

When he first left France, in 1955, it was to go to Sweden, where he remained for three years as director of the Maison de France at the University of Uppsala. Thereafter, in 1958, he moved to Warsaw as a cultural attaché to the French embassy. He spent only a year in Poland, but nevertheless this experience of a Communist-run country can I think be said to have influenced him politically, inasmuch as it convinced him once and for all that Communism did not offer much of an alternative to Western capitalism, that the problems that concerned him in the West were found similarly in the East. As he himself later put it: 'I lived in Sweden, a country of liberty, then Poland, a country quite to the contrary, and these experiences showed me that whatever the legal system, mechanisms of power constrain the individual and direct his conduct in an effort to normalize him' (Foucault, quoted in Friedrich 1981, 148).

This experience could be seen as seminal to Foucault's perspective. Certainly, after his youthful flirtation with the pro-Soviet PCF, the position he adopted was one that was effectively cynical in relation to all real existing political powers. His overall orientation throughout his work emphasises and criticises the shared history and assumptions of both the right and the left within Western political thought, though I will argue he remained himself distinctively on the left, seeing himself ultimately as within the tradition of left-wing modern Western political thought rather than that of the right.

I think one factor in informing Foucault's cynicism towards both sides of the Cold War was his homosexuality, though it is hardly the main factor. Homosexuality was for much of Foucault's life an issue beyond left and right, which is to say that the left were almost as homophobic as the right. It was not until relatively late in

Foucault's life that fighting for the rights of homosexuals became a fashionable component of left-wing politics, and that this concern became a left–right shibboleth. Not only the PCF but also French Trotskyist groups held negative attitudes towards homosexuality (Berry 2004, 20).

Foucault was not alone in criticising both sides of the Cold War. This indifference to East and West was shared by those who might be characterised as the political ultra-left, such as the Trotskyist and post-Trotskyist groups mentioned above which Foucault shows no signs of awareness of. In the domain of critical thought, as opposed to political militancy, the German Frankfurt School are an example of a tendency that saw things somewhat similarly to Foucault, with their critique of an instrumental rationality common to all contemporary political systems, as indeed, in their ways, did two major influences of theirs, Heidegger with his critique of technology and Nietzsche with his critique of massifying modernity. Foucault encountered the Frankfurt School's work only rather late in his career, but both he and they had a string of German philosophical influences in common: Kant, Hegel, Freud, Marx, Heidegger, Nietzsche. A difference between Foucault and the various leftists who rejected both Soviet Communism and Western capitalism is that, rather than couch his rejection of socialism in terms of an adherence to a true socialism not seen in Russia, he simply rejected both capitalism and socialism per se. Foucault posited no ideology of his own, but rather criticised both sides – crucially by pointing out their similarities – while refusing to propose any alternative of his own. This puts him closer to Heidegger and Nietzsche, although Foucault remains on the left, I will argue, whereas Heidegger was essentially right-wing and Nietzsche deeply politically ambiguous.

The History of Madness

Foucault left Poland in 1959 for a three-year post at the French Institute in Hamburg, West Germany. It was in Hamburg that he put the finishing touches to his first major work, The History of Madness, though it did not appear till 1961. Only a year later, in 1960, he was appointed to a permanent teaching position at the University of Clermont-Ferrand, and thus returned to France (DE1 28–9).

The History of Madness was the fruit of his period of exile, written mostly during his time in Sweden and Poland, though its themes clearly owed much to his studies and experiences of psychology and psychiatry in the years before in France. It was his primary doctoral thesis, though the doctorate in France at that time was a more stringent, higher qualification than it is in academia today. It required not one but two theses, a primary and a secondary one, with the former having to be published commercially. The sheer length of *The History of Madness* is vastly in excess of what would ordinarily be accepted as a doctoral thesis today, weighing in at close to seven hundred pages in its original edition. It is indeed Foucault's longest book by far, close to twice as long as his second-longest book, *The Order of Things*, itself a compendious volume.

It is therefore hard to do justice to Foucault's argument in *The History of Madness* here then, or to boil it down to a simply stated set of claims. Its historical range is vast, dealing with Western Europe over a period between the fifteenth and nineteenth centuries. Its aims are similarly grand. Foucault wanted to reconstitute an experience of madness, that is, what it felt like to be mad. This focus on subjective experience shows a debt to phenomenology, and differentiates the book from Foucault's later work.

To reconstitute such an experience implies a hermeneutic project that was in effect impossible. This does nothing to detract from the thoroughness of Foucault's researches, however, and indeed could be said to have in its impossibility pushed him to go as far as possible in this asymptotic direction. The guiding thread of the study is the concept of 'madness' (or, to be more precise, of *folie*, a French word that is very close in meaning to 'madness', but also encompasses the comparatively innocent domain of what we in English call 'folly'). What was considered mad, how the label of madness was applied, have changed over time. So the people and behaviours that are classified as mad have changed. But this change is deeper than merely a list of what is considered mad. It rather is a change in what madness is taken to be, what the classification as mad means, which entailed changes in the way the mad were treated. These changes in what people considered madness to be and the way the mad have been treated together have made the experience of being mad quite different at different times, Foucault argues. Indeed, one could go further and say that it changed not only the experience of being mad but the experience of being sane.

To understand these changes, Foucault marshals a broad array of sources: archival, empirical, literary. He is studying them both at the level of concrete, institutional history and at the level of the history of ideas. Indeed, he does not draw a distinction between the two.

A study of such breadth has enormous political implications, though without being explicitly about politics at all.

The History of Madness details a number of distinct historical phases. In this, and in other respects, it sets the pattern for almost all of Foucault's later studies (the exceptions being his *Archaeology of Knowledge* and his book on the author Raymond Roussel). Most of Foucault's books are historical, proceeding through the study of texts of the relevant period, and focusing on disjunctures in the way people talked about certain things.

These phases are not laid out with any great clarity, however. The book is not itself tightly structured, or well sign-posted. The earliest period Foucault discusses in any detail is the late Middle Ages. In this period, the mad are considered alien. The mad are excluded, yet remain highly visible. This changes with the Renaissance. During this period there is a certain valorisation of madness. Madness comes to be seen as harbouring a special kind of wisdom, as being on the side of spiritual revelation. Madness then went through a dramatic reversal in what the French call the 'Classical Age' (*l'âge classique*). This is Foucault's primary focus here and named in the original subtitle of the book. It is not a term with currency in English. Its meaning in French is somewhat imprecise, referring in a narrow sense to the great flourishing of French art and literature at the end of the seventeenth century, but it can refer to a longer period encompassing the sixteenth to eighteenth centuries. The period Foucault is talking about in relation to madness has its beginning in the sixteenth century, but begins decisively in the mid-seventeenth century, with what he calls the 'Great Confinement'. This Great Confinement was targeted at a variety of undesirable social elements. In one year, from 1656 to 1657, fully 1 per cent of the population of Paris was confined, an undifferentiated shutting away that quite abruptly arose as the solution to all of society's ills. In this event, the mad, along with the poor, are quite suddenly herded into vast institutions. At this point, the attitude towards the mad shifts diametrically. They are thought no longer to have a special wisdom but rather only to lack reason. For Foucault, this attitude is connected to the dominant attitude of the period, stemming from what is often called the Age of Reason, the rationalist philosophy of the early seventeenth century. This led to the Age of Enlightenment in the late seventeenth and the eighteenth centuries. Throughout this period, reason became the dominant intellectual virtue, eclipsing earlier tendencies towards religious mysticism. Madness was the opposite of reason, the *déraison* ('unreason') of Foucault's original title. As such, it was seen as utterly without merit, and indeed became something of a guilty secret, to be banished both from intellectual life, and ultimately from society at large. Those deemed mad were literally locked away from society en masse.

The Enlightenment itself in turn led to challenges to this undifferentiated treatment, as men of reason turned their attention to the conditions that obtained in the houses of confinement. In the late eighteenth century, a new attitude emerged, one that saw madness, and other causes of confinement such as poverty and criminality, as different conditions that could be cured through the application of reason. This differentiation seems to occur via an automatic mechanism. That is, the people who do not adapt to the disciplinary regime of confinement are labelled mad. Those who play the game of punishment and confinement adequately, most of the time, are by contrast considered sane. This is, in itself, a merely practical question, a division between two groups who need different conditions of confinement. What attaches to one group, however, is a much older notion, madness, now turned to a new purpose in a new social configuration. People in these different types were first separated out from one another in distinct institutions. Then, within the asylums which now housed the mad, they were 'liberated'. Where previously they had simply been chained up, treated in effect as non-human, they were now freed and processes were established aimed at restoring their sanity. Madness now became a medical problem, a disease, to be treated by the new discipline of psychiatry. Where once reason had simply banished madness as its irreconcilable opposite, it now sought to understand, control and eliminate it.

As with most of Foucault's historical studies, *Madness* stops well before the present. As with those other studies, though, I would argue that it stops precisely when it has got more or less to the point where the contemporary situation can be described. That is, by the nineteenth century, with the invention of psychiatry, we have more or less the current situation in relation to madness. Of course not everything has remained the same since that time by any means. For one thing, even in the time since Foucault wrote *Madness*, the mad have been freed once more, with the asylums being closed for the most part in favour of 'care in the community'. On the other hand, the pathologisation of madness has continued and indeed become more entrenched. We do not indeed speak of 'madness' any more in a medical context, but of 'mental illness'.

This indeed seems to people today to be simply the way things are: some people are at some times mentally unwell, and need medical treatment. Foucault's historical studies, however, disturb such assumptions. They show that people have had entirely opposite ideas about things. They moreover show how things came to be seen as they are now. The mad were not confined because they were sick. They were confined because, like criminals and the poor, they had come to be seen as morally bad, abandoned by God, and an offence against nature. The medicalisation of madness when it came, represented a more sophisticated view that sought to ask questions about why people acted in such ways. But it continued to be based in a moral outlook, that is, in the attitude that it was bad to be mad. While it might seem obvious to us today that the behavioural 'disorders' characteristic of mental 'illness' are objectively problematic, no other society has found it necessary to treat them in the same way ours does.

It is worth here referring to the work of an important influence on Foucault, the French philosopher of science Georges Canguilhem, and his explorations of the medical concept of the normal. Canguilhem explored various possible bases for distinguishing between normal and pathological states, and concludes that there is no objective basis for doing this. Rather, judgements of what is normal are always normative, value judgements. Thus, for Foucault, when we call someone mentally ill, it is not because there is something objectively wrong with them, but because they are transgressing the norms of our culture. The attempt to cure the 'sickness' is thus not objectively necessary, but a requirement of a culture that cannot tolerate their behaviour. Psychiatry has clothed a moral prejudice in the garb of science.

THE HISTORY OF MADNESS AND FOUCAULT'S OEUVRE

In my first book on Foucault, I passed over *The History of Madness* almost completely, because, as I said there, everything that Foucault says in that book he says again in a clearer and more precisely thought-out way later in his work (Kelly 2009, 7–8). This is true, but it also implies its inverse, that everything Foucault says in his subsequent work is either already contained in *The History of Madness* or is an attempt to think through the problems broached in that work. Foucault's entire life's work is, I would now argue, a continuing attempt to think through and actualise the enormous project of *The History of Madness*, to understand the way in which experiences have been constituted through political and social changes. *Madness* is, in this sense, Foucault's key work. Most of Foucault's other major works can be understood as sequels to it. *The Birth of the Clinic* is one most obviously, coming directly after *The History of Madness* and dealing with medicine in the late eighteenth and nineteenth centuries, expanding from the analysis of psychiatry involved in *Madness*. So too is *The Order of Things*, dealing with transformations in academic knowledge at the same time as *The History of Madness*, extending that dimension of the book. *The Archaeology of Knowledge* is clearly a sequel to *The Order of Things*, not *The History of Madness*, but these three works, from *Birth of the Clinic*, through *The Order of Things*, to the *Archaeology of Knowledge*, studies of the 1960s that can be grouped under the rubric of 'archaeology' that Foucault gives to his methodology at this time, represent an attempt to think through the methodological implications of *Madness*. An abrupt change occurs in 1970, with a new methodology, 'genealogy', in which the focus becomes more concrete, a turn back towards history and politics. The two major studies of this phase, *Discipline and Punish* and the first volume of *The History of Sexuality*, are each again sequels to *The History of Madness*. *Discipline and Punish* tells the story of what happened to a different form of confinement from that dealt with in *The History of Madness*. *The History of Sexuality* took up another prominent theme of *The History of Madness*, sexuality, and focused on it. Indeed, Foucault (PK 184) had planned a history of sexuality as a parallel companion to his history of madness when he was writing the latter, though in the event fifteen years intervened between the two.

Foucault begins with psychiatry and psychology in his first efforts, which lead to his magnum opus, *The History of Madness*. He then works on various tangents from this: a supplementary medical history, *Birth of the Clinic*, the examination of 'mad' literature in *Raymond Roussel*. But he gets drawn into lengthy methodological reflections, which results in a tighter examination of academic discourses in *The Order of Things*, and a book of methodology during a period of intense introspection, *The Archaeology of Knowledge*. With the 1970s, we get a methodological turnaround in *The Order of Discourse*, followed by a return to the matter of *The History of Madness*. The researches of the 1970s are various forks of *The History of Madness*. The research on the history of the prison is very close to *The History of Madness*: punishment and madness are intertwined historically, in a complicated way (actually, they pass almost like ships in the night: till the eighteenth century, the mad were 'confined', as part of a general mass including the poor and indigent, as well as criminals, but criminals were not generally confined; rather lawbreakers generally received punishments of a physical type, where they were punished at all. From the eighteenth century, two institutions are established in respect of criminals and the mad. The former are incarcerated in prisons, the latter in asylums. The undifferentiated confinement ends, but confinement becomes a more dominant solution in general. *Discipline and Punish* centres on the prison, but is a history more generally of disciplinary institutions, which indeed means all institutions from the eighteenth century onwards in Western Europe, including the asylum). There is even a supplementary lecture series on *Psychiatric Power* that is a sequel to the *History of Madness*, and a lecture series, *Abnormal*, that marries this history to that of the prison, and to a third history, connected closely to both the other two but particularly to that of psychiatry and madness, the history of sexuality. This history provides the general framework of work for the last ten years of Foucault's life. His lecture series of this period might seem quite eccentric from this point of view, notably the series on governmentality, *Security, Territory Population* and the *Birth of Biopolitics*. The former, however, deals with questions raised prominently in *The History of Madness* of statecraft in early modernity, of police, and the second series follows from the first. The question of subjectivity Foucault raises in the 1980s in relation to Antiquity is perhaps the most distant from the *History of Madness* in both its theme and its chronology, but still questions of subjectivity are utterly fundamental to *The History of Madness*. In short, I think it is not hard to see Foucault's entire intellectual career unfolding quite organically from *The History of Madness*, and never straying far from it. There is no break, but only an attempt to master questions first raised there. So many questions are raised there that to untangle them easily became a life's work.

The importance of *The History of Madness* is generally underestimated in the English-language literature on Foucault. The book is in this respect effectively a victim of its own greatness. That is, it was so important that it was quick to appear in translation in English (only four years after its initial publication in French, quite a feat given that Foucault was at that time a virtually unknown figure, even in France), but in an abridged version, which thus was all that was read in English from its publication in 1965 until 2006. As Jean Khalfa put it in his translator's introduction, the '*History of Madness* has yet to be read' (HM xiii).

The problem that Foucault encounters in this his first major book, which remains important for his entire career, is how to deal with an essentially elusive object. He wants to write the history of madness. Madness is defined by Foucault as an experience. Yet it is impossible to actually recreate the experience itself. Rather, we must study this object, madness, via textual traces, via a variety of forms of fact and discourse, none of which allows us actually to get to the experience itself, the very thing we want to know about. Foucault will deal with this problem initially by moving further away from the problem of experience. He reintroduces the concept in some of his last work, but never again openly makes the reconstitution of a historical experience the stakes of his researches.

The focus on experience is almost transparently the survival of a filiation to phenomenology. Phenomenology, even in its Heideggerian fork, is effectively a philosophy of experience, which begins with the investigation of our experiences of the world. It is this form of philosophy that Foucault had shown an affinity for in his study of Binswanger, and which he does not excise from *Mental Illness and Personality*.

History, however, poses two problems for this form of philosophy. On the one hand, how to understand history itself without direct access to the experiences that people used to have. On the other, by suggesting that our experiences have a history which is important to understanding them, but which cannot be found within them. The desire to understand phenomenologically the experience of the past spawned the discipline of hermeneutics, which attempts to enter into the spirit of the past by a study of and reflection on the evidence we do have of past experiences, producing a 'hermeneutic circle', by which we come closer and closer to past experiences. Heidegger took up hermeneutics, and those who have followed him have developed it in diverse directions. Foucault would seem to have been unaware of hermeneutics as a solution, however, despite his interest in Heidegger. As with other trends in German- and English-language philosophy that had not enjoyed popularity in France (most notably Critical Theory), he seems to have become aware of hermeneutics only late in life, as a result of exposure to it during his increasingly frequent visits to America during this time. He seems to have been enthusiastic enough about the idea of hermeneutics to name a Collège course *Hermeneutics of the Subject*, but this would seem to be the first time he ever used the term, two years before his death. He perhaps, perversely, encountered the idea first from the American scholars Hubert Dreyfus and Paul Rabinow, who were writing a book about him in the early 1980s, with the thesis that Foucault's work in then-recent years had been hermeneutical. The pair, however, concluded after interacting with Foucault that he was in fact *beyond* hermeneutics (Dreyfus and Rabinow 1983, xi). Indeed, Foucault had abandoned any attempt to understand history phenomenologically, and this abandonment is palpable already in *The History of Madness*. Hermeneutics might be able to get us closer to understanding a historical experience, but it cannot actually reconstitute it fully. Foucault's starting point in *Madness* is the impossibility of reconstituting an historical experience. His conclusion is that, since we cannot reconstitute it, we must do something else to understand it.

With madness, we have a peculiar problem in this regard, a problem that bedevils the discipline of psychology. Madness is an experience, yet we are required to identify it by non-experiential markers. And as an experience, it can scarcely be untouched by historical changes. The way mad people are treated might not be the sole cause of madness, but it nevertheless drastically alters the experience they have. What actions see one categorised as mad change historically. The kind of behaviour people exhibit varies historically. People's mentalities vary historically. The reciprocal effects of categorisation, behaviour, mentalities and the treatment of people according to their behavioural categorisations contribute correlatively to the production of the phenomenon of madness in any given period. The kind of experiences people have thus can be expected to vary significantly. Today, one might find oneself unable to cope with various demands of life that are highly specific to the modern world – school, work environments quite unlike those that have existed in the past – developing feelings of persecution. One may thus be referred to a psychiatrist who diagnoses 'schizophrenia' and prescribes 'antipsychotic' medications. One will believe one has a persistent 'illness', characterised by a 'chemical imbalance' in the brain, which can be remedied with drugs. No part of this picture can in its specificity be found in any experience people had hundreds of years ago. The word 'mad' might be applied (colloquially) to the schizophrenic, but this does not mean that schizophrenia is the same thing as what was called madness circa 1700. This is not to say that Foucault denies any similarities or substantial identities between the two conditions.

It is rather a matter of stating the extent of the absence of a basis for asserting that the two are identical.

The notion of experience is a continuing preoccupation during Foucault's career (Lemke 2011a, 28). The extent of this can be missed by Anglophone readers because the French word *expérience* can be translated into English as either 'experience' or 'experiment', and frequently in Foucault's works of the 1960s is translated inappropriately in the latter way. Foucault really only ceases to talk about experience in the mid-1970s – the term is almost absent from *Discipline and Punish* and the first volume of *The History of Sexuality*. This is odd, because these books seem to relate much more to human experience than do the relatively staid works of the late 1960s, *The Order of Things* and *The Archaeology of Knowledge*. The extent of Foucault's reference to experience in these volumes is indicative of the extent to which the problem of experience animates his entire archaeological project, even though archaeology is largely about dispensing with actually giving an account of experiences. The guiding idea here would seem to be that an experience is constituted in large part by the conceptual framework given to one in one's culture with which to understand it. Since Foucault as an archival historian has lots of evidence of that conceptual framework, but the experience itself is very hard to access, it makes sense to focus on the conceptual side. There is never much work written by those on the receiving end of the discourse, as it were, in this case the mad. When there is writing from them, moreover, it necessarily avails itself of the conceptual vocabulary of the day, regardless of the experience itself. This is then Foucault's difficulty here: on the one hand, a plausible and deep intuition that discourse is constitutive of differentiated experiences; on the other, a lack of any confirming evidence.

Madness and Politics

Foucault was disappointed not to reach a wider audience with the *History of Madness*. However, it proved to be something of a political time-bomb. He recounts that, at the time he was writing it, questions around mental illness were not seen as political. The political field during the postwar period was dominated by concerns about foreign policy, the state, and class. Questions about the treatment of marginal groups were not taken seriously within politics. On the left, such issues were seen as distractions from the important question of workers' power. Of course, there was some variation in the attitude towards different issues: anti-racism and feminism were to some extent identified as left-wing causes (since they had a much longer history on the left, and indeed are covered to some extent by Marx), unlike the struggles of homosexuals or the mentally ill. The PCF was particularly prickly about both these last two issues, since homosexuality was illegal in the Soviet Union, and its psychiatry did not differ in its essentials from that practised in the West, and indeed it was used as a form of persecution of dissidents. The left in general changed its attitude in the late 1960s, however, and Foucault's book belatedly connected with a larger audience than it had found on publication (RM 79). The confinement of the mentally ill was now understood as crucial to understanding the operation of contemporary society in general, which is an insight that Foucault had arguably had many years before.

For Foucault, the study of the mad connected to a larger concern with limits and abnormality. There was nothing marginal about the significance he attributed to the treatment of the mad. For Foucault, the exclusion of the mad from society was nothing short of a constitutive component of Enlightenment rationality, producing modern society and thought.

Madness is moreover not just one marginal issue among many, but rather related to the others. The crucial linkage here is the concept of 'normality', later the subject of a series of lectures by Foucault (1975's *Abnormal*). Madness is linked as a form of abnormality to criminality and sexual perversion. This is decisive from the perspective of Foucault qua homosexual man: the abnormality of being considered mentally ill qua depressive can only have exacerbated feelings of abnormality already foisted on him by a homophobic society in relation to his sexual preferences. This is the basis of Lynne Huffer's recent queer feminist rereading of *The History of Madness*, *Mad for Foucault*.

Foucault was aware of the political stakes of his study of madness and was surprised and disappointed that it was not taken up by more Marxists. While we can adequately explain their lack of interest and even hostility in terms of their desire to conserve a rigorous focus on class politics and not to attack the Soviet Union, there is nothing in Marxism itself that conflicts with an attention to mental illness, as demonstrated by Foucault's own earlier Marxist perspective on the subject, and the work of the German Freudo-Marxist school, with which he would later engage marginally in the first volume of his *History of Sexuality*. Yet Foucault's perspective in

The History of Madness can be seen as defying Marxism in its specifics. Its focus on literary evidence and cultural shifts might seem idealist, denying the importance of political, material imperatives in imprisoning the mad. This would, however, be a misreading. *The History of Madness* posits no causal priority, either of the cultural shift over the institutional, or vice versa. It simply notes the coincident transformation, without aetiological speculation. For most Marxists, this ambiguity itself was tantamount to heresy, of course: if a writer did not affirm the correct, economistic order of things, they were to be considered bourgeois. The lack of such an affirmation is, moreover, genuinely indicative of Foucault's disagreements with Marxism.

The History of Madness represents a liminal position in the abandonment of Hegelianism by Foucault. On the one hand, it is still somewhat Hegelian; as Khalfa notes in his introduction, 'Hegelian vocabulary' is still 'present throughout the book' (HM xv). Foucault (2004, 87–8) himself admits as much, averring that he was still caught up on Hegelianism in that work. On the other hand, the book contains criticism of Hegel, specifically the claim that '*homo dialecticus*' ('dialectical man' – an allusion to Hegel's 'dialectical' method) is 'already dying in us' (HM 543). Of course, this implies that it is still present, merely declining. But it also sees Foucault looking forward to the extinction of Hegelianism.

The context of this meditation is extraordinarily interesting. It is, namely, Foucault imagining how things will look for people in the future. This is a quite Hegelian device: imagining things from the perspective of the end of history, where all things are known. Such reflections are common in our time; politicians frequently claim that history will bear out their decisions. This is, indeed, a device Foucault continues to employ much later in his career, namely in the *History of Sexuality Vol. I*. The specifics of what he imagines people in the future thinking of the past are quite different from a Hegelian determination, however. Whereas for Hegel, and our politicians, everything should be clearly understandable from the point of view of the end of history, for Foucault the perspective of the future will be marked with incomprehension of the past. Whereas our political leaders claim in a Hegelian way that they will be vindicated by the judgement of history, Foucault invokes the future only to point out how absurd and nonsensical the present would seem from any point of view outside of itself. The point of his invocation of the future then is to allow criticism of the present by making us see how contingent our contemporary arrangements are. As Khalfa points out, there is no trace even in *Madness* of a Hegelian vision of history as having a set logic (HM xix).

What we see in *The History of Madness* then is a new way of thinking about society based on an understanding of the reciprocal historical constitution of experiences and political institutions. Institutions are not merely something created by humans. Rather, humans are shaped by institutions, just as they shape those institutions in turn. Politics and subjectivity are bound up in a complicated, reciprocal relationship, which is prone to change in all kinds of unexpected directions. While the notion of a reciprocity between history or politics on the one hand and subjectivity on the other is to be found in a long German philosophical tradition from Hegel to Marx to Heidegger, Foucault breaks with this in seeing things as much more free-form. For Hegel, subjectivity is engaged in a progressive movement towards knowledge. For Marx, it is engaged in a progress of self-emancipation. For Heidegger, it is called back to a lost awareness of Being. For Foucault, there is no clear teleology. He is rather a historical relativist, for whom even these teleological conceptions of the history of subjectivity are artefacts of historical thinking. Relativism itself is not original to Foucault, by any means (see Baghramian 2010). Relativism is not a popular philosophical position, however. It is often held to be a nonsensical paradox. That is, it is typically said that relativism is itself a non-relative, absolute position, and thus contradicts itself. We must be clear that Foucault is not a relativist about everything, which would indeed be paradoxical. He does not believe that the sun rises in the morning only because people believe that it rises. He does not hold that reality is dependent on thought, or discourse (which would be idealism, rather than relativism, strictly speaking). Rather, he maintains that human experience is relative to thought and discourse, in addition to a dependence on external reality (here we may point out that the sun does not have to be seen as 'rising' at all, and indeed by our modern scientific worldview does not 'rise', but rather the earth rotates such that the sun comes into view in the morning). Indeed, all these things reciprocally affect one another: experience, discourse and reality. While reality presumably exists without the other two, and not vice versa, giving it a certain ontological priority, if we are interested in doing human history, the history of experiences and society, we cannot ignore these complicated reciprocities. It cannot be the case that 'madness' is simply an invariant thing, given that it is a human phenomenon, experienced and constituting itself the same way in all historical and social contexts. It is thus relative to the core. The same may be said of sexuality, punishment, or knowledge itself as such.

Criticism of Madness

There is much to criticise in *The History of Madness*, however. One aspect which most of Foucault's works have been challenged on is their historical accuracy. This is not a critical viewpoint I will examine at all in relation to Foucault in this current book, for a number of reasons. One is that I am not in a position to do the historical research required to verify or falsify Foucault's claims. Suffice it perhaps to say that it is not the case that there is an expert consensus among historians either for or against Foucault, that the status of Foucault's historical research is debated within history. To this extent, Foucault's is little different essentially from any other particular historical research. Another reason why this criticism can be bracketed from discussion is that historical accuracy is not really our concern, but rather the accuracy of his descriptions at describing the political *present*.

One can also criticise *Madness* on formal grounds. It is not set out in a particularly clear way and it is very easy to confuse the various periods it covers, since Foucault jumps back and forth through time incessantly. Demarcations are not clearly made, and references are frequently to broad historical moments. This lack of clarity can be found in some of Foucault's later works too, though it is perhaps to be expected that his first major study would also be his least organised. I have the feeling that it would have benefited greatly from an able and sympathetic editor, and presents a daunting and challenging read, such that most readers are best advised to read later works of Foucault's first.

The most famous criticism of the content of *Madness* came from someone who is himself a notoriously difficult read, Foucault's sometime student, Jacques Derrida. Derrida's (2001) challenge to Foucault is primarily in relation to the latter's interpretation of the history of ideas, specifically Foucault's contention that seventeenth-century French philosopher René Descartes excluded madness from consideration in his *Meditations*, thus performing an absolute exclusion of madness from reasoned discussion. Derrida on the contrary thinks Descartes does take the possibility of madness seriously, whereas Foucault thinks that Descartes's position, and those of men of his time, was that to even think one might be mad was inconceivable; by contrast, for Descartes, thinking that the world around him might not exist at all and that he was being deceived in his perceptions by an evil demon was a perfectly acceptable thing to consider. In terms of the history of philosophy, this question is significant: the *Meditations* is credited widely with being the text that inaugurates modern philosophy. However, it is hard to see what the political repercussions of this disagreement could be. Although Foucault was to defend his reading of Descartes vigorously, he also argues against Derrida that the case of Descartes is not crucial to his general argument in *The History of Madness*, because philosophy is not as important to history as Derrida holds (HM 576). Here Foucault positions himself between a quasi-idealist such as Derrida, who thinks language is all important, and Marxism's tendency to ignore the significance of words and culture.

A more general criticism made by Derrida is that, for Foucault, madness is conceived of as a primitive, natural thing, trapped and distorted by linguistic classifications. In this, Derrida I think subtly but significantly misunderstands Foucault's position on madness and its silence. Foucault thinks madness has been silenced, and as such it's very difficult for us to understand it as a historic experience, because we lack linguistic accounts from the mad, though it is still difficult to understand an experience even if we do have first-person accounts. Derrida takes Foucault to be saying that madness is a pure experience beyond language. This is also Ian Hacking's interpretation in his foreword to the current English edition of *The History of Madness*, seizing in particular on a phrase – also quoted by Derrida (2001, 43) – that Foucault uses to describe madness, 'inaccessible primitive purity' (HM xi, xxxiii). It seems to me that this phrase is actually a reference to madness qua experience, rather than being a specific description of madness. Our experiences are primitive and pure in the sense that they have not been mediated by verbal interpretation – but for this reason they are inaccessible.

Derrida thinks that Foucault's evident ability to talk about madness clearly shows that madness is not inaccessible or pure, and indeed it is not. But nor does Foucault think it is, only that pure experience is.

If Derrida is not right that Foucault is overly reificatory about madness, making madness into a pure thing existing outside of history, however, might the opposite not then be said to be true, that Foucault is too relativist about madness? I think this is by far the more likely objection to Foucault. He seems to imply that madness is *just* a culturally constituted experience. But, in point of fact, he does not make any such claim either. He neither affirms nor denies that madness is a real thing that exists transhistorically.

If madness does exist objectively, however, could it not be said that we can produce an unproblematic definition of madness that simply accords with its reality? This is a difficult question. Ultimately, no matter how objective our basis for a categorisation, a description is never merely neutral where human beings are concerned. Even an objective description will produce a specific experience, a different one to any that existed before that description was formulated. The best one could hope for here presumably would be a description that constitutes an experience that accords with the description. It is also possible however that we will never pin down madness in this way. This does not of course mean that we should not try to find new ways of thinking about madness. Foucault is not trying to forswear new ways of doing this, to end the conceptualisation of madness. But neither is he interested in producing any definition of madness himself. This differentiates this stage of his career from both *Mental Illness and Personality* and his piece on Binswanger, where he was trying to produce or contribute to an understanding of madness. His project after *The History of Madness* is, by contrast, entirely critical. This purely critical attitude is a hallmark of all his mature work. In *Madness*, then, his purpose is to expose what is happening now for what it is, to show how it works, not to produce a positive conception of what we should do or say instead, but only to undermine. Thus, we end up with a critique of the contemporary attitude to madness which exposes that attitude as a moral condemnation couched in scientific language. This simple point is easily missed in the maelstrom of ideas and evidence that comprises the *History of Madness*.

This does not mean that Foucault denies that some people actually have psychic 'issues' that distinguish them from others. He means only to describe, and to some extent thereby effect change in respect of, our current ways of treating and thinking about madness. To some extent, one might say that he was successful in this. *Madness* was taken up by a movement that Foucault did not know existed when he wrote it, British anti-psychiatry. It was due to this connection that Foucault's book found such a rapid passage into English. Critiques such as Foucault's, together with the work of many theorists, writers, practitioners, artists, patients, family members and activists, led internationally to a discrediting of the institution of the asylum, and to the widespread closure of asylums. However, it did not lead to a fundamental change in the treatment or conceptualisation of the mad or of madness. And so, as Foucault later put it, the closure of the asylums simply led to 'new problems' (EW1 256). Foucault resolutely rejects any idea that these new problems are any kind of indictment of anti-psychiatry: the asylums genuinely were previously the problem, whereas now there are new problems. Foucault's critical practice will be conceived as an unending battle against the emerging status quo. This is not made apparent until many years later, and then only in interviews, however.

Derrida (2001, 52) also questions Foucault's methodology in the *History of Madness*, describing it as 'a method that presents itself precisely as structuralist, that is, a method for which everything within the structural totality is inter-dependent and circular in such a way that the classical problems of causality themselves would appear to stem from a misunderstanding'. The stakes of this notion of 'structuralism' will be examined in the next chapter. Derrida's idea here is that for Foucault all the elements in society or in language constitute a hermetic system where everything supports everything else and no element can be given any priority over any other. Derrida rightly notes that the problem of causation is absent from the *History of Madness*. Derrida 'wonders whether' it is possible to avoid aetiology in history. It is worth pondering this question as we proceed through Foucault's corpus.

Derrida's complaint about the absence of aetiology would seem to be quite opposite to the Marxist complaint: where the Marxists might worry that the importance of economics in shaping ideas is being underplayed, Derrida worries that Foucault does not accord enough importance to the influence of philosophy on history. Foucault, I think rightly, ridicules this suggestion. Foucault grasps this nettle and effectively accuses Derrida of idealism (though he does not actually use that term – HM 577). Foucault criticises Derrida here for embodying the typical French academic prejudice that philosophy is the essential motor of historical development. Derrida ignores the existence of 'events' in favour of a pure attention to texts (HM 573, 577). Derrida is, in effect, guilty of the thing that Marxists will repeatedly accuse Foucault of, that is, taking language and ideas to be more important than things.

For Foucault, Derrida is the 'most radical' of a conservative philosophical tradition which is closed in on itself. Foucault seeks to 'free himself' from this perspective. He thus on the one hand rejects

Marxism's privileging of certain aspects of materiality – economics, class, revolution – but seeking to retain the baby of these insights while dispensing with its bathwater. In particular he retains the idea that philosophy is a product of an historical and political context, and that it must be criticised as such, rather than offering a safe, transcendental harbour for thought.

Derrida (2001, 53) also seems to pose questions about the seeming totalisation of Foucault's approach, suspecting the older man of not allowing for the great diversity of views about madness at any given time. This strikes me as quite unfair, at least in relation to *Madness*. Foucault is quite explicit that there are many overlapping, interlocking tendencies. The decisive shifts in relation to madness occur at a subterranean level, involving wide changes, which cannot be read off individual texts, but can be discerned across them. This contrasts with Derrida's deconstructive approach, which is deeply particular in relation to individual texts. Now, it is hard to adjudicate between these two perspectives, but they are trying to do quite different things. Derrida is trying to analyse and subvert the presuppositions of individual texts. Foucault is trying to do a broad-scale history with a social component, for which Derrida's method would be entirely inappropriate.

Notes

1. Quoted in Huffer 2009, 23. Huffer's reference is to p. 29 of the unedited transcript of Roger-Pol Droit's interview with Foucault.
2. For an account of the changes to the title see HM ix. In English it has been best known as *Madness and Civilization*, though the edition with this title, the only English edition available from 1967 until 2006, is in fact a translation of a significantly abridged paperback edition.

3

Words and Things

This chapter deals with Foucault's thought of the 1960s after *The History of Madness*. During this period, he became increasingly concerned with language. One might say that his thought underwent a 'linguistic turn', a phrase used to describe a general reorientation towards language in Western philosophy during the mid-twentieth century. French philosophy in the 1960s provides a pronounced example of such a turn.

Most of this chapter will deal with the methodology Foucault formulates during this period under the rubric of 'archaeology'. It will also deal briefly with his reflections on and relation to literature during this period.

The Birth of the Clinic

Foucault's follow-up to *The History of Madness* was *The Birth of the Clinic*, which appeared only two years after. The two books are closely thematically and historically related. *Birth of the Clinic* deals with the history of medicine, which relates to the previous book's study of the roots of psychiatry, and begins at approximately the same point in the eighteenth century that the history in the earlier book left off. The book itself is not methodologically different in any particularly obvious way from *The History of Madness*. The differences are that it deals with a shorter time period, and has a tighter structure and narrower focus, namely the foundation of institutional medicine.

The Birth of the Clinic is not overtly political. Its focal concept is that of the medical 'gaze' (*regard*). This concept might at first glance seem to be a political one, and Foucault will use the same word in a political way in later work, particularly *Discipline and Punish*. In *Birth of the Clinic*, however, Foucault is not talking directly about the way patients experience the medical gaze, or even the relation between doctors and patients. Rather, his point there is simply that modern medicine has become essentially observational, teaching doctors to observe, monitor and then make judgements. In that much, he has diverged from the grand ambition of *The History of Madness* of reconstituting an experience, though his overall method of relating institutional changes, history, discourses and practices remains largely similar. He is, moreover, still trying to understand how experience was reduced to silence, that is, how the empiricism of the dispassionate medical gaze came to conquer the experience of the patient (BC xiv). And this is certainly not without political ramifications.

There is substantial specific political-historical content in the book, but this is mostly overshadowed by more detailed later work done by Foucault that develops similar themes in the 1970s, which we will examine in later chapters of this book. Foucault here for the first time identifies, for example, medicine as taking over functions previously the province of the Church (BC 39), and the emergence of modern medicine as closely related to the growth of the state (BC 38–9). There are some slightly Marxist inflexions here that will be lost in Foucault's later work, such as his use of the phrase 'political ideology'. He also uses class categories in his analysis, although this is something he will never cease to do or call into question in any of his work, despite his later pointed rejection of Marxism. Specifically, in this case, he explains the creation of a relatively inclusive and egalitarian public health care system by reference to the usefulness to the rich of having a large population of poor patients on whom treatments could be tested and developed (BC 85). He draws this explanation, however, simply from the historical texts he is reading, rather than inferring it himself.

There is furthermore something very noteworthy from a political point of view about the historical divisions he posits here, specifically in relation to the French Revolution of 1789, which occurs early during the timeframe covered by the book. While the Revolution certainly had palpable effects in disrupting and transforming the French medical establishment, the most crucial changes according to Foucault began somewhat *before* the Revolution, and after the tumult of the Revolution's early years the situation stabilises to be more or less the same as that before it (BC 101). What is crucial about this is its implication that different institutions (medicine and government in this case) and different discourses (medical and political in this case) are relatively autonomous from one another in their historical dynamics, rather than all following the same script, or rather than one of them being the fundamental historical force that the others follow.

Archaeology

Still *The Birth of the Clinic* is as an historical study rather staid, if an important contribution to scholarship. The most radical moment of the book is, I think, found not in the historical study of medicine itself but in the book's preface. This preface really amounts to the first systematic methodological statement of Foucault's career. Here we see him trying for the first time to set out a distinctive methodology, an effort which will increasingly preoccupy him during the remainder of the decade. He will come to call this methodology 'archaeology'.

This somewhat surprising word is first used by Foucault in his original preface to *The History of Madness* to describe his project there (HM xxviii). What Foucault does is of course not what we ordinarily think of when we think of archaeology: he does not dig trenches in mud. He does dig up artefacts, however, in the form of old texts out of libraries, so one might say that it is still technically a form of archaeology in its literal sense. We may also say that his invocation of 'archaeology' is a play on words. The word derives from the Greek word *arkhaios*, meaning 'ancient', such that 'archaeology' means the study of ancient things. The French *archéologie*, like the US English spelling 'archeology' (lacking the second 'a'), however, could in principle have been derived from the Greek word *arkheia*, 'records', whence the English word 'archive'. Foucault may have intended this etymological pun, since he is studying ancient archives.

How does this 'archaeology' differ from any ordinary historical enquiry? We have already considered various facets of the *History of Madness* that might be distinctive in relation to other kinds of history. Foucault specifically says in his first invocation of the term 'archaeology' there that he intends to do the archaeology of the 'silence' that madness has been reduced to, counterposing this with the simple 'history' of the 'language' we use today to speak about madness. Thus, what is distinctive about Foucault's approach is that he is asking not so much how ways of talking about madness might have changed, as how it is that mad people's speech has been devalued to the point that it is ignored and doctors speak for them. Thus, it is not so much a work of the positive history of ideas or of science, but a negative history of a form of exclusion, a specifically political form of history. As I have indicated, *The Birth of the Clinic* also follows this essentially negative, hence political, pattern.

The theme of archaeology becomes more prominent in Foucault's work as the 1960s wear on. In *The Birth of the Clinic*, the word appears in the subtitle, *An Archaeology of Medical Perception*, though nowhere else in the book. The next book after that, *The Order of Things*, follows suit with its subtitle, *An Archaeology of the Human Sciences*, but also contains a discussion of the archaeological method as such. Finally, Foucault ends the decade with a book about method itself, with archaeology at the front of its title, *The Archaeology of Knowledge*. I will present the methodological reflections that Foucault makes in these books – in the prefaces of the first two, and throughout the third – as a concatenating construction. I think this methodology is crucially important, both because it is the focus of much of Foucault's intellectual attention during this period (though by sheer volume his excavations of the archives take up the bulk of his books) and because it proves to be surprisingly politically controversial.

THE BIRTH OF ARCHAEOLOGY

His methodological reflections begin in earnest with the preface to *The Birth of the Clinic*. Here he claims that 'In order to determine the moment at which the mutation in discourse took place, we must look beyond its thematic content or its logical modalities to the region where "things" and "words" have not yet been separated. We must re-examine the original distribution of the visible and invisible insofar as it is linked with the division between what is stated and what remains unsaid' (BC xi).

There are two binary divisions here, which seem to be synonymous for Foucault: invisible words are distinguished from visible things. The use of the vocabulary of 'visible and invisible' seems to me to signal a debt to the then-recently deceased French phenomenologist Merleau-Ponty, a sometime teacher of Foucault's.[1] This terminology is most prominent in his posthumously published work, *The Visible and the Invisible* – but this had not yet appeared when Foucault was writing. Merleau-Ponty (1964, 21) had used it as early as 1960, however, as an alternative to the dualist ontology expounded by his sometime close friend and collaborator Jean-Paul Sartre. In Merleau-Ponty's usage, the distinction of visible and invisible refers to the difference between the specifically human pole of existence, what might be called subjectivity, and the non-human, objective pole. Merleau-Ponty's point in using the terms, and presumably Foucault's in following him, is to avoid the vocabulary of subjectivity and humanness, which Merleau-Ponty had himself used copiously in his earlier work, and by avoiding this vocabulary to minimise the difference between language and material reality, between humans and things. For Merleau-Ponty, humans are a 'fold in being', by which he means that our consciousness is essentially a permutation of reality, rather than a substantially different element to physical things. We are an invisible side of the same nature as visible things.

In the above-quoted passage in the *Birth of the Clinic* preface, Foucault is arguing that everything begins with an originary unity, and only then can we effect the division that produces both things qua objects of perception and the language that subjectively describes them. He thus posits a '"carving up" of things', introducing a division between what can be said and what cannot (BC xviii). As linguistic beings, we cannot completely recover the viewpoint provided that existed prior to the carving up, since any attempt to describe it presupposes its having been carved up. It is only once the original unity has been fractured that language, 'words', come to exist. This entails that there is no transcendent language by which to assess the different divisions of the visible and the invisible that manifest at different times. The best we can do is attempt to understand the emergence of these different economies of visibility and invisibility from the original unity by reference to the existence of that original unity. In this Foucault diverges crucially from a standard approach to language and truth, in ways that will be played out in later books, examined below within this chapter. The typical modern way of thinking about the relation of language to reality is to see words as 'referring' to things either successfully or unsuccessfully. Successful reference produces true statements, which describe the true nature of material reality. Not least among this mainstream is orthodox 'scientific' Marxism.

What does this divergence of Foucault's mean in practical terms? What Foucault says here, in relation to medicine, is that 'We must place ourselves, and remain once and for all, at the level of the fundamental *spatialization* and *verbalization* of the pathological' (BC xi). That is to say, that we must attend to the production of words and arrangement of things in space which constitute medicine, and to the interrelation of the two, the way the two are related to one another at different times and in different places. This basic methodology never ceases to operate after this point in Foucault's thought. It could be called a matter of having an *objective* assessment of words and things. 'Objectivity' is often used to refer to a specific way of relating words to things, trying to suggest that words can match adequately to things. *The Birth of the Clinic* in fact details precisely such an 'objective' method in medicine, namely empiricism, an objective method for relating words to things which pretends to derive the former from the latter via experience. Foucault, by contrast, we might say has a meta-objectivism. The methodology Foucault proposes in *The Birth of the Clinic* is specifically 'a structural analysis of discourses that would evade the fate of commentary by supposing no remainder, nothing in excess of what has been said, but only the fact of its historical appearance' (BC xvii).[2] This means looking at language as a fact, rather than in terms of what meanings or motives might be said to lie behind it. He is objective about words *and* things, taking the former also as objects, real objects which have their own existence and power vis-à-vis material objects in the ordinary sense.

The reference to 'structural analysis' is crucial. Foucault goes on to talk in terms of the 'signified' (that is, things) vis-à-vis 'signifiers' (that is, words). He is using here the jargon of what is commonly called 'structuralism', then a movement much in vogue in Paris, thus in effect declaring his allegiance to this movement. We may call this more precisely 'French structuralism', to distinguish it from other movements bearing the name of 'structuralism'; Foucault himself refused to use the term 'structuralism' to describe the French movement at all because it was already in use in Eastern Europe to refer to something else (DE3 884). This did not stop him being readily identified as a structuralist by others.

French structuralism comes out of linguistics. Its effective progenitor was the French-speaking Swiss linguist Ferdinand de Saussure, who introduced the vocabulary of 'signified' and 'signifier' in his structural linguistics.[3] His key insight was that language worked primarily as a system of signifiers, with each word deriving its meaning from its place in the system, via the differences between itself and the other words. However, Saussure's conception of the relationship between words and things was relatively conservative, seeing signifiers as relating to signifieds in a one-to-one correspondence, that is, seeing words as referring to things.

Foucault follows Saussure in advocating an analysis of a discourse itself as a system. In an earlier treatment of the *Birth of the Clinic*'s preface (Kelly 2009, 9), I read Foucault as indeed proposing to look at discourse in itself without examining the institutional context of its production. But I now think this was a misreading. He rather is arguing only against attempts to read discourses in terms of other discourses (that is, reading past discourses as true or false according to the notions of our contemporary discourses), advocating instead looking objectively at what they say and how they are produced. In this, Foucault develops his own idiosyncratic method under the influence of structuralism via Merleau-Ponty. He proposes to describe the 'conditions of possibility of medical discourse' (BC xix). This means understanding how institutional medicine has 'carved' up things to produce its discourse (BC xviii). He hopes thereby to produce 'a systematic history of discourses' (BC xvii). The *Birth of the Clinic* is not this history but it is not long in coming, appearing in 1966 in the shape of his next major work, *The Order of Things*.

ORDER AND THINGS

The French title of *The Order of Things* is 'Words and things' (*Les mots et les choses*), invoking the same basic conceptual division established in the preface to *The Birth of the Clinic*. Despite the invocation of things, however, this book is concerned almost entirely with words, to a much greater extent indeed than *Birth of the Clinic* is. Still, he maintains in principle a perspective whereby words and things are correlative.

Even without things, *The Order of Things* was enormously ambitious in its scope. He now invokes the idea that 'the fundamental codes of a culture – those governing its language, its schemas of perception, its exchanges, its techniques, its values, the hierarchy of its practices – establish for every man, from the very first, the empirical orders with which he will be dealing and within which he will be at home' (OT xxii). This amounts to the claim that the way words and things are distributed constitutes particular human cultures.

Foucault distinguishes between the cultural production governed by cultural codes and the philosophical and scientific inquiries which interrogate the being of cultural order. He suggests moreover that

> between these two regions, so distant from one another, lies a domain which, even though its role is mainly an intermediary one, is nonetheless fundamental: it is more confused, more obscure, and probably less easy to analyse. It is here that a culture, imperceptibly deviating from the empirical orders prescribed for it by its primary codes, instituting an initial separation from them, causes them to lose their original transparency, relinquishes its immediate and invisible powers, frees itself sufficiently to discover that these orders are perhaps not the only possible ones or the best ones; this culture then finds itself faced with the stark fact that there exists, below the level of its spontaneous orders, things that are in

themselves capable of being ordered, that belong to a certain unspoken order; the fact, in short, that order *exists*. As though emancipating itself to some extent from its linguistic, perceptual, and practical grids, the culture superimposed on them another kind of grid which neutralized them, which by this superimposition both revealed and excluded them at the same time, so that the culture, by this very process, came face to face with order in its primary state. (OT xxii)

Foucault seems here to be saying that there are both things and order which exist objectively beneath the contingent orders of culture, that there is a primal order in the universe which is the basis of all the orders that humans may articulate. This might seem to contradict his previous position that words and things are both based on a single division imposed on an undifferentiated reality. But Foucault did not earlier claim that the reality beneath words and things is intrinsically undifferentiated, only that the particular division we make between words and things is not found prior to the articulation of that division in language. He continues to think in terms of a certain kind of critical operation that can call the contingent cultural order into question on the basis of experience – but not perfect knowledge – of an order beneath that, which one might call 'reality'. What distinguishes Foucault from phenomenology and other more conventional forms of philosophy is that he does not believe we can know what is beneath knowledge, whereas the project of phenomenology, described by its founder Husserl as going 'back to the things', is about knowing things foundationally.

The specific object of study in *The Order of Things* is the 'human sciences'. This, Foucault notes, is an obscure area even in France (OT ix). In the English-speaking world the concept has still less currency. What unites the human sciences is their object, the human, what was until recently in English called 'man', and in French continues often to be thus gendered: *homme*, hence remains as 'man' in translations of Foucault's work. They thus include anthropology, economics, linguistics, psychology and medical biology, meaning that both *The History of Madness* and *Birth of the Clinic* had in effect been concerned with particular human sciences. The human sciences are humans' attempt to know *themselves*, by constituting humanity, or 'man', as an object of knowledge that was at the same time the subject of that same knowledge. This for Foucault instantiates in our society the 'middle region' of 'a pure experience of order', between everyday culture and philosophy, invoked in the long quotation above (OT xxiii). It is thus a privileged area for the analysis of experience.

He takes up three specific disciplines of the human sciences – biology, economics and linguistics – and traces their development from precursor disciplines, which had different names and different objects.

Like *The Birth of the Clinic*, though rather more drastically, *The Order of Things* disturbs an accepted historical story about science. The conventional view in this case is of a single, progressive 'scientific revolution' producing the modern worldview, but Foucault complicates this by pointing out the very different scientific methods which have come to the fore at different times over the last few centuries. Foucault found that the 'Classical' age's thinking was much more different from contemporary thought than is normally allowed. The differences are not explicitly formulated in what has been said, hence the ease with which the history of science has missed them. They occur rather at a level that can only be excavated by digging beneath surface layers of discourse for its structure, adding a further sense in which Foucault's method can be said to comprise an 'archaeology'.

This substrate Foucault dubs the *episteme*. An episteme consists of the differential 'rules of formation' (OT xii) for making a true statement in a particular discourse at a particular time. What Foucault shows in *The Order of Things* is that the precursor disciplines of the human sciences, and the human sciences themselves, share a common episteme between them in the period in which they occur, and that the episteme changes across all these disciplines in similar ways at similar times.

The Order of Things was a drier and more scholarly book than his previous ones, but, to Foucault's surprise, it was contemporaneously the most widely read and most controversial of any of his works. The controversy derived primarily from its conclusion. It ends by proclaiming a new shift in knowledge, which Foucault traces back to the German philosopher Friedrich Nietzsche at the end of the nineteenth century, and which he identifies as being carried forward by his French structuralist contemporaries. These thinkers depose the subject from its sovereign position, rejecting the notion of the human that guides the human sciences as such. Far from being a universal category, Foucault famously alleges, 'man is an invention of recent date. And one perhaps nearing its end' (OT 422).

The broad cultural tendency of humanism had since the Renaissance placed humans at the centre of the world, emphasising their ability to know the world, and to shape it. By suggesting that the category of the human was a limited and spent one, *The Order of Things* was seen as a landmark challenge to the progressive 'humanism' characteristic of French intellectual life, and indeed European intellectual culture more generally, including Marxism. It was as such that the book became a bestseller and brought Foucault's name to national prominence in France.

Another point of crucial controversy rather earlier in the book is his association of Marxism with an obsolete episteme: 'Marxism exists in nineteenth century thought like a fish in water: that is, it is unable to breathe anywhere else' (OT 285).

The combined rejection of humanism *and* Marxism constituted a major challenge to hegemonic views on the left and in academia. In particular, the book was taken as a challenge to the position of France's most prominent philosopher, Jean-Paul Sartre (1946; 1948), who presented his own phenomenological philosophy, 'existentialism', precisely as a variety of Marxist 'humanism'.[4] Sartre's fellow travellers were hyperbolic in denouncing *The Order of Things* and Foucault himself, which drove the sales of the book as readers clamoured to see what all the fuss was about.

This controversy was above all political, from Marxists who accused Foucault of being reactionary, attacking historical progress itself. Although *The Order of Things* is not an overtly political book, this is indeed something that made it controversial: it seems to condemn politics (that is, Marxism) in favour of an apolitical view of ideas, and it seems to denigrate the role of praxis in relation to discourse. In short, Foucault seemed to be an *idealist*, rejecting Marxist materialism in favour of a rarefied study of ideas. This is not his position, however. Foucault does not claim that ideas are independent from, or that they determine, historical events. Rather, he simply declines to speculate at all about the aetiology of changes in the history of ideas. For him, there simply was no satisfactory way of explaining how these changes were caused, so he bracketed the question of causation from consideration entirely, in order to focus simply on describing what had happened.

From a Marxist perspective, this was already in itself heresy. For Marxists, at least for most Marxists of Foucault's day, all of history must be understood from a narrowly materialist perspective, which means explaining what happens in the realm of theory from the point of view of economics and class struggle. According to the Marxist orthodoxy of the period, 'bourgeois' (i.e. non-Marxist) science was an ideological distortion in the service of the ruling class, and Marxism itself was the undiluted scientific appreciation of reality as it really is. By casting Marxism as a fundamentally outmoded form of theory, and simultaneously refusing to privilege any historical perspective, Foucault completely repudiates the theoretical armature of this Marxism.

This is not to say, however, that Foucault actually rejects every element of Marxism. He affirms that developments of discourse answer extra-discursive institutional and political imperatives. He is on the side of Marx's nineteenth-century move towards economics and away from philosophy. But he argues that there is a gap between any discourse, including Marxism or natural science, and reality, such that new forms of knowledge do not 'discover' things that were already there, so much as constitute these things as objects of knowledge (OT 375–6). One might say here that Foucault is neo-Kantian in distinguishing between real 'things in themselves' and the way we represent things in our discourse.[5] Immanuel Kant, on whose anthropology Foucault had written a secondary thesis for his doctorate, argued that human psychology required the representation of the world in terms we could understand, and thus our understanding does not correspond to the reality of the world, which is beyond our comprehension. Foucault is fundamentally in accordance with this picture, though he rejects Kant, like Marxism, for being a thought of 'finitude' in relation to the human, which is to say, for claiming that humans are limited in their capacities and can be captured definitively in an anthropological theory, at least in principle. For Foucault, unlike for such universalists, the way we understand the world varies historically, even if each historical knowledge maintains a certain relationship to extra-discursive reality. Specifically, Foucault counterposes 'things that are in themselves capable of being ordered' to the cultural ordering in which they have to be placed for human beings (OT xxii). For Foucault, innovation in knowledge comes about through the criticism of previous orderings via reference to the things that exist stubbornly beneath the order. This of course can only serve to produce a new order, which is never final.

This insight can even be applied to Foucault's methodology itself. It is often not understood, though Foucault is quick to point it out (OT xiv–xv), that archaeology is not meant to be a privileged methodology. It is rather meant to be an additional mode of approach to knowledge, adding to what is known already through more conventional forms of history and analysis (though he does make a point of rejecting phenomenology tout court – OT xv). Even as an addition, what Foucault is doing disturbs, not by showing all pre-existing views to be false, but by pointing out that what was presented as a final answer was actually only one possible way of looking at things. In *The Order of Things*, he denounces both the old dream of a complete knowledge and the newer one of a definitive knowledge of where the limits of our knowledge lie.

Foucault rejects any kind of universalism, the idea that there is a single, transcendent correct perspective on things that can be expressed in language. In this much he diverges from the stock account associated with Western thought, including Marxism. This does not mean, however, that Foucault is a historical relativist. His position is not simply, as it is sometimes imagined to be, that we are caught in the concepts of our historical era, trapped in its perspective. Rather, he thinks we can escape it, through an act of negation of our limited historical perspective. Thus Foucault is neither a universalist (advocating what he sees as the single ultimately correct perspective) nor a relativist (advocating an awareness that we are trapped within our perspective). His position may be characterised as a version of realism, since he believes a pre-linguistic reality exists, even if he does not believe in our ability to describe it. He believes we can leverage this reality to get a critical distance on our cultural perspective, though this does not imply that we can escape it entirely. We cannot simply live in the pure reality beyond words and things. What we can do is criticise any particular perspective whatsoever, including our own. We ourselves do indeed have to have a perspective, but our potential to criticise our own point of view is limitless.

The political implication of Foucault's critique of humanism in *The Order of Things*, though he does not draw this out himself explicitly until many years later, is that any attempt to produce a vision of an ideal political system, since it must be based on a constraining conception of human nature or of the operation of society, is both passé and inadequate. The latter point follows from Foucault's methodology itself: any attempt to produce a vision that adequately answers human needs is based on the false belief that it is possible adequately to represent reality. Rather, the political implication of Foucault's views is that reality will always contain a substantial remainder that has the potential to disturb any culture or society. This political implication is not stated in Foucault's works of the mid- to late 1960s, but it is certainly in line with the position he had already taken about madness and literature. While Foucault did not draw such conclusions yet, the extremely negative and political response that *The Order of Things* garnered indicates a quite immediate awareness of its implications. Foucault's diagnosis of an end to finitude implies the end of any historical certainties, along with an end to the ability to diagnose a solution to society's problems (thus indeed threatening not only Marxism but conservatism and liberalism too, that is, all traditional politics).

THE ARCHAEOLOGY OF THINGS

The controversies around the methodology of *The Order of Things* pushed Foucault to a level of introspection never before or again seen in his work. They thus led to his only book primarily about method. This book, logically enough, is the only one to wear the name of a methodology as its title: it is called *The Archaeology of Knowledge*. It was the product of another period of self-imposed exile Foucault took in the wake of *The Order of Things*, this time in Tunisia.

The Archaeology of Knowledge is Foucault's most abstract work. Its central concept is the 'statement'. Foucault uses this word to mean any actual instance of language, from which all discourses must be composed, as opposed to language qua all the possible statements that could be formulated (AK 85). Foucault now reorients archaeology through the prism of this concept.

Now, it is common enough in philosophy to break discourse into individual statements. The statement is thus the building block of discourse. But Foucault's approach goes further than just breaking down speech. There is also the matter of what makes one statement identical to another. For Foucault, even though exactly the same words are used to make a statement, it does not make it the same statement. The identity of the statement is also constituted by the medium used (written, oral, etc.), and the context in which the statement is made. This includes the institutional context of its production (AK 115).

The statement's materiality relates to that of institutions: it is based in the existence of material things, but it itself is not a spatially located object, any more than an institution is (AK 116). Discourse is seen now as a matter of concrete 'practices' (AK 51). In this he is following the thread of an 'objective' study of discourse that I previously indicated is found as early as *The Birth of the Clinic*. It seems to be something of a departure from the less concrete approach to language seen in *The Order of Things*.

Another apparent departure for Foucault in *The Archaeology of Knowledge* is the positive attitude he now expresses towards the thought of Karl Marx. He credits Marx with originating a significant change in the way history has been viewed, one which is still contemporary, towards discontinuity (AK 13–14). Foucault specifically here distinguishes Marx from Marx*ism*. He attributes to the Marxist tradition the attempt to build on the back of Marx's thought a form of historical analysis which is rather more clear-cut and traditional than Marx's own was. Thus here, unlike in *The Order of Things*, Foucault views Marxism as a distortion of Marx, rather than suffering from allegiance to Marx's nineteenth-century thinking.

That Foucault now feels the need to make such a distinction does seem to suggest a shift in his political perspective, one which can be readily explained by his experiences during the last years of the 1960s, which will be dealt with in the next chapter. While this might seem to be a dramatic turnaround from his attitude towards Marxism in *The Order of Things*, it does not actually contradict his earlier position. For one thing, one should also bear in mind that he is dealing now with the discipline of history, not of the human sciences: it is perfectly possibly for Marxism to be obsolete in the latter context while remaining relevant in the former. As he makes clear now in the *Archaeology of Knowledge*, epistemes change in different ways in different scholarly disciplines, and history's current transformation can be traced back rather further than that in the human sciences. This explains how the disjunctive picture of medicine and politics in *Birth of the Clinic* can be compatible with the apparently monolithic epistemes in *The Order of Things*: these epistemes were not really monolithic, nor do they govern the entire of culture and society, but only specific sets of discourses. He wants now to correct a misunderstanding of *The Order of Things* as implying that discourses and epistemes were monolithic, by emphasising discontinuity in history. Discontinuity is the theme of the introduction of the *Archaeology*, but he claims now that it was also the point of *The Order of Things* (the word certainly appears in that work often enough), since it highlights how suddenly knowledges can shift. He thinks that there was a prevalent misreading of that book that epistemes are stable and neat, when really they are neither.

The Archaeology of Knowledge was thus a reaction to the criticism levelled at *The Order of Things*, which for a relatively young academic such as Foucault must have been hard to bear. He begins the book by reconsidering *The Order of Things* and its reception. His more sympathetic remarks about Marx might be seen in this light, as an attempt to correct his previous dismissiveness by showing he did see value in Marx's thought.

Foucault reacts to the misunderstandings of his previous work by adopting a halting style, by which he hopes to exclude the possibility for confusion at each step (AK 19). The book culminates in a dialogue in which Foucault defends himself against various accusations made by an imaginary interlocutor.

Something particularly important that comes out in this terminal discussion is the modesty of Foucault's ambition for his project. He offers it only as one possible useful mode of analysis and, though he brackets the subject from consideration in it, he does not believe that this means that the subject does not exist, or can be abolished. He means rather only to suggest the limitations of the concept of the subject (AK 231). His archaeology diminishes the role of the sovereign subject in the production of discourse, by showing the extent to which we are governed by constraining rules we scarcely suspect exist, and the extent to which we say the same things as other people in the same discourse, no matter how original each person thinks they are being (AK 232). The point here is not though to produce a limited conception of humanity. Rather, this is what Foucault accuses humanism of doing in *The Order of Things*. He wants rather to indicate the limits of the notion of the subject, because he thinks our notions of subjectivity and humanity have served to give us peculiarly constrained conceptions of ourselves.

The political import of the view of language espoused in *The Archaeology of Knowledge* is never made explicit by Foucault, but it can be seen in work he does in the following decade. Foucault conceives of the statement as a unit of language that is repeatable, but is determined by its production and materiality, not by its meaning. Traditional views of language, including understandings of the political operation of language, focus by contrast on the meanings of words and sentences. Foucault's view allows us to understand the way language is used in politics differently, in particular what Foucault calls the 'strategic' unification of discourses which are superficially incompatible (AK 64–7). Conventionally, it is assumed in political theory, as by lay persons, that the words one utters define one's political position. From Foucault's point of view, however, it is not a matter of the inherent 'meaning' of a statement – this is something he bracketed from consideration already in *The Order of Things*. Foucault's position is not that meaning does not inhere in words, but rather that we can see new import to language by setting this aside and considering the other way in which it operates, what it does, how it combines with different elements, both linguistic and non-linguistic. This is not to say that language is without importance, subordinate to other considerations. In fact, Foucault is emphasising the importance of language as a real thing in its own right: contrary to what we might think, its reality is not exhausted by the interpretations of those who hear or even those who use it. In this way, Foucault points away from attempts to see discourse as merely the 'expression' of some deeper tendency, be it psychological, political or historical: 'Discourse must not be referred to the distant presence of the origin, but treated as and when it occurs' (AK 25). In both *The Archaeology of Knowledge* and *The Order of Things*, he rejects the search for the hidden origin, for some ultimate knowledge behind what is said. Nevertheless all kinds of contextual facts in relation to the discourse's utterance are important: who says a thing remains important, as does the place where it is said and the manner in which it is said (AK 41–2). There is clearly no meaning which is independent of context.

Literature

There is another book written by Foucault in the 1960s, which I have not thus far mentioned, and is often ignored. It was published simultaneously with *Birth of the Clinic* in 1963. It was a study of the work of the relatively obscure French avant-garde author Raymond Roussel, translated into English as *Death and the Labyrinth*. This is the only monograph of literary or artistic criticism Foucault wrote.[6] He found Roussel peculiarly interesting for at least three reasons. One of these is Roussel's technique: he was an experimental author, whose work revolved around technical games with language. This gels with Foucault's increasingly formal interest in language. Another thing that is important is the extent to which Roussel was a somewhat mad author, an eccentric who committed suicide. Lastly, we can say Foucault was attracted by the obscurity of Roussel as a figure: his work has never been well known, even in his own country. This doubtless is one reason why Foucault's book on him is not widely read.

While forays into literary criticism were common among intellectuals of his generation in France, an orientation towards literature is a key part of Foucault's specific orientation during the 1960s. This interest in literature is already palpable in the *History of Madness* in its plethora of literary examples. In *The Order of Things*, Foucault assigns a particular significance to literature's tendency to overflow, to show the way beyond the straitjacket of thinking in any particular historical period (OT 44). In this it is not dissimilar to madness itself. Foucault towards the end of his life credits theatre and literary criticism with showing him a way out of the intellectual limits of phenomenology and Marxism that had marked his thinking in his student days (DL 176).

In the 1960s, Foucault can be counted within circles where it was widely believed that literature was a genuine revolutionary force in itself. Indeed one may say that in his seemingly apolitical period in the 1960s, his radical hopes were placed in literature rather than political activism. The way in which these hopes were invested in literature may be appreciated via the concept of *transgression*. This is the subject of an extraordinary meditation on the work of the writer Georges Bataille, called 'Preface to Transgression' (EW2 69–87). 'Transgression' is a major concept in Bataille's work, and one that appears in Foucault's vocabulary relatively frequently throughout his own career. To transgress is to break the codes and taboos of a society, though Foucault, after Bataille, associates it specifically with breaking the codes of a society which, like our own, has no notion of sacred taboos (EW2 70). Transgression is significant in relation to literature because literature can transgress the boundaries that our society imposes without requiring any of the more physical activism normally associated with political activity. However, Foucault later came to doubt the radical force of literary transgression. Speaking to Roger-Pol Droit in 1975, he effectively criticises himself in relation to his earlier interest in literature, though he does not entirely repudiate it. He begins by giving a brief history of literature, outlining a trajectory by which literature went from being a classical production of the universities to being the opposite, a remainder left over outside of serious, scholarly discourse, to again become, in the form of avant-garde literature in the twentieth century, something read only by university students. He says that his work since 1970 ignores literature, dealing with it only as a historical artefact. For him this is a matter of correcting a tendency he had to some extent found himself drawn into, that of 'sacralising' literature. This is a process, which he thinks has not been studied, by which certain books and authors are sacralised as the literary canon. Foucault's interest in avant-garde writers, though tending in the opposite direction by valorising literature that broke with traditional literary conventions and called into question concepts such as the canon and the author – he specifically chose to write on Roussel because Roussel was obscure

(DL 186) – nevertheless tended in the direction of the promotion of this work as a new canon. For Foucault, the assignment of a great political importance to literature (in a broad sense, including philosophy) precisely led to its sacralisation, teaching it in schools etc., which in fact robbed it of whatever political force it had, leading to a 'political blockage' (Droit 2004, 85). This disillusionment perhaps informs Foucault's decision to assign what we might call a non-canonical status to his book on Roussel, saying of it that 'it doesn't have a place in the sequence of my books' (DL 187), though of course the book on Roussel is straightforwardly quite different from any of Foucault's other books.[7]

Foucault however distinguishes the investment in literature per se that he wants to distance himself from from the literary critics and writers who were in this crucial for his intellectual development, such as Bataille, Blanchot and Klossowski. He defines such figures as 'extra-philosophical' rather than literary, which is to say that their writing dealt with philosophical problems, albeit outside of philosophy itself and on the margins of literature (Droit 2004).

Author and Oeuvre

One of the most widely read and influential pieces of Foucault's 1960s output is the essay 'What Is an Author?', which appeared in 1969, the same year as the *Archaeology of Knowledge*. Its perspective is similar to that of the *Archaeology*. Where that book examined statements in their anonymity, this essay probes the necessity of indexing statements to a subject, the author, who makes them, pointing out the extent to which historically texts have circulated anonymously. The political import of this is to take attention away from who is saying something, just as Foucault had downplayed the question of the content of the utterance, and rather to ask how the statement functioned. This is not to say that such things are of no importance, however. Foucault is not, as is sometimes imaged, trying to abolish the notion of the author. Rather, he is simply asking critical questions about how such things are historically constituted. As he concludes by saying, 'the subject should not be entirely abandoned', but rather only deposed from its role as the sovereign source of meaning (Foucault 1998, 333).

A similar misconception arises from another essay, a 1964 piece entitled 'Madness, the Absence of an Oeuvre', in which Foucault picks up the literary dimension of *The History of Madness* immediately after *Birth of the Clinic* and the book on Raymond Roussel. The article's eponymous 'absence of oeuvre' is a concept found in the *History of Madness*, especially in its later stages. Foucault indeed defines madness in the *History of Madness* preface as 'the absence of an œuvre' (HM xxxi). We should be clear here, however, that, although this is for Foucault the 'most general form' of madness, it is not a transhistorical or transcendent definition, but rather a description of how madness appears to people who try to grasp it. What those who would study madness encounter is the absence of an oeuvre. The 'oeuvre' which is absent here might be a clear body of work *about* madness, or a body of discourse *from* the mad – it is not clear which. Perhaps it is both. Certainly, the fact that madness is not included within the narrative we have about 'the history of the world' is being referred to here (HM xxxi). Madness is then a remainder, that exceeds our historical narrative (*histoire* in French means either 'history' or just a 'story'), that is excluded from it because it does not fit into its neat, closed ordering. These points are often misunderstood by Anglophone readers owing to the foreignness of the word 'oeuvre' to us. The word has come into English exclusively to refer to the work of an author or similar artist. In French, however, it has a broader meaning, namely anything that is manufactured.

Foucault does indeed however end *The History of Madness* by indicating a moment of the inclusion of madness into the oeuvre of the West, in avant-garde art and literature. Madness actually at this point is no longer the absence of an oeuvre, but rather something with its own oeuvre. Foucault's *History of Madness* is precisely in this direction: the bringing of madness into the oeuvre.

Foucault is sometimes interpreted as being opposed to oeuvres, but he never says as much, nor does he think he was mad. Rather, as I have tried to demonstrate elsewhere (Kelly 2009), there is a great deal of deliberate cohesiveness to his body of work. His meticulousness in deciding what could and what could not appear under his name is indicative in this regard. He attempts to think about madness, not to think madly.

Conclusion

Effectively, as Foucault tries to formulate his methodology and clear up the confusions of the sprawling *History of Madness*, he spirals inwards centripetally around the question of the status of language, in closer and closer circles of methodological self-examination. This ends with an explosion, one apparently caused by extrinsic political events in 1968, rather than the logic of his thought itself. One could say that Foucault was awoken by these events, but that is not to say that he had been in a dogmatic slumber. There is little trace of self-satisfaction in Foucault's thought of the 1960s. He never ceased to probe the limits of what he was doing or his subject matter; the spiralling was driven by self-dissatisfaction. His approach to his research employed a meta-methodology, a mode of construction of books, that had self-criticism at its heart, a method calculated to produce a distance from the ideological background of received opinion that we all have. Moreover, the events of 1968 did not awaken him to problems he had never seen before, so much as bring him back to an awareness of the concrete, political reality that had previously animated him. The *History of Madness* is the key to seeing this as a *reawakening*. In this first full-scale work, we see in embryo all the concerns that would occupy him later. In the course of the 1960s, most of this disappears from view, but it returns with a vengeance in the 1970s.

Notes

1. Merleau-Ponty's best known use of these terms is in the posthumously published text *The Visible and the Invisible*. This text, however, appeared only in 1964, so presumably cannot have influenced Foucault's *Birth of the Clinic*. Merleau-Ponty already uses the same vocabulary, however, in his 1960 essay collection *Signs*.
2. Foucault was to have the word 'structural' removed from the second edition of the book, published in 1972 (Eribon, 185).
3. Foucault tells us of being introduced to Saussure's structural analysis in lectures by Merleau-Ponty (EW2 436), which helps to explain the combination of their respective concepts in the *Birth of the Clinic* preface. Foucault sees here Merleau-Ponty as leading a move in French philosophy away from phenomenology and towards structuralism.
4. The English title of this essay is *Existentialism and Humanism*, but the French original bears the more pointed title *L'existentialisme est un humanisme* (Existentialism is a humanism).
5. Foucault identifies himself as Kantian, though for rather different reasons, and somewhat less than directly (EW2 459). For a comprehensive, if tendentious, treatment of Foucault's relation to Kant, see Han 2002.
6. Two essays of Foucault's on a French artist, one each on Manet and Magritte, have been published as short books in English translation but were not published as books in French.

7. I should, for the sake of honesty, note that both of the interviews I am citing here are dubiously placed within Foucault's canon: the Droit interview was blocked from publication by Foucault, and the other interview cited here, which appears at the end of the English edition of *Death and the Labyrinth*, was extraordinarily not edited by Foucault prior to its publication. Nevertheless, I don't think it was the remarks about literature that led these interviews to have this anomalous status, and I think what they reveal is a true and unique insight.

4

Genealogy and Discipline

This chapter deals with Foucault's political turn after 1968 and the new perspectives it led him to adopt, specifically his new methodology, 'genealogy' and his first major work utilising it, *Discipline and Punish*.

Events

The Archaeology of Knowledge appeared in 1969, but he would seem to have more or less completed the manuscript by the end of 1967 (DE1 41). Certainly it seems likely the book was finished by early 1968, because things changed for Foucault in 1968 such that it is hard to imagine him writing so abstract a book during that year.

In May 1968, quite unexpectedly, there had been a student uprising in Paris, the so called Events of May. It began in protests about conditions in the universities, but tapped into a deeper well of discontent. Students fought police on barricades in the streets of Paris, masses of workers went out on strike and revolution seemed a real possibility. President Charles de Gaulle fled the country. In the end, though, substantial popular support rallied to the President, the army indicated it would back him in the event of a revolutionary seizure of power and slowly the revolt died away over the succeeding months, with the incumbent right-wing forces of order winning legislative elections in June by a landslide.

Foucault was living in Tunisia during this period, though he visited Paris for some of it, and was closely informed via phone conversations and radio broadcasts from the city when absent. He himself played down the impact the revolt had on him, however. He considered himself to have been much more affected by experiencing a much more serious, if less well known, student rebellion in Tunis already in March of the same year. The greater seriousness he imputed to this rebellion, in which many of his own students were involved, was due to the much greater stakes and more violent repression they faced. In contrast to liberal democratic France, where police fights with students were almost a kind of theatre, without fatalities, Tunisia was an authoritarian regime where dissent was illegal. Foucault's assistance to his students led to him being harassed.

Overall, I think we can see the experiences of Tunis and of Paris as complementary in politicising Foucault, with the Tunis experience providing an initial stimulus, but Paris providing additional and ongoing impetus. When Foucault returned to Paris full time late in 1968, he found himself in an environment that was intensely politicised. Though the revolution of that year had been abortive, it spawned a general climate of militancy, and repression, which bubbled away for years afterwards.

Foucault was brought to reassess Marxism by these experiences, and this perhaps did happen early enough to influence the introduction to *The Archaeology of Knowledge*. Whereas in Poland he had been disillusioned with Marxism by encountering it as an official doxa, met by most people with tired cynicism, in Tunisia Marxism was still a radical, forbidden doctrine adopted by young revolutionaries prepared to risk everything for social change (RM 135). Foucault began reading a series of Marxist militant writers he had not read previously. This began in 1967 when his Tunisian students influenced him to read Trotsky, leading him once, privately, to declare himself a Trotskyist in 1968 (DE1 39). Under the influence of his Marxist Tunisian students, during 1968, he read Marxist writers such as Rosa Luxemburg, Che Guevara (DE1 42), and the Black Panthers (DE1 44). These figures all represented rather different Marxisms from the PCF version he had rejected as a young man.

In France too, new forms of Marxism emerged as ideologies of the revolt, perhaps most prominently Maoism. Inspired by Mao Zedong's contemporaneous Cultural Revolution in China, where Mao claimed that Marxism could be encapsulated in the formula 'it is right to rebel', many young militants in France came to see Mao as representing the true spirit of Marxism, which had become corrupted in the Soviet Union and the PCF (Badiou 2005).

The overall effect during this period, as Foucault himself saw it, was that politics had come around to his pre-existing way of thinking (DE2 524). A clear example of this is that, where his work on madness was ignored by political people at the time, his concerns being seen as outrageous distractions from the serious business of working-class politics on the left, after 1968 people were suddenly intensely interested in the kind of issues of marginalised experiences that Foucault had been interested in all along. These issues entered the field of what was considered political and political parties felt obliged to take a stance on them.

Returning to Paris, partly because of the political repression in Tunis, he was offered the job of setting up the philosophy department at a new experimental university being opened at Vincennes, on the outskirts of central Paris. This new university was designed to get students away from the historic student district on the Left Bank where the Events of May had erupted. It was also designed to answer many of the grievances that had incited rage in May: students had a major stake in governance, and the curriculum was much freer in form than that of the traditional universities. Foucault put together a department almost entirely composed of young, militant Marxist philosophers, including several collaborators of Althusser (Étienne Balibar, Alain Badiou, Jacques Rancière), who would go on to be among the most prominent philosophers in their generation in France. The Marxists among the recruits represented contrary tendencies: the Trotskyist Henri Weber, the Maoist Badiou and Balibar, who, though he was part of the small intellectual opposition around Althusser, remained a member of the PCF.

One might take the recruitment of such a radical group as indicative of an incipient reconversion to Marxism on Foucault's part. While he was certainly more sympathetic to Marxism than he had been for a long time, he kept 'aloof', as he put it, from the Marxisms of the moment, however (RM 139). While many of his colleagues taught nothing but Marxism, he was teaching Nietzsche. Compared to the serious militancy he had seen in Tunis, he found Marxism in Paris a matter of middle-class students engaged in fractional bickering over matters of dogma, taking relatively minor risks with their careers and freedom, rather than risking their lives. This disdain was somewhat mutual: French leftists were suspicious of Foucault in turn. The Maoists in particular were suspicious of anyone who was even slightly less extreme than themselves, including other Marxists, let alone someone historically as anti-Marxist as Foucault.

Nevertheless, in this setting, Foucault became drawn into activism to a greater extent than had been possible in Tunisia, participating actively at the beginning of 1969 in a student occupation and physically resisting the police when they came to break it (Macey 1993, 226). A companion in this escapade was his partner Daniel Defert. The two had been involved since 1963, and Defert had been in Paris during May 1968, serving as a point of contact for Foucault with the Events.

Genealogy

His newfound militancy found reflection in Foucault's thought, though there would seem to have been some significant time lag in this. A decisive change is quite explicitly flagged by Foucault only in 1970. This theoretical shift coincided with a decisive change in his life, his election to the Collège de France. This is France's highest educational institution. Its professors are required to give an annual series of lectures detailing their work in progress. This is their sole responsibility. Foucault would do this every year but one between 1970 and his death in 1984, producing thirteen book-length courses, which are now appearing as print books, with most at the time of writing already published.

The job began with an inaugural lecture, itself published contemporaneously as a book, called in French *L'ordre du discours* (The order of discourse, which is one title under which it has appeared in English, though it has also been published as 'The Discourse on Language'; it has never been published as a book in English, possibly because of its brevity). Foucault took this opportunity to announce nothing less than a new methodology, which he called 'genealogy'.

As with 'archaeology', 'genealogy' is a word to which Foucault gives quite an eccentric meaning. 'Genealogy' of course ordinarily means tracing a person's descent, that is, their family tree. Foucault's usage of the term comes from Nietzsche, who himself used it in an eccentric way. Nietzsche's 'genealogy of morals' involved tracing how morality descends from non-moral, even immoral, motivations, that is, from a 'will to power', though Foucault instead prefers to focus on a related but often overlooked concept in Nietzsche, the 'will to knowledge' (EW2 446). Foucault proposed to do something broadly similar to Nietzsche's genealogy, a historical investigation of our contemporary society which traces the impetuses that have produced it. What distinguishes this investigation from archaeology is a broadening of his approach beyond discourses. While the analysis of discourses remains central, Foucault proposes to incorporate the analysis of institutions into his approach, analysing discourses in their relations to concrete social and political forces, to understand how they are *produced*, and what they produce in turn.

Much of what he says in 'The Order of Discourse' repeats *The Archaeology of Knowledge*, and some even *The Order of Things*. We can thus think of genealogy as incorporating archaeology within a more complete historical methodology. He retains its emphasis on discontinuity, but seeks to expand this to a correlative history of institutions. Foucault (1983) indeed remarked later that he never stopped doing archaeology.

The framework Foucault proposes for analysing the production of discourse is one of mapping the various *prohibitions* placed upon speech: what may be said, by whom, where and at what times. In this, he sees himself as returning to the problematic of his *History of Madness* a decade before, though it is true that *The Order of Things* also fits within such a project, by mapping what could be said within certain scientific discourses in different periods. Still, the focus on prohibition implies a fresh concern with the negative functioning of institutions, rather than with the positive episteme. Yet this focus on prohibition will be rejected by Foucault within a few years, and genealogy will in a more mature phase be conceived as a method that sees power as essentially productive rather than prohibitive. More indicative perhaps of the way his thinking will develop is Foucault's focus on the nebulous Nietzschean concepts of the 'will to knowledge' and 'will to truth', which cover the variable ways people have as subjects related to knowledge at different times, even if for Foucault this is here understood as a form of exclusion (OD 11).

The shift of focus of Foucault's here is unmistakeably *political*. It is indeed a *politicisation* of archaeology, investigating how discourses fit into politics and society. This is a logical enough turn in Foucault's thought in light of his recent experiences.

Importantly, Foucault in 'The Order of Discourse' invokes the concept of 'an incorporeal materialism' (OD 23). This in effect is nothing more than a new name (which he will never mention again) for what he had already done throughout his archaeological work, which was to take language as a kind of material thing, albeit one whose materiality is not purely 'corporeal', that is, not reducible to its concrete embodiment. With this concept, though, Foucault in effect takes up a position in relation to debates within Marxism around the 'base–superstructure' model. Marxist orthodoxy required the maintenance of a distinction between a material, economic base and the culture and ideology which are deemed to have been built on it. Foucault refuses any prioritisation here and, while declaring his 'materialism', a term used repeatedly by Marxism to define itself, circumvents the problem of having to subordinate ideas to matter by declaring language itself to have a materiality. He thus sidestepped problems that had bedevilled his old friend Althusser (1971), whose earlier classic treatment of ideology was marked by a tortured attempt to conform to the doctrine of base and superstructure.

While genealogy does represent a relative move towards the concrete and political, its key reference is not someone in the Marxist tradition but Nietzsche. Nietzsche's overt antipathy for socialism and sometime use by the far right (though he in point of fact himself had at least as much antipathy for nationalism as for socialism) made him an unpopular figure for the militant left. Foucault's affiliation to Nietzsche marks a continuing distance from the militant climate around him in Paris.

In an essay first published in 1971, 'Nietzsche, Genealogy, History', Foucault marks genealogy out by its difference from conventional history. By adopting the word 'genealogy' rather than 'history', he was taking a position about the nature of history itself. For traditional historians, the aim is to be impartial, which means trying to control for biases and give a single, true version of the history of whatever they are dealing with. For Foucault, this is disingenuous, because it means trying to elide the very motivation that leads them to study history in the first place. In genealogy we are trying not simply to do the history of a thing but to deliberately pick one thread, for reasons of our own particular to our present situation, to do what he will call a 'history of the present' (DP 31).

A history is a 'story' ('history' and 'story' are indeed the same word in French, *histoire*, as in many European languages – the English words both ultimately come from the same Latin root, *historia*). Foucault remarked that his works are 'fictions' (PK 193 / DE3 236). This does not mean, however, that he just makes things up. Foucault's works are not fictional in the same sense that novels are fictional. Foucauldian genealogy is still *objective*. It's just that it has an agenda which it is open about in picking up pieces of information. His historical references are at least supposed to be accurate. His point is not that his work is peculiarly unhistorical but rather to highlight the selective fiction of the exercise of writing history in general.

Foucault's archaeology had tried to bracket all these debates, to try to understand at a deep level what shifts had gone on, objectively, without the need to produce a question-begging narrative.

Foucault's first lecture series at the Collège de France, *Lectures on the Will to Know*, beginning a week after 'The Order of Discourse', saw him take quite a surprising direction. It represented an isolated foray by Foucault into ancient Greek philosophy – a period which he had not broached before and to which he would not return in earnest for a decade. The point here, indicated in the title of the series, is to investigate the Nietzschean roots of genealogy. The move back to the Greeks is a Nietzschean gesture (Nietzsche himself having begun as a scholar of classical philology), and the question Foucault now asks is what the 'will to knowledge' is that lies behind our scientific inquiries. This inquiry pushes in inevitably political directions, leading to an analysis of Greek political thought, for one thing.

So, the ball of politics has been set rolling in Foucault's thought, but does not initially have much pace. It gathered momentum quickly thereafter, however, correlatively with a deepening of Foucault's militant involvements. He from 1970 became closely associated with a Maoist group, the Gauche Proletarienne (Proletarian Left – hereafter GP). The GP was an unusual formation: though nominally dedicated to Mao, its members were extraordinarily anti-authoritarian, abandoning some Leninist practices advocated by Mao himself. This made it a natural group for Foucault to gravitate towards inasmuch as his political inclinations were relatively libertarian. The GP has moreover been described as 'the most dynamic movement on the French Far Left' at that time (Fields 1988, 87).

The GP, like many far-left groups, fell foul of government banning in the post-1968 period. The GP in particular became a cause célèbre, garnering the patronage of Jean-Paul Sartre, the most prominent public intellectual in France. Sartre assumed nominal editorship of the group's paper, La Cause du Peuple (The people's cause). The government was unwilling to arrest Sartre because of his prominence, and hence his patronage allowed the paper to keep going to a certain extent. It did not prevent hundreds of members of the group being rounded up and imprisoned, however.

Another who rallied to the cause was Foucault's partner Defert, who joined the GP in 1970 after it had been banned (Miller 1993, 186).

The association with the GP was to be very important to the trajectory of Foucault's thought in the early 1970s. The importance was not so much any direct cognitive influence: while Foucault certainly once again used Marxist vocabulary during this period, he did not use specifically Maoist concepts, except where he is brought on to this terrain in direct discussions with GP militants, for example when discussing the theme of 'popular justice'. Rather, the big influence came through his activities in support of them in relation to their imprisoned members.

In the prisons, the GP began to agitate for better conditions. They demanded 'political' status for themselves, but also became active in trying to foment discontent among prisoners more generally. It is via his association with the GP that Foucault began to take an interest in the struggle for prisoners' rights. This led in early 1971 to Foucault becoming the prime mover in the setting up of an initiative called the Groupe d'Informations sur les Prisons (Prisons Information Group – hereafter GIP). The similarity of the 'GIP' abbreviation to the 'GP' (now banned, hence referred to as the 'ex-GP') was not coincidental: the GIP was a collaborative effort between GP members and intellectuals like Foucault. Foucault quipped that the GIP stood for the insertion of the intellectuals in the GP (Defert 2004).

The GIP was an unusual proposition. Unlike the GP, it was not a direct activist organisation, trying to organise people. Rather, it operated solely as a conduit for information. Its business was to send surveys out to prisoners, to collate their responses detailing their problems and conditions, and then to release a report on this basis, before handing its role over to an organisation composed of prisoners themselves. It thus also refused the usual role intellectuals arrogate to themselves of interpreting a situation in favour simply of bringing to light first-hand testimony.

This project was begun during the time of Foucault's first lecture series at the Collège de France. By the next academic year, the prison system had become the object of Foucault's research itself, the focus of two years' lecture series, leading up to his next monograph, *Discipline and Punish*, published in 1975, which was on the prison system. Thus, from 1972, for a couple of years, for the first and only time in his life, Foucault's historical researches fused with political activism.

Discipline

Discipline and Punish then was Foucault's first full-scale genealogy, one indeed of only two books that I think can unambiguously be so categorised. These appeared in two consecutive years, 1975 and 1976. *Discipline and Punish* was the first full-length book (so not counting the very short 'Order of Discourse') Foucault had published since the *Archaeology of Knowledge*, six years before, marking a much longer publication gap than any he had left between books in the 1960s – even the four-year gap between 'The Order of Discourse' and *Discipline and Punish* was longer than any such gap since *The History of Madness*.

Discipline and Punish was in certain respects unfamiliar to readers of Foucault's earlier work. It is a historical study, dealing specifically with a period covering the eighteenth and nineteenth centuries, a period also dealt with in several of his other works to date. This approach, studying relatively recent history to show the roots of contemporary phenomena without approaching the present day too closely, is typically Foucauldian. Moreover, the specific issue of confinement was already a central issue in the *History of Madness*.

Stylistically, it begins with a jolt, however: it is certainly the most striking beginning to any of Foucault's books, and one of the most forceful beginnings to any academic work. It opens, without any preamble, with a graphic description, ranging over multiple pages, of a man being tortured to death. Foucault here sets up an extreme contrast between two different ways of punishing, one which had existed for centuries and was still being practised in the early eighteenth century, and another which came into existence only in the late eighteenth century and which is still practised today. The first is the use of violence as the paradigmatic form of punishment. Punishments were usually public, and usually corporal or capital, targeting the body. The use of imprisonment, the dungeon, locking people away, hidden, without hurting them, was highly unusual in Europe before the mid-eighteenth century. But then came a sudden change, which occurred in quick succession throughout the Western countries, in which imprisonment replaced corporal punishment as the main way of dealing with criminality. As in the cases of the treatment of madness, the development of medical techniques and the scientific knowledge of human beings, so too with punishment Foucault finds an astonishingly sudden discontinuity.

Why did this happen? Part of the answer perhaps is that the earlier forms of punishment were ineffective. Criminal justice in the early modern period was a matter of the use of exemplary violence on a small number of people who were caught, while most lawbreakers simply got away with it. There was no police force in the modern sense anywhere during this period, so the authorities tried to make up for their inability to enforce laws effectively through the extremity of their violence. This did not work, however. The arbitrariness of the system combined with the publicness of the punishment (which was required for it to have its supposed deterrent effect) was apt to make heroes and martyrs out of criminals and to stir up disorder. As Foucault notes, public executions often turned into riots (DP 61–2).

However, it would be wrong to think that our system of punishment, based around imprisonment, is much better in terms of effectiveness at discouraging criminality. Indeed, there is reason to think it is worse. This is Foucault's central concrete claim in *Discipline and Punish*, in fact. Now, ostensibly, the opposite is true. With the invention of the modern prison, the idea of punishing is complemented by new ideas about deterrence and rehabilitation. The prison is supposed to be a 'house of correction', where individuals go after committing crimes for a period of time to 'learn their lesson', before coming out as reformed individuals. The problem is that, consistently since the birth of the prison, what has actually happened in prisons has been more or less the exact opposite of this. It became manifest almost immediately: people who come out of prison are predisposed to nothing so much as committing more crimes and going back to prison. The prison does nothing to equip someone to live a non-criminal life in society. It rather simply serves to acclimatise people to prison and make them relatively incapable of living in the free world outside its walls. For Foucault, prison ultimately has the objective function of constituting a social layer of criminal delinquents, of providing the infrastructure to bring into existence a new social layer made up of criminal recidivists. That is, put simply, *prisons cause criminality* (DP 265ff.). The facts of this are incontestable, the correlation between imprisonment and subsequent criminality being so well attested, evident from the earliest days of mass imprisonment. And yet these facts have not been faced up to by our society.

The normal way of dealing with these facts is to say that prisons need to be made better. Foucault is scathing about this discourse of prison reform. He points out that this prison reform discourse has been around as long as prisons themselves. That is, as long as there have been prisons, there have been people with schemes for making they them work properly. This leads Foucault to conclude that the discourse of prison reform is not opposed to, but part of, the failed 'carceral' system. That is, schemes for the perfect operation of the prison have always been the basis for the operation of actual prisons. The initial impetus for mass imprisonment involved ideas of the moral perfectibility of humans through institutional interventions. All modern imprisonment is thus a consequence of the urge to reform. The way the ideal scheme of prison operation works is as an excuse for the real prison which never lives up to that scheme in practice.[1]

The prison assuredly does not serve a need to reduce criminality, then, though it is certainly supported by a *desire* to do so, since most people continue to believe that imprisonment will prevent crime, and this popular belief is necessary for the prison system to continue. There is here an important disjuncture between perception and reality. A hallmark of Foucault's genealogical approach is to reveal this disparity. While the bare facts about the ineffectiveness of prisons at reducing criminality are well attested, it is essential to grasp that Foucault is here revealing effects that occur even without anyone explicitly intending them to. In this case, no one actually intends to create a subculture of criminal recidivists. The criminals themselves do not: they simply commit crimes from personal motivations. The prison guards are simply doing a job. The political leaders who preside over the system are largely genuinely concerned to try to deal with crime, or at least placate voters who want crime dealt with. Yet the net effect of all these people interacting together is to produce a system for generating criminal recidivism.

Why then did this occur? The invention of the prison must be understood as part of a larger social-political shift. This is where the 'discipline' of *Discipline and Punish* comes in. The prison was in effect the application of the invention of something much more general, what Foucault calls 'discipline', which quickly transformed all the social institutions of the West over a couple of centuries.

Discipline is a way of dealing with bodies in space. This sounds like a very general idea, but it is none the less something quite historically novel. A key example given by Foucault of how discipline changes things is the military, in the passage from medieval to modern warfare, spurred in particular by the adoption of firearms. In the Middle Ages warfare was conducted in a relatively disorganised way. While troops were organised into blocks based on type, with foot soldiers, archers and knights fighting in distinct groups, organisation within these groups was relatively lax.

Guns changed things, particularly once relatively rapid fire became possible. Effective use of muzzle-loading firearms required co-ordination, in particular the invention of line infantry, utilising the technique by which soldiers were lined up such that one line could crouch and reload while the line behind them fired over their heads. This, however, required a kind of co-ordination of bodily movement and placement that had not previously been necessary: large numbers of soldiers had to do exactly the same thing at the same time. Moreover, the military efficacy of the rifleman could be greatly increased by teaching him the precise movements required to maximise the rate of fire. Every single physical movement that he made was now a matter of a prescriptive method that he was to be taught.

We should not exaggerate the extent of the novelty here. Disciplinary techniques of this type, governing the movement of individuals, had been around for millennia, for example 'in monasteries, armies, workshops', as Foucault noted (DP 137). What happens at this time is not the invention of discipline per se but a mutation in its application, by which a quite sudden impetus arises to try to maximise efficiency across a range of fields of human activity. Still, as Foucault points out, the spread was uneven, sometimes rapidly moving from one area to another, sometimes very gradual and subtle (DP 138).

In this way, disciplinary institutions were established in which bodies are arranged in precise ways. These are familiar to us; indeed our society is largely composed of such institutions: the school, the hospital, the factory, the office, the barracks, the prison; all of these involve the arrangement of individual bodies in particular positions to allow for precise activities of (or upon) those bodies. The atom which is produced in all these systems is what Foucault calls 'the docile body'. We must be reduced to bodies that are pliable, tame. This happens to us early on in educational institutions. Once broken in this way, we are then ready for insertion into other disciplinary institutions, which operate on similar principles, throughout the rest of our life, as workers, and finally, perhaps, as retired people in nursing homes. Although all of these institutions seem absolutely natural to us now, and although they all had predecessors before late modernity, as mass disciplinary institutions in their contemporary form they are mostly innovations of the late eighteenth and nineteenth centuries. Schools, for example, have existed for millennia, but the kind of schools we are used to, with classes organised by precise age groups, with pupils sitting in regimented rows, have not: schools in the past were smaller and less formal institutions, which only a small minority of people ever passed through.

This transformation relates closely to the contemporaneous industrial revolution. Modern factory production is disciplinary to the core, involving the precise distribution of workers, and the control of their activities. One might think that discipline could be characterised as serving an economic imperative, specifically that of the capitalist class's drive for profits. Foucault certainly does allow that such economic motives do exist and drive the application of discipline. He cites the Marxist treatment of imprisonment from a predictably economistic point of view by Rusche and Kirchheimer, *Punishment and Social Structures*, as the landmark reference in the area for *Discipline and Punish* (DP 24). However, the technical necessities for discipline must exist for it to be applied at all, and these are not simply produced by capital (cf. DP 162–3). Disciplinary techniques are adopted 'in response to particular needs' that emerge historically (DP 138), but there could have been no industrial revolution without these techniques: it is perhaps more a matter of the two coinciding to produce industrialisation than one causing the other. Here, Marxism falls down, and Foucault outflanks it in his materialism. He is talking here about something Marxists have not recognised, what he calls 'political technologies', which are as potent as industrial technologies in changing society. Like any other technology, political technologies relate to things, but circulate as sets of ideas for the production of things. Of course, the stock in trade of political technology is human bodies rather than manufactured goods.

Political technology is hardly indifferent to concrete materiality, however. For example, architecture, both qua technique and qua built environment, is key to the disciplinary reorganisation of bodies. The arrangement of bodies in space is achieved in part by structuring space itself. Great attention was paid to architectural questions during this crucial period of transformation. Even the home, which one might not think of as a disciplinary institution, was transformed during this time: for the first time in history, in the nineteenth century ordinary people's homes were subdivided into rooms with specialised functions, something previously commonly found only in the homes of the wealthy. Previously the poor had lived and slept together indifferently in undivided spaces. This in the nineteenth century came to be seen as a moral scandal, this mixture of ages, and sexes, often all sleeping in a single communal bed. Indeed, it is not going too far to see the family as transformed into a disciplinarised institution during this period, in which each individual has their precisely defined place.

In relation to the prison, architecture is particularly vital, and an exploration of prison architecture is perhaps the best-known figure of *Discipline and Punish*, or even of Foucault's entire body of work. The architectural figure in question is that of the *panopticon*. 'Panopticon' implies universal visibility, and was the name given by the British philosopher and social reformer Jeremy Bentham to his design for an ideal prison. This design involved a central guard tower surrounded by a ring of cells, stacked one on top of another, with windows providing back lighting. In each cell there would be a single prisoner. The main purpose of this design was to allow the guard to see all the prisoners. The guard, indeed, was to be invisible to the prisoners, such that the prisoners could not know whether they were being watched, but would always have to assume that they were under surveillance and act accordingly.

The Panopticon was never built exactly as Bentham envisaged it, but it was immensely influential on real-world prison design, such that some prisons, in various parts of the world, have very closely resembled it. Foucault takes this figure as emblematic of a much wider and older effect, which Foucault calls 'panopticism'. This thesis has been taken as a precursor of more recent work on the so-called 'surveillance society' of today, where everyone is watched, with CCTV turning the streets into a panoptic space, and the internet putting a greater portion of our lives in a forum that is easily monitored invisibly. Certainly, Foucault's idea is that surveillance is an important aspect of disciplinary institutions: the original French title of *Discipline and Punish* is *Surveiller et punir*; while the last word of the title means the same thing in both languages, *surveiller* does not mean 'discipline', but rather is the French verb from which our word 'surveillance' is derived.

For Foucault, panopticism, rather like the great confinement he details in *The History of Madness*, originates in medieval practices of disease control. Imprisonment partakes of both genealogies. On the one hand, as detailed in the earlier book, the technique of confinement grew up around leprosy in particular, as a way of quarantining lepers and ostensibly protecting the healthy from their disease. The leper houses were thus the forerunners of the insane asylums. Panopticism, on the other hand, first emerged not with leprosy but with a different disease, the plague. Plague was much more contagious than leprosy. It spread rapidly through settlements, infecting people who either died or recovered within a relatively short time. It thus could not be dealt with by quarantining people for life. It required rather an immediate micro-management of people, spaces, and movement within a settlement to control the spread of infection once it had appeared.

CRITICISM OF DISCIPLINE AND PUNISH

I wish to focus here on a particularly biting and sensitive critique of *Discipline and Punish* by C. Fred Alford (2000). The focus of Alford's criticism is the figure of the panopticon in relation to the prison. Alford brings into question both Foucault's conclusions and his methodology. The centre of Alford's critique is his own direct experience of the American prison system. Alford notes that, in rare instances, there is an element of panopticism in the design of US prisons, but feels that there is nowhere the intense disciplinary surveillance that Foucault talks about. Rather, prisoners are largely left to their own devices by indifferent warders. Alford goes on to argue that Foucault has mistaken the archival texts he has read in which ideal schemes for prisons are propounded for the reality of prisons themselves.

I do not know how intentional this is on Alford's part, but his critique seems quite Marxist in complexion. It largely amounts to an accusation of idealism of the type that Marxists levelled at Foucault's archaeological work, and goes so far as to accuse him of confusing the material 'base' reality of the prison with its 'ideological superstructure', mistaking the latter for the former (Alford 2000, 124). Alford can surely not be unaware of the resonances here, of the challenge to Foucault's project of moving beyond this base–superstructure distinction and the concomitant concept of ideology.

Now, where with Foucault's archaeological work one can exculpate him from such criticism by pointing to his deliberate bracketing of the concrete from what is essentially an inquiry at the level of ideas, this is not a possible defence in the case of his genealogies. Foucault quite deliberately sets out in *Discipline and Punish* to 'analyse rather the "concrete systems of punishment", study them as social phenomena' (DP 24). Indeed, his methodology is quite different from the high archaeology of *The Order of Things*: he cites facts and figures in support of his argument (e.g. DP 266). The accusation of Alford's that Foucault's researches do not match empirical reality might seem quite devastating then, although Alford himself allows that the problem he thinks he identifies really only pertains specifically to the understanding of the institution of the prison and that Foucault's analysis of discipline retains some usefulness.

I think Alford's criticisms fall flat for at least two reasons, however. The first problem is the locus of Alford's evidence, namely America in the recent past. While he is careful correctly to note the relevance of American research to *Discipline and Punish*, he fails to note the temporal disjuncture between Foucault's research on the nineteenth-century prison and his own experiences well over a century later. That is, there is no consideration that prisons might have functioned differently in the past. And there is some reason to think they might have, not least because of the great changes in incarceration in the United States in recent decades, with massive privatisation of prisons, and enormous growth in the rate of incarceration to the point where nearly 1 per cent of Americans are imprisoned. These changes might well change the way that prisons are run in the direction of a cheaper and more laissez-faire attitude by prison authorities.

Something else needs to be pointed out here, moreover, which is the extent to which these conditions are not so much unprecedented as anachronistic. Prisons have been considerably more laissez-faire in the past. One per cent was the incarceration rate seen in the Parisian Great Confinement, which was a historic case of a largely undifferentiated incarceration of all kinds of people without due process or close monitoring.

So, is it the case that Foucault's picture of panoptic imprisonment was valid for a period but has now ceased to operate in the United States? Actually, my point is that there has always in prisons been an uneasy compromise between the laxity of simply confining people and the attempt to control them individually. Prison reform, the ideal schemes of men like Bentham, in effect comprise one side of a see-saw which moves backwards and forwards. I do not believe Foucault ever meant to imply otherwise. He does not claim that the prison is a perfect panopticon, only that discipline is one technology in operation in modern prisons (unlike in earlier dungeons), as in all contemporary social institutions. This is what Alford himself concludes, believing wrongly that this constitutes a major correction to Foucault's idealism.

Abnormal

In the prison, one sees a combination of both confinement and micro-management, though brought together to deal with the problem of criminality. But panopticism, the heritage of plague management, is in late modernity not specifically about criminality, but a broader category that includes both the criminal and the sick, namely the *abnormal*. Since the nineteenth century, the social body has been widely monitored for signs of both ill-health (physical, mental or moral) and criminality.

After focusing on the prison for a couple of years, Foucault's researches moved on to these broader questions. The GIP was effectively wound up late in 1972 (Macey 1993, 288), and Foucault's lectures on prison questions ended early in 1973. The first draft of *Discipline and Punish* was completed at around the same time (DE1 58). Foucault then took up a different research object, though by no means a new one: his lecture series of the winter of 1973–4 was entitled *Psychiatric Power*. This series takes up where the *History of Madness* had left off chronologically, applying the new genealogical method. However, the development of psychiatry can be seen in the new context as of a piece with the development of discipline. This is made clear in *Discipline and Punish*, and in his lecture series of 1975 (the same year that *Discipline and Punish* appears), *Abnormal*, which combines his older concern with mental and medical pathology with newer focuses on criminality and sexual perversion.

There is indeed considerable overlap between the two lecture series of 1973–4 and 1975, *Psychiatric Power* and *Abnormal*, and *Discipline and Punish*. Quite whether this is a matter of Foucault expanding on material from a book already written in lectures, or incorporating material from his fresh researches in the final draft of the book, is not important. What can be presumed, since Foucault never intended the lecture series to be published, is that whatever is most important in these lectures made its way either into *Discipline and Punish* or into the first volume of Foucault's *History of Sexuality*, which appeared only the following year.

Foucault makes clear across these various sources that the move towards mass, systematic imprisonment is inseparable from the rise of the discourse of psychology, and that of medical psychiatry. On the one hand, psychiatrists are brought into the judicial process from the nineteenth century to determine whether an accused person was compos mentis. They were made responsible in effect for deciding whether people were to be sent to prison or to a different disciplinary institution, the asylum (DP 22). Thus, people are segregated between criminally culpable and morally insane (DP 19).

On the other hand, psychology was deeply involved in the prison system. Despite this segregation of criminal from mad, in both cases psychology inserts itself by promising to search for a 'cure'. Where punishment had previously been a solely moral and political concern, it now becomes a scientific one. Prisoners must be categorised not only by their crimes but according to their personalities and possibilities for rehabilitation. Somewhat eccentrically, Foucault refers to this problematic in *Discipline and Punish* using the word 'soul'. The background to this usage is the early modern distinction between body and soul, which was later displaced by the more contemporary distinction between body and mind. 'Soul' and 'mind' are both possible translations of the Greek *psyche*, which is the object of study that gives us the word 'psychology'. Foucault's point is that where punishment had previously focused on the body, had been corporal, with the emergence of discipline it comes to focus on the psyche instead. This is not to say that it seeks to punish the psyche, to inflict psychological torture, so much as to change, to reform the psyche. While punishment remains focused on the body in a practical way, since discipline is indeed primarily about arranging the body, the soul none the less becomes the new target of punishment. The psyche is not merely targeted but actually *produced* in this process. While the soul is not new per se, Foucault argues that a new soul is created at this time, different from the previous, Christian soul. In Christianity, there was a soul 'born in sin and subject to punishment' (DP 29). The new soul 'is born rather out of methods of punishment, supervision and constraint' (DP 29).

One must be careful to understand what Foucault is saying here. The belief of those who invented disciplinary techniques was presumably that there already existed a soul that they targeted – particularly since many of the pioneers of the prison system were deeply religious. For Foucault, this unwittingly produced a real thing called the soul. But the soul that was produced was not what the people involved thought a 'soul' was. It was 'not a substance' (DP 29) – Foucault is not, in invoking the soul, implying that there really exists what is ordinarily connoted by this word, which is to say a spiritual essence of the human being that exists independently of the body. It is actually rather unclear exactly what it is for Foucault; he calls it an 'element' upon which power and knowledge have effects, and which is the basis for the construction of subsequent concepts of psychology: 'psyche, subjectivity, personality, consciousness, etc.' (DP 29–30). The soul for Foucault is less substantial than it was considered by dualist metaphysics, but it is not merely an ideological illusion that we can forget about either: it is a historical reality, one that has become an actual part of what we are. The rub here for Foucault is that our demands for freedom are articulated on behalf of a soulful individual produced by discipline, and therefore inadequate in so far as they fail to address this production. Foucault has a different agenda, in effect to demand the liberation of the body from the soul – at least, this is the obvious implication of his claim that 'the soul is the prison of the body' (DP 30). Interestingly he suggests also that the soul provided a base for humanism, indicating a continuity with the critical target of *The Order of Things*, with the soul now standing in for 'man'.

Note

1. We should perhaps here distinguish between the consistent calls for prison reform that we have heard for hundreds of years now – calls to end overcrowding, to improve rehabilitation, to respect the inmates, to segregate inmates more effectively from one another – from genuinely new trends in imprisonment. I have in mind here the contemporary Norwegian model in which imprisonment is made as similar to life outside prison as possible, and the boundaries between prison and the outside made as porous and gradual as possible, with enormous support given to prisoners to ensure a successful transition to freedom. This relative indistinction between prison and its outside is not typical of historic prison reform, which indeed has often made a point of demanding prisons be made into highly distinctive spaces.

5

Power and Resistance

This chapter is the heart of this book. It deals with Foucault's account of power. After briefly contextualising this account, we first deal with the account itself, before exploring the consequences of the account for political action.

Power

CONTEXT

In the previous chapter, I dealt with *Discipline and Punish* at varying levels of specificity: at its most specific, its historical analysis of the carceral system; less specifically, the techniques and social forms associated with discipline. There is a higher level of generality at work here, though it is not made explicit in this work; it emerges into the full light of day only with the first volume of the *History of Sexuality* the following year, and even then in a rather unprepossessing garb. This more general concept is that of *power*.

While power is not thematised as a concept in *Discipline and Punish*, it is a word that Foucault makes free use of there, and its implicit significance is such that Foucault would later conclude that his genealogical project in the 1970s did not fulfil its early ambition of providing a history of the will to knowledge, but rather amounted only to 'a history of power' (RM 145). Between roughly 1972 and 1978, peaking in the middle of this period, power became Foucault's central preoccupation. This can be clearly seen from public remarks of Foucault's going back as early as 1971 (Kelly 2009, 32). It is the theme on which he begins his lectures on *Psychiatric Power* in 1973. Though he does not discuss it explicitly in *Discipline and Punish*, he does much here to hone his views of it. Discipline will later be understood as one form of power, but for now Foucault characterises discipline in ways that will be taken later to be general characteristics of power itself (DP 26–7). While there are other treatments of power by Foucault during this period – such as at the beginning of his 1976

Collège lectures, *Society Must Be Defended*, and in a 1977 interview, 'Powers and Strategies' (PK 142) – by far the most comprehensive single account he ever gives of power appears in the first volume of his *History of Sexuality*.

This is the unprepossessing appearance I spoke of above. It is entirely without fanfare. There is nothing earlier in the book, in the title of the book or in its table of contents to indicate it is coming. It appears at the beginning of the second half of the book, in two cryptically titled chapters, called simply 'Objective' and 'Method' in the English edition. Foucault's claims for his views when they appear are extraordinarily modest. Ostensibly, he introduces his account of power as a methodological manoeuvre in his attempt to give an account of the history of sexuality in the nineteenth century (with which account we will deal in the next chapter). But it clearly greatly exceeds that purpose, as a sledgehammer does the cracking of a nut. It had been formulated by Foucault over many years, not specifically for this purpose, but in order to correct a deficit in contemporary understandings of politics.

He begins his treatment of power in the first volume of the *History of Sexuality* logically enough by criticising all previous attempts to analyse power. Indeed, he actually criticises not so much previous attempts to think about power as all previous attempts to think about politics for failing to appreciate the dimension of power. What could be more fundamental to understanding politics than power? Yet, no one in the history of political thought has paid it adequate attention. Political thought has primarily concerned itself with the state and law, asking questions of legitimacy and justice, that is, of what the state and law should be like. It does not ask about the more general phenomenon of which the state is merely one instance, which is to say, power. When it does pose the question of power, political thought usually does so in a way that is artificially constrained within the horizons of state and legality. Foucault, in relation to this established horizon of political thought, is launching a conceptual revolution, though one completely without fanfare.

At base, as Foucault sees it, the problem with existing conceptions of power is their essential negativity. That is, power is taken as essentially negative, as repressive, constraining. The state and the law are seen as primarily constraining institutions, and such constraints taken as the model for all power. While conventional views of power allow that power exists in other places than just the state – in institutions and families, for example – it understands all power as part of a single structure and operating on the same model. This single model of social power is 'hierarchical'. It sees power as pyramidal, flowing from a single apex: a sovereign, a king, a president. The power of the boss, of the father in the family, is seen as simply replication of this sovereign power at a micro-level, and indeed part of a single hierarchical pyramid supporting the power of the great boss, the great father at the top.

The law is itself something specific for Foucault. It is no more reducible to power than power is to law, but power is clearly the more primitive and more important of the two, lurking always behind the superficial way in which power relations are encoded in the law. The law tells us who has a right to do what to whom. But power extends well beyond that: all kinds of people have all kinds of ways of influencing others that are not acknowledged in the law.

DISCOURSE, KNOWLEDGE AND POWER

It is useful, not least because it shows the political stakes and usefulness of Foucault's 1960s work covered in Chapter 3 above, to understand how Foucault's cogitations on power relate to his earlier ones on discourse and language, and how the two thematics come together in a new concern with knowledge.

Discourses are understood by Foucault as structures that emerge in response to a variety of historical pressures, but cannot simply be reduced to that response – there is more to them than that. They are specific in their importance, and relatively autonomous in relation to other social forces and in relation to any individuals. Discourse had previously been thought of as the production of sovereign human consciousness. Foucault tries to understand it otherwise. As Foucault's approach in *The Order of Things* implies, while discourses may seem to be founded by individual persons, the biggest shifts in knowledge occur as it were in the background without an author. Even if Foucault (1988) does admit that certain authors like Marx and Freud inaugurate new discursive possibilities, knowledge has a particular dynamics and influence of its own, not reducible to economics, politics, society, or to individual authors. This means that it influences economics, politics, society, culture, just as they influence it in turn. Foucault now essentially says exactly the same things of power that he said then of discourse. It is relatively autonomous, and not reducible to the actors that produce it.

Foucault actively incorporates his concern with discourse into his concern with power, moreover, introducing a hybrid concept of 'power-knowledge' to indicate that the two are frequently almost synonymous. This concept allows us readily to imagine the political implications of some of his earlier cogitations regarding knowledge. Note that the point here is not, as it sometimes seems to be misread, simply to imply that 'knowledge is power'; rather, 'power-knowledge' implies the opposite, that power and knowledge are on an equal footing as specific, similar, related, but ultimately always distinct things.

STRUCTURE

What is power, if not negative and hierarchically organised? The answer can only be that it is positive and non-hierarchical. But what can this mean? Foucault's positive account of power follows a pattern already established in his earlier attempts to understand discourse. Though he does not himself make this link explicitly, his archaeological position in relation to discourse both resembles and intersects with his position in relation to power.

Foucault is shy in presenting his positive account, putting it forward only as a tool, a 'method', for doing the history of sexuality, defeasible in relation to the data he may later find. He is tentative as to its scope, moreover, refusing ever to describe anything he puts forward during his career as a 'theory' of power. As we have said, however, what he gives us emerges all but complete, since it almost entirely follows from the basic insight of looking at an ensemble of relations in their specific autonomous interrelationships. This insight gives us what we have already dealt with, the dismissal of traditional state-centred accounts of power, with their reference to sovereign subjects as the holders of power, with their centripetal structuring. The new paradigm is the decentred network.

Key here is the idea that power is not a substance but a *relation*. Though this relationality is not something that is much emphasised in Foucault's earlier archaeologies, it is straight out of the French structuralist playbook. Foucault at his most structuralist, in an interview immediately after *The Order of Things*, characterises both his project and that of his 'French structuralist' contemporaries as a search for 'an ensemble of relations which is maintained and transformed independently of the things that bind these relations' (DE1 514). If French structuralism has a single core idea, it is that structures are systems of differences, composed by the relationships between the elements more than the elements themselves. When it comes to discourses, then, it is not so much what is said but how the things that are said interrelate. Foucault defines power in turn precisely as a functioning in a 'system of differences' (PP 4). Power for Foucault is entirely relational. He claimed that his usage of the term 'power' was only ever a 'shorthand' for the fuller term, 'power relations' (EW3 291).

Foucault's alternative conceptualisation of power closely follows the model he adopted for understanding discourse in his high archaeological period. Principally, he follows a method similar to that of *The Order of Things*, seeking to understand how formations come together. Other aspects of his approach to power are more analogous to the *Archaeology of Knowledge*, with Foucault looking at repeatable materialities composing power, analogous to statements. Indeed, the two approaches by this stage are melded into one: there is no attempt, as in *The Order of Things*, to simply map formations without trying to deal with the materialities that compose them. Moreover, unlike his treatment of discourse in these earlier works, Foucault does not attempt to study power in splendid isolation. Rather, he studies it in all its complex interrelations with other types of relation, principal among which is discourse/ knowledge.

In a sense, then, Foucault's analysis of power is off-the-peg. It did not simply spring from the deep well of his great and profound genius – but then Foucault would never claim any such thing; it would be quite at odds with his whole perspective. In fact, *The Order of Things* implies that radically new perspectives essentially come about precisely through the application of new paradigms across a range of different discursive contexts. Foucault casts himself there self-consciously as a partisan of a new, anti-humanist episteme that he conceptualises in terms of looking at the autonomous ensemble of self-organising relations. Though Foucault does not talk in such terms in the 1970s, that does not mean it is no longer so.

It is not so much the model he applies that is the radical choice then but the choice of power as the phenomenon to apply it to. This choice is radical in the literal sense that it goes to the most fundamental problematic imaginable, beneath the more superficial problematics with which contemporary political thought was, and continues to be obsessed, problems of the state and its laws: sovereignty, legitimacy, democracy, equality. Doubtless, Foucault was primed conceptually to make this leap to power by his repeated reading of Nietzsche, for whom power is nothing if not a central theme. But Foucault credits the primary influence in his discovery of power as the experience of historical events themselves, of revolt in Tunis and Paris, which he saw retrospectively as producing something akin to a chemical reaction, producing the concept of 'power' in his mind (EW3 329). We may say that what it reacted with to produce this concept however were his theoretical influences, 'French structuralism' and Nietzsche.

That it should have emerged only in Foucault's thought, rather than in any of innumerable other French minds of the time, can be explained I think by reference to the combination of Foucault's interest in politics with his lack of adherence to any dogma. The political structuralists, principally Althusser, were generally committed Marxists, hence hidebound by a perspective that prevented all-out conceptual innovation, constrained as they were to think in familiar terms of economy, state, ideology. Most structuralists were simply not that political, for instance the anthropologist Claude Lévi-Strauss, or the literary critic and sometime companion of Foucault's, Roland Barthes. Another prominent 'structuralist', the psychoanalyst Jacques Lacan, was himself almost aggressively apolitical. His followers, like his son-in-law, Foucault's Vincennes colleague Jacques-Alain Miller, were often politically inclined, but they were like Althusser constrained by dogma, albeit in their case based on Freud and Lacan rather than Marx. Not coincidentally, Lacan's position comes in for some lightly veiled criticism in Foucault's *Will to Knowledge* chapter on power, with Foucault lambasting psychoanalysis for conceptualising things only in terms of the law. Though he names only psychoanalysis and not Lacan, it is the Lacanian psychoanalysts who particularly focus on the importance of the unconscious 'law' in the formation of the psyche.

Thus, where Foucault had previously, in *The Order of Things* and the *Archaeology*, been able to situate himself within a movement, French structuralism in the first instance and (French) historiography in the second, when it comes to political theory, he found himself on his own out on the leading edge. Foucault bemoans the fact that no one has thought to do what he was doing when he says that 'in political thought and analysis, we still have not cut off the head of the king' (HS1 88–9). The allusion here is to the decapitation of King Louis XVI in the French Revolution at the end of the eighteenth century. The imputation is that, while we have been able to dispense with monarchy in practice, we retain a conception of power that is as hierarchical as ever. Political theory, it would seem, lags behind fields such as anthropology, linguistics, psychoanalysis and history. But this is not so much a problem of political theory as a discipline, as it is for Foucault a problem of inadequate thinking about politics infecting all contemporary thought.

CONCATENATION

The relationality of power implies that power is not something that can belong to an individual. Rather, it takes place *between* individuals. The relationship of individuals to power we will deal with in due course. The point is for Foucault that power is primarily something relatively autonomous, which goes on in the interstices between individuals. Power thus has a kind of life of its own. This life of power is encapsulated by Foucault in his use of the word 'strategy'. Power has its own 'strategies'. What this implies, Foucault puts in confronting terms by saying that power is 'both intentional and nonsubjective' (HS1 94). Here, Foucault treads a tightrope. On the one hand, he is careful not to make power into an agent in its own right, some political demiurge with its own intelligence capable of tricking people. It is to avoid such a metaphysics of power that he stresses that power is 'nonsubjective'. Conversely, however, he wants to say that power does have a kind of *logic* of its own, does have discernible modes of operation, targets, even aims. For this reason, he says it is 'intentional'. In making this distinction, Foucault flies in the face of received philosophical wisdom, by which intentionality and subjectivity are synonymous: ordinarily, intentions are said to be the province of subjects who intend things. For Foucault, what happens in power is precisely the detachment of subjectivity from intentionality. On the one hand, it is a phenomenon with its own intentionality that lacks subjectivity. On the other, power is the running on of *our* intentions beyond our subjectivity. We intend things, but the things we intend take on a life of their own in the relational space in between individual subjects.

These claims are of course confusing and require further explanation. We already have at our disposal a perfect concrete case of this effect from *Discipline and Punish*. How does the prison system operate? Certainly, it involves subjects and their intentions, indeed a wide array of subjects and intentions. It involves criminals and their diverse motives for their crimes. It involves judges and their intentions, for example to punish. It involves guards and their intentions, for example to maintain an orderly prison. It involves politicians and bureaucrats and their intentions, for example to reduce the crime rate. Power happens where all these intentions intermingle and interact, in the space beyond their subjective intenders. The mechanism by which this occurs, to use a word Foucault does not, is the *concatenation* of power relations (HS1 93).[1] This much can already be found in Nietzsche, as Foucault would surely have been aware: 'My idea is that every specific body strives to become master over all space and to extend its force (its will to power) and to thrust back all that resists its extension. But it continually encounters similar efforts on the part of other bodies and ends by coming to an arrangement ("union") with those of them that are sufficiently related to it: thus they then conspire together for power. And the process goes on' (Nietzsche 1968, §636). Power is a matter of minor power relations, distributed throughout the social body, found everywhere where people interact, meeting one another and producing new and unexpected combinations. It is important here to note what Foucault calls the 'tactical polyvalence' of relations (HS1 100). He actually uses this term in relation to discourses, but as we will see it can be said also to apply to power by that token. 'Tactical polyvalence' means that things can combine with one another in many difference ways for tactical reasons. In the case of discourse, it means that apparently opposing ideas can none the less complement one another within a strategy of power, such as the discourses of prison reformers and those who advocate harsher punishments. We can say something similar about apparently opposing power relations.

Thus, a coherent strategy of power which is quite different from any of the subjective intentions feeding into it is produced. No one involved can have been said to intend to produce a device that would regularly produce a class of criminal recidivists. Many of those involved explicitly intend to combat criminality. For Foucault, the point is to take up 'the viewpoint of the objective', rather than the point of view of the law which says how things are supposed to work (HS1 102). This means both not assuming that anything, including the law, actually operates the way the law says it should, and also more broadly that there is no guarantee that the way things work corresponds to what anybody involved at any level intends, nor that anybody involved necessarily explicitly understands what is happening.

WAR GAMES

This is not to imply, however, that power is a kind of static structure. Indeed, the implication is precisely the opposite: since all the people's actions and intentions which constitute the strategies of power are themselves constantly changing, so too are the strategies of power themselves. One critical reading of Foucault, that of Jürgen Habermas (1987), is that Foucault is a social 'functionalist'. This is to say that Foucault is alleged to see society as like a machine in which each part plays its own 'function'. Hence, in the social totality, the prison system would function to produce criminality. Now, Foucault does use the term 'function' in precisely this context. However, this is a loose way of speaking: Foucault never problematises or thematises the notion of function. We can talk about the prison system as having the *effective* function of producing criminality. This functioning of prisons is essentially accidental, however, even if it is regularly reproduced. While such social effects have considerable inertia, for Foucault they are prone to rapid and unpredictable change. He moreover explicitly distances himself from functionalism, arguing that his model is strategy, not function (STP 119–20).

For Foucault there is no such thing in the real world as stability in absolute terms. Stability is a superficial and temporary phenomenon, a relative stability only within the maelstrom of reality. Systems then are not stable, but rather processes, things already changing, moving targets for analysis. For Foucault, to use an analogy from mechanics, we should be looking at the motion of power relations, not their position. Power relations, being relational, don't have a substantial existence of their own, like material objects. This is similarly true of discourse. While artefacts of discourse – statements – may have a sedimented existence, discourse itself does not subsist entirely in such things. Discourses and power may be structured in a sense, but they are not 'structures' in the sense of stable and inflexible frameworks. Foucault does talk about a kind of power, domination, which is inflexible, but it is only relatively so. In this respect, again, Foucault takes structuralism in a rather Nietzschean direction, though indeed the systems described by structural linguistics, languages, are themselves hardly static and unchanging. Foucault is in any case consistent in this regard, speaking in the preface to the *History of Madness* of 'continuously mobile and obstinate forms of repression'.

This quotation indicates multiple things. On the one hand, it reveals the extent to which, in his early work, Foucault had a conventional conception of power as repression – though he would later defend this retrospectively on the basis that repression was indeed the primary form of power during the time period and domain of analysis of *The History of Madness* (PK 183–4). On the other it shows that from the outset he understood a certain solidity – here described as obstinacy – to be of a piece with mobility in power relations.

In his classic, early-to-mid-1970s reflections on power, Foucault repeatedly conceptualises power as war. 'War' has, since the dawn of Western philosophy, been a metaphor for the absence of staticity: the pre-Socratic Greek philosopher Heraclitus, who famously said that one never steps into the same river twice, also expressed his belief in the ever-changing nature of reality by saying that war is common to everything. Since Foucault will say that power is everywhere, and since he identifies power with war, we can say that he would agree with this assessment.

Foucault's full formulation is that 'power is war, the continuation of war by other means' (SD 15). The last part of this, the phrase 'continuation of war by other means', is an epigrammatic paraphrase of the famous dictum of the nineteenth-century German military theorist Carl von Clausewitz: 'war is diplomacy by other means'. Foucault deliberately inverts this dictum. Clausewitz's idea is that we try to do things by peaceful means in politics, but, when these fail, we resort to war. This is a conventional way of looking at things. Foucault's idea is that on the contrary the political contestation that we experience as 'peace' is the continuation of war by other means. War is where politics begins, but the open violence historically became coded as 'peaceful' politics.

This position resembles, but crucially differs from, the positions of other political thinkers. Thomas Hobbes, for example, believed that peaceful politics emerged from an earlier state of war. The difference between Hobbes's position and Foucault's, the latter explains in *Society Must Be Defended*, is that Hobbes believes that political society is absolutely unlike the state of war, indeed is justified as an alternative to the horrors of war. For Foucault, on the other hand, political society is suspicious, representing not the rational choice of individuals to leave the state of war by establishing a state, as classical liberals have thought, but rather simply the victory of certain forces over others in war leading to the establishment of a state to serve the interests of the victors. Another classic figure of political theory worthy of mention in comparison with Foucault's position is Niccolo Machiavelli, who does see peaceful politics as involving strategic manoeuvring, but Foucault thinks he is too focused on the state (see Holden and Elden 2005 for detail).

Foucault's position also differs crucially from Nietzsche's, though Foucault never talks about his differences from Nietzsche, preferring to the end to think of himself as 'simply Nietzschean' (PPC 251). In Nietzsche's *Genealogy of Morals*, we see civilisation as emerging from a warlike culture by a trick of the oppressed, who use language to subvert aggressive tendencies, and produce peace, the suppression of warlike urges. Nietzsche is thus a kind of opposite to Hobbes: in Nietzsche, the state of war is valorised and peace is seen as a victory of weakness and ill health. While Foucault does not explicitly pass any comment on Nietzsche's historical thesis, the picture he offers in his turn is rather different, inasmuch as it straightforwardly involves a position of physical advantage accreting into a political system in which the powerful become the ruling class. In this much, Foucault is self-consciously closer to Marxism, seeing the state as a tool of class power. This is not necessarily incompatible with Nietzsche's position, inasmuch as Nietzsche's idea of the priestly caste taking control within the state from the warriors who originally ruled is not precluded in Foucault's picture. Indeed, Foucault's claim that politics remains war implies that, under the surface calm, society remains a churning mass of contestation, in which everyone strives for power – this last insight is straight out of Nietzsche, as we have seen. Out of such a politics, new rulers may emerge. It is worth noting a continuing distance of Foucault from Marxism, even if he is more inclined towards a conventional class analysis than Nietzsche is, because the war he imagines is one in which everyone struggles with everyone else to some extent (PK 208). While this certainly does allow us to understand groups, such as classes, locked in struggle, it also implies that there are any numbers of struggles which cut across these divisions, within groups, bringing allies together across groups. This means that Foucault's conception of power undercuts the exclusive focus on class divisions that has typified Marxism, though it does still allow class analysis.

There is a clear problem with Foucault's invocation of war, however, if it is taken literally. As Jacques Derrida (1982) points out, all metaphors are essentially imperfect: if they were perfect, they would be literal descriptions, not metaphors. The pronouncement that 'power is war' makes sense only if construed metaphorically, as is the case also with Heraclitus's pronouncement about war's ubiquity. Speaking more precisely in the first volume of the *History of Sexuality*, Foucault indicates that one can think of 'war' and 'politics' as two different ways in which 'force relations' (which in his vocabulary seems to be an exact synonym for 'power relations') can be integrated. Now, this might seem odd, inasmuch as one might tend to think of war as being chaotic and that, of the two, only politics is truly integrated. But we should remember that war is highly organised. War involves sides, sides that are themselves structured internally. It involves balances of forces: much of war involves a kind of mutual threat and enticement that is not actual battle. Indeed, battles, actual physical violence, may be the exception rather than the rule of war. Historically, wars lasted many years with only rare battles occurring. In the twentieth century with its enormous, unprecedentedly deadly wars, while battles seemed to be almost continuous for long periods, they occurred only rarely in space: despite their being 'world wars', most of the world at any given time remained peaceful. The conception of war as total chaos, as Hobbes's war of all against all, is a mythic state of which there is no evidence of it having existed.

Foucault did move away from talking about war. The problem of course with comparing politics to war is that war is necessarily marked by deadly violence. We do not want to encourage insouciance about deadly violence. Foucault in fact avers as much when he specifically condemns the 'model of war' as such in a 1978 interview (RM 180). It should be noted that this condemnation is limited in scope: it condemns using war as a model for understanding ideological disputes, not as a model for understanding society at large. Still, if war were a good model for understanding society at large, it would presumably by that token also apply to ideological disputes. Some scholars, in particular Thomas Lemke (1997), have seen there as being a very substantial change in Foucault's attitude towards power around this time. My position, by contrast, is that, since Foucault never says his views of power have changed, and since the formulation that 'power is war' was only ever a metaphor, this is not of crucial importance.

There is another metaphor that Foucault uses that becomes more and more prominent. One could even say that it displaces that of war. This is the metaphor of the *jeu*. This word in Foucault's usage is routinely translated as 'game'. Thus, in English one reads Foucault talking about 'games of power' and 'games of truth' (e.g. EW1 296).

The metaphor of the game in relation to power seems to me to be a less accurate description than that of power. This is because games are essentially legalistic: a game is always governed by a set of rules which constitutes it. That said, I don't think Foucault means 'game' by *jeu* at all. In English there is a distinction, absent in French, between the 'game' and 'play'. Foucault means *jeu* not in the sense of a structured 'game' but, at least in the case of power, in the sense of a freewheeling kind of 'play', in the sense of a child's play. In English, we talk about a child 'playing' when they are engaging in an activity that has no discernible rules and can go in any direction. One might also refer to Immanuel Kant's notion of the 'free play (*freies Spiel*) of the imagination': for Kant this is a state in which our mind effectively wanders in boundless, enjoyable freedom. In German, as in French, there is no distinction between 'play' and 'game', only one word, *Spiel*. What I am suggesting then is that effectively Foucault's *jeu de pouvoir* has been consistently mistranslated as 'game of power'. It should be 'power play', a time-worn English phrase. The notion of a play of power captures its complete multidirectionality, and how a certain form emerges from something that has no form imposed from above. It also captures, in a way that the metaphor of war perhaps fails to connote, the extent to which much power is often banal, while retaining the implication that it is question of manoeuvring to get something.

The shift in rhetoric between the florid vocabulary of war and the emphasis on playfulness undoubtedly relates to shifts in Foucault's milieu and its politics during this time. In the early 1970s, Foucault's milieu was composed of post-1968 Parisian revolutionaries. From the middle of the decade on, things change dramatically. This milieu itself declines and transforms into one in which violence and revolution are talked about far less, or indeed in which the mood changes decisively against these things, revolutionary enthusiasm gives way to the vehement anti-Marxism of the Nouveaux Philosophes (the 'New Philosophers'), mostly young Maoists known to Foucault who performed a 180-degree ideological turn in the mid-1970s. So the politics of Foucault's associates changes, and he also begins to associate with quite different people, particularly by spending more and more time as a visiting scholar in the United States. The notion of the 'game' in Foucault can be associated with an Anglophone influence, though not a particularly new one, but rather one that he first encountered seriously in Tunis in the 1960s, with speech act theory and the concept of the 'language game'. This too is a part of what Foucault sees himself as doing at this time, a way of conceiving his political thought as an 'analytical philosophy of politics', doing with power relations something akin to what he saw Oxford philosophers as having done with language, which is to say analysing them (DE3 534ff.).

THE SUBJECT AND POWER

In his last years, as we will see in subsequent chapters (particularly Chapters 7 and 8), Foucault changes focus away from power. However, he never entirely stopped talking about it, and indeed significantly extended his account of power in an extraordinary essay, 'The Subject and Power', which was published as an appendix to one of the first books to be written about Foucault's thought, *Beyond Structuralism and Hermeneutics*, by two Berkeley scholars known to Foucault, Hubert Dreyfus and Paul Rabinow. As the title of the essay suggests, it situates power in relation to a new focus on subjectivity in Foucault's work.

Here, he clarifies that violence is the 'primitive form' of power, but that in fact violence and power may be distinguished by the fact that the former acts directly on bodies, whereas power acts mediately (EW3 340). That is, power is what happens not when people act directly on other people but when we act on their *actions themselves*. Power is thus defined as 'a set of actions upon other actions' (EW3 341). This seems to leave open the possibility that there are other actions upon actions which do not constitute power – perhaps actions out of genuinely altruistic solicitude – but Foucault does not say as much. It is thus unclear how far Foucault follows Nietzsche's (2006, §34) cynicism in declaring that 'where there are sacrificing and favors and love-looks, there too is the will to be master'. What is made clear is that to be acting on the actions of another is a minimum condition for something to count as power. In this, he follows a theme he had been exploring since 1979 at least of 'conduct' (STP 194–5), defining power in terms of how people 'conduct' themselves and other people. Foucault thus now makes clear exactly what the relation of power consists in, what it is that concatenates into power: attempts by people to influence one another to do things, with our interrelating attempts all to influence each other into doing things producing unexpected patterns of influence. Violence thus gives rise to power only when it is used to threaten and cajole, to produce behaviour in people.

Typology

'Generally', Foucault tells us in 'The Subject and Power', 'it can be said there are three types of struggles: against forms of domination (ethnic, social, and religious); against forms of exploitation that separate individuals from what they produce; or against that which ties the individual to himself and submits him to others in this way (struggles against subjection, against forms of subjectivity and submission)'; and, of course, there are admixtures of the three (EW3 331). Of course, here Foucault is taking 'struggle' to mean 'resistance struggle' – the attempt to dominate others could be characterised as a form of struggle, but this is clearly not what he means to refer to here.

The second form of struggle here is the most surprising of the three. The first form is the most obvious: the struggle for freedom *simpliciter*. The third is obvious in the context of Foucault's work: the struggle against interpellation, against a form of power we have seen in the case of the constitution of the soul in *Discipline and Punish*. The second form is also familiar, but not from Foucault's work – rather, it is distinctly Marxian. Not that this form of struggle is, at least as Foucault couches it, the same as economic exploitation in the Marxist sense – it could also apply, say, to the appropriation of one's culture. Still, the fact that Foucault makes the struggle against exploitation one of the three fundamental forms of struggle so late in his life demonstrates a continuing taking into account, an attempt to incorporate and not dismiss, the central insights of left-wing thought.

Similarly, Foucault, in an interview from the last months of his life entitled 'The Ethics of the Concern for Self as a Practice of Freedom', subdivides power into three distinct types, providing a differentiated spectrum from the most banal to the most pernicious, categorising power according to the degree of freedom it accords. At one end of this spectrum of power is a situation he calls 'freedom'. Freedom is not, as one might imagine, the absence of power, since for Foucault power is never absent in human relations. Indeed, in a certain sense, freedom is never absent either, since control is never total, and if it were complete this would be a situation where it is no longer power (qua influence) we are dealing with, but simply an automatic process. 'Freedom' in Foucault's vocabulary, however, refers to a situation where different participants are approximately equal to one another, with none of them really compelling one another. This is the kind of power one finds in a standard, friendly social situation: people influence one another, but there is nothing particularly pernicious about any of this. The second, less flexible situation Foucault calls 'government'. In this situation, power is asymmetrical, with one party having more power than the other, but with all parties having some room for negotiation. This of course is how a democratic government relates to its people: we can contest the actions of government, protest them, but in the end the government has more power than any individual and has the authority and means to compel us. The last, least flexible situation, Foucault calls 'domination'. In such a situation, there is an asymmetrical relation in which people are not allowed to negotiate or contest power. Needless to say, this characterises totalitarian regimes. It also, for Foucault, characterises class relations in capitalism. While the working class are allowed to demonstrate, demand change and act collectively to pursue demands for improved conditions in our society, they are not allowed to negotiate their status as employees vis-à-vis their bosses. Thus one class, the owners, *dominate* the other, their labourers. And thus Foucault maintains and develops a key insight of Marxist thought within his schema.

Now, these three types of power might seem to correspond to the three types of struggle outlined in 'The Subject and Power', but I do not believe they can be mapped directly. Rather, all three types of struggle are essentially against power in general, tending to break down structures of power and move towards freedom. This is true not only of struggles directly aimed at domination but also of those aimed at exploitation and subjection, in so far as exploitation and subjection are often supported by domination. This is certainly the case in our society.

Resistance

This explains too why power is quite so ubiquitous in the social body for Foucault: whether I am asking someone to make me a cup of tea, or trying to get them to marry me, this can be construed as power. The question then is raised of where resistance to power can fit into this picture.

This is an extraordinarily vexed area of Foucault commentary. Foucault makes relatively scant remarks about resistance, though he also makes clear that it is centrally important to his conception of power. What he says has caused controversy, namely that 'where there is power, there is resistance, and yet, or rather consequently, this resistance is never in a position of exteriority in relation to power' (HS1 95). The controversy focuses on this idea that 'resistance is never in a position of exteriority', that is, is never *outside* power. Does this mean that resistance is *inside* power, or is there some position that is neither inside nor outside? Is power similarly not outside resistance, or does power have the outside position?

People have read Foucault to be saying here that resistance is subordinate to, or produced by, power. However, Foucault is actually quite explicit, in the rest of this brief paragraph dealing with resistance in the first volume of *The History of Sexuality*, that he is *not* saying we are trapped inside power. He explains that what he means is that every power relation involves resistance (HS1 95). This makes resistance *neither* exterior *nor* interior to power, but, to use a word Foucault does not, *immanent* to power relations. Nor is resistance subordinate to power, he tells us, nor is it produced by power.

It is indeed truly remarkable the extent to which Foucault has been read in relation to the notion of resistance in a variety of ways which he specifically tries to anticipate and disavow in his main published remarks on the topic. The reason for this I think is that people have not understood how it is possible for resistance to be the way that Foucault says it is. People are used to a binary picture in which power and resistance are polar opposites. Charles Taylor (1984) for example reads Foucault as indeed giving us a moral account of politics in which power is bad and resistance is good, but being unable himself to recognise this due to a pedantic insistence on an amoral position. But Foucault's position is extraordinarily simple. It is there in *The Will to Knowledge*, but is explained further in a series of interviews in which Foucault tries to answer the various misunderstandings that had immediately arisen (these were in fact published well *before* some of the better-known misunderstandings by major scholars such as Taylor, however, though it is not clear whether these scholars had read Foucault's clarifications).

Perhaps most important of all to clarifying matters is a remark of Foucault's in a 1982 interview that 'resistance comes first' (EW1 167). One of the problems with Foucault's view of resistance is that it was unclear how it could escape being produced by power, not least because Foucault has often been interpreted as saying that individuals are themselves produced by power. However, Foucault tells us in this interview that 'power relations . . . refer to the situation where you're not doing what you want' (EW1 167). That is to say, power occurs when someone is influenced to do something they otherwise would not do. This means that the resistance is presupposed: if there were no resistance to the power there already, there would be no power. If someone offers me something I really want, there's no power involved in getting me to accept it (though there may of course be power involved later on, in influencing me to do other things out of feelings of gratitude and obligation; and power might have been exercised earlier in cultivating my tastes, and so on). By contrast, if someone gets me to do something I don't really want to do, there is a form of power involved, precisely because I am already resistant to the suggestion.

Resistance then is everywhere, but also begins at an absolutely local level. This is not to say it is located particularly at the level of the individual, however. As we will see, for Foucault individuality is indeed something constituted by power. We may conceive of resistance as even more local than that, a matter of things that are going on within the individual, underneath our individuality, out of our control (cf. PK 208). Since Foucault does not believe in a universal human nature, resistances may occur in any number of different ways. Indeed, for Foucault part of the point about resistance is its sheer unpredictability. This implies that you cannot tell from looking at a political situation what people will do.

Resistance is unpredictable moreover because people *react* to power (EW1 325). While Foucault talks about resistance existing in advance of power, this does not mean that we always know in advance what we want, but rather that we exist, as individuals or sub-individual drives, such that when power comes along we will react. We react dynamically: power doesn't control how people react to it, or, at least, resistance is a part of the reaction it doesn't control. We moreover get fed up with things we previously tolerated, producing new and surprising resistances seemingly out of nowhere. Foucault notes the propensity of international resistance movements to arise that manifest themselves in radically different political settings in similar ways: he notes that the global prison movement was prominently manifested in Sweden, despite the fact that Sweden had amongst the most favourable prison conditions in the world, and that feminism went through similar evolutions in countries where women's roles were quite different (DE2 545). Foucault notes that occasionally such resistances crop up massively, become strategically co-ordinated between many participants, produce revolutions – but this is comparatively rare (HS1 96).

This does not mean other resistance is simply futile, however. We can presume we locally combat and emerge victorious over power relations all the time.

Resistance for Foucault is always specific. 'I do not think that the will not to be governed at all is something that one could consider an originary aspiration,' he says. 'I think that, in fact, the will not to be governed is always the will not to be governed thusly, like that, by these people, at this price' (1997, 72). The point here is that, although one might well avow the desire not to be governed at all – anarchists do – Foucault believes that such an ideology originates in something more proximate. That is, we experience power in immediate and concrete instances, which may lead us to adopt a blanket, pedantic opposition to all forms of government, but there is always something local and direct that we are originally concerned to resist. Thus, in a real movement, there may be many ideologies, but there is also a direct target, a specific nexus of power relations that people wish to dismantle.

Something that might make Foucault appear pessimistic about resistance is his castigation of prison reform as an internal element of the prison system in *Discipline and Punish*. This is merely a particular case, however. Movements demanding reform might be successful in other cases. We must also ask, moreover, whether the prison reform movement is really a case of resistance. While a prison riot, for example is clearly a form of resistance – indeed, prisoners clearly resist the conditions of their imprisonment routinely in a expansive variety of ways – the demand for prison reform is something we can characterise precisely as a form of power, because it is a demand that typically comes from people who want to run prisons better, to imprison people better, to change prisoners into model citizens.

This is not, however, to say that it is not possible to resist the prison system. We can take Foucault's own activities, and those of the Prisons Information Group, as a paradigmatic form of resistance, even though they were on behalf of others. For one thing, his activism and scholarship are always explicitly intended as offering help to others in their resistance, rather than resisting by proxy for someone else. Offering help in these ways is designed to open up new possibilities, rather than to close them down by suggesting solutions. It is, in short, the polar opposite of the reform movement.

A worry with Foucault is doubtless that, without normative bases, it is unclear what resistance to support and what to deny support to.

Foucault indeed seems to suggest that this is only a tactical question, only a matter of discerning as best we can what forms of resistance are likely to be fruitful and supporting those. But are there not bad forms or resistance? I think it is at most unclear as to whether there are. It seems to me that forms of resistance one would not wish to support are typically not really forms of resistance, but merely classify themselves as resistance.

An example would be the far right, who help themselves to the language of resistance, and of revolution, from the left in the service of reactionary aims. For example, racists may think of themselves as a 'resistance' against multiculturalism, or Jewish domination, etcetera. The essential problem with this is that the structures they themselves believe to be existing do not exist, or at least are not as they believe them to be: there is no Jewish conspiracy to impose multiculturalism. But can they not 'resist' multiculturalism itself? To the extent that there is a strategy of power here to be resisted, then it is possible to resist it. Indeed, it may be resisted from the left: 'multiculturalism' could be said to be a divisive politics that keeps people segregated in groups, something that all kinds of people may want to resist. Right-wing 'resistance' here, however, is directed not against multiculturalism per se but against people of other cultures, and not against any power these people might have over racists, but simply against the existence of the cultural or racial other in the same space as the racist. This is, in a word, not resistance, but power, power masquerading as resistance.

Truth and Power

One thing Foucault is adamant about is that the distinction between power and resistance does not simply coincide with the distinction between truth and falsehood. It is not true in particular that the truth is something that simply works against power, or conversely that falsehoods always play into power's strategies. His major example of how this is not so is the figure of confession, central to the argument of the first volume of his *History of Sexuality*. For Foucault, the demand for truth, specifically the demand to *confess* our sexuality, rooted in the Christian practice of confession, is implicated in manufacturing our identities. That is, though when we tell about our sexual desires we appear simply to be reporting something that is already true, Foucault argues that we are in fact being made to constitute our desire in a certain way. Thus, power involves a complex interplay of silences and statements, the production of specific discourses. To lie in such a situation may indeed therefore be a form of resistance.

This introduces an apparent paradox in his argument, however, since he is himself telling a certain truth by pointing this out, and is trying to reveal something that is hidden. The solution to this paradox is a simple one: though it is not true in general that truth and transparency militate against power, it is true in this case. This is precisely because Foucault is telling a truth that undercuts and undermines power. By contrast, the truth of sex is not what it seems to be. While it appears to be liberatory, it is not really liberation, nor indeed really the kind of truth it appears to be: it masquerades as natural, when it is in fact artificial. Yes, you do have the desires that you confess to, but not independently of the impulse to confess them – at least, this is Foucault's argument, as we will see in the next chapter.

For Foucault, power is capable of existing as it does only on the condition that it masks itself (HS1 86). The focus on the politics of the state and its institutions is thus a smokescreen that obscures the deeper operation of power, for example the disciplinary 'micro-physics' of power detailed in *Discipline and Punish* (DP 26). The masking of the power of confession might seem like something specific to a new, post-sovereign form of power. The real difference between discipline and the sovereign power that came before it is precisely the invisibility of the new form of power (DP 187). Before discipline, power operated through spectacular displays, the public execution, corporal punishment that leaves a mark. Discipline marks the realisation that power can be more effective when it is concealed, silent, unexceptional; it is a power that requires secrecy (DP 129). Thus, as Foucault remarks, 'It is wrong to consider power as essentially linked to the effects of ignorance' (AB 50). Power can, after all, be utterly blatant.

Still, the spectacular displays of earlier sovereign power were a matter of protesting too much: they were hysterical displays, insisting on power in order to try to mask the yawning vacuum behind sovereignty. Monarchical power was always a kind of ruse: though the political system was premised on the principle that all power flowed to and through the monarch, that the king was the linchpin of society, this was never the reality. A passing familiarity with medieval history is enough to realise that the king's power was always highly conditional, depending on the goodwill of a nobility who manipulated and overthrew kings. Something similar could in turn be said about noblemen's need to account for the politics in their own camps, down to the lowest level of society, where the peasant rebellion was a constant concern of all constituted power. In the early modern period, when kings, particularly in France, took more power unto themselves, this represents not so much a genuine concentration of power in the person of the king as a displacement of the power of nobles in favour of the power of a new state bureaucracy which was identified with the central monarchy rather than the regional nobility.

This tactic was a failure. What evolved instead was a strategy of understatement, power that blends into the background, appearing grimly inevitable, natural. This is a sign not of its lesser power but if anything of a power so great it appears to be simply part of nature even more than earlier forms. However, this power can be said to appear, like the earlier sovereign power, to be more monolithic and substantial than it really is. The state in particular can appear all-powerful today, but in reality politicians with their democratic mandate are largely beholden to the whims of corporations whose executives are wealthier and more powerful than any politicians.

Now, this problematic has been well known to Marxists for a century, so it is not just this that Foucault hopes to reveal. While Marxists see beneath the ostensible conduits of power in liberal democracy, from people to government, the machinations of the market that determine much of what happens, Foucault thinks they remain much too focused on the state, that is, on either seizing control of or smashing the state. From a Foucauldian point of view, this insight does much to explain the failure of Marxism, by failing to understand the extraordinary complexity, multiplicity and promiscuity of power relations. Marxism understands power as formed underneath the level of the state, in an economic infrastructure. Still, it can also be said that Marxism retains a hierarchical view of power, with a class, rather than a single sovereign, at the top. While outstripping more conservative, liberal approaches in the depth of its analysis of politics then, it does not go far enough for Foucault.

He thinks there is a key failing of both these conventional views of power, what he calls their economism, which he outlines in *Society Must Be Defended*. In the more traditional, liberal view, power is seen as a quantitative commodity, which can be possessed and indeed traded (SD 13). Power is thus seen as a thing: people have it or lack it. By contrast, Marxists see that power is not a thing, but rather governed by relations, as Foucault himself does. However, the relations in question are economic ones: power is reduced to economics rather than being treated in its specific nature (SD 14). It is worth noting that this is true only of contemporary Marxist theory, which he contemporaneously distinguishes from Marx's work, specifically his magnum opus, *Capital*, which Foucault views as a precursor to his own work on power (Foucault 2007, 157–8).

Foucault's antidote, as we have seen, is the analysis of power not in terms of who the real rulers are but in terms of relations of power. This moves us beyond a familiar impasse. Most people point the finger at politicians, more astute leftists accuse business leaders, right-wing populists bemoan the power of 'cultural elites', conspiracy theorists see monsters lurking in the shadows. But the truth is that even the putative '1 per cent', the bourgeoisie, the Bilderberg Group, who control our society are themselves imbricated within wider strategies of power that they scarcely understand. It is the illusion that someone is in control, this specific, pervasive falsehood, that Foucault seeks to unmask.

Foucault produces his discourse about power and resistance precisely as a form of resistance to power. By showing power at work, Foucault's project in his 1970s output unmasks power. It does not do so decisively, however. Rather, power continues to mask itself anew. Indeed, to this end even Foucault's own thought can be co-opted; certainly, power as a Foucauldian concept can be and has been turned to the services of power, and not just counter-power. The very usage of Foucault's work in management theory would seem ample evidence of this. Nevertheless, I think I have now demonstrated the basic relation Foucault's conception of power has to his concrete political engagements, and thereby elucidated its meaning as a concrete political intervention in itself.

Critique

Foucault insists that the role of an intellectual like him should be specific and limited. He forswears intellectuals taking on any leadership function, or the function of saying how things should be or will be (a utopian or prophetic function, respectively – on these categories see Kelly 2014): 'the role of the intellectual today is not that of establishing laws or proposing solutions or prophesying, since by doing that one can only contribute to the functioning of a determinate situation of power that to my mind must be criticized' (RM 157). This puts Foucault completely at odds with much of the tradition of political theory, including contemporary 'political philosophy', which is primarily concerned with 'normative' pronouncements: that is, with saying what should be done (or at least with what should be the case, if not always how to realise disiderata). 'If I don't ever say what must be done,' he tells us, however,

> it isn't because I believe that there's nothing to be done; on the contrary, it is because I think that there are a thousand things to do, to invent, to forge, on the part of those who, recognizing the relations of power in which they're implicated, have decided to resist or escape them. From this point of view all of my investigations rest on a postulate of absolute optimism. I do not conduct my analyses in order to say: this is how things are, look how trapped you are. I say certain things only to the extent to which I see them as capable of permitting the transformation of reality. (RM 174)

This entails a conception of critique different from the dominant way of understanding it. To criticise something is understood to be a matter of opposing it to a superior alternative, or to a normative standard which that thing does not meet. Foucault, however, not only refuses to suggest an alternative but opposes any attempt to do so by anyone. He never posits anything like a normative stance, moreover.

Now, on this point, Foucault finds himself opposed to almost all existing political theorists. Such a radical stance is of course already flagged in his explicitly radical position vis-à-vis pre-existing political theory. It is held that it cannot make sense to criticise something unless someone has a normative standard or an alternative in mind. Since Foucault's critiques do seem to make sense, it is held by some commentators, most notably perhaps Taylor (1984), that Foucault is relying on normative standards, ones which his readers share, but does not state them. That is to say, it is held that Foucault thinks, and we all know, that the effects of power Foucault describes are *bad*.

There are reasons to think that Foucault genuinely eschews such a normative stance, however. For one thing, he never says explicitly that anything is 'good' or 'bad'. One might argue he does not need to because it is so obvious. However, Foucault is committed to a position that we might loosely describe as a form of 'historical relativism' about norms; that is, that norms are not something that we can use to criticise contemporary society, since they are an artefact of that society. Indeed, for Foucault this is true in an unusually strong sense, since he believes that not only specific norms but, as we will see in the next chapter, norms as such have a unique significance in our society.

Yet, it is often held that relativism is an intrinsically paradoxical position. If everything is relative, including truth, how can we say anything at all? Isn't everything just a matter of our personal opinion? This objection to relativism involves understanding relativism as meaning its most extreme form imaginable. In practice, relativisms are always limited in the things they categorise as relative. For Foucault, there are things that are not relative, what we might call 'reality'. Power, for example, is not in itself relative, though the concept of power might be; something similar might be said of the body. When it comes to truth, Foucault thinks there are 'regimes of truth' which determine what may be held to be true in any particular discourse, but that does not mean that these claims are not constrained in any way by reality – it's rather that different discourses have differential relationships to reality. This is indeed precisely the crux of Foucault's archaeological analysis. Similarly, when it comes to genealogy, Foucault is constrained by reality in his analysis: he doesn't just make things up. Norms, however, are held to be culturally contingent.

We will deal with what Foucault has to say about morality and ethics in more detail in the final chapter, but what is crucial in both cases is that Foucault in both cases, despite attempts to revive them, declares them both not to exist, and indeed to be impossible to revive. In the case of morality, which he comments on in a brief paragraph in *The Order of Things*, he is definitive about this impossibility (OT 328), though by the time of his reflections on ethics, in his *Hermeneutics of the Subject* lectures in 1982, he has renounced prophetic pronouncements and thus cannot pronounce definitively on the impossibility of its revival, so limits himself to 'suspecting' it (HS 252).

Foucault thus permits intellectuals to offer strategic advice based on their analyses of historical facts, but since they cannot normatively prescribe, they must leave the final decision up to others: 'My role is to address problems effectively, really: and to pose them with the greatest possible rigor, with the maximum complexity and difficulty so that a solution does not arise all at once because of the thought of some reformer' (RM 158). He thus suggests that the work of intellectuals is to furnish tools for others to use, which it is then up to them to take up or not as they see fit – certainly this is how he sees his own work operating (DE2 523). His own works in light of this he sees as being in principle available to anyone, but only finding their real audience in people to whom they are directly relevant. In the case of the *History of Madness*, Foucault sees it as finding its audience among psychiatric professionals and the mentally ill (DE2 525).

Now, one might note that Foucault appears to have his own morality here, since he is prescribing what people should do. Indeed, Foucault did admit that he is 'a moralist, insofar as I believe one of the tasks, one of the meanings of human existence – the source of human freedom – is never to accept anything as definitive, untouchable, obvious, or immobile' (Foucault 1988, 1). But this amounts to a morality which defies any kind of morality as usually construed, any set values. There is nothing inconsistent in Foucault's stance, which amounts to a rejection of specific prescription, a prescription not to prescribe. We cannot prescribe not because there is a higher moral order which forbids it but because the moral order which would allow specific prescriptions does not exist, lacks any empirical or metaphysical grounding.

We must moreover point to the extent to which this help for others' resistance is not a pure act of altruism, as one might conventionally think moral acts should be, but a form of strategic, blocking resistance. As Foucault indicates in his genealogies, we are all imbricated in the same broad strategies of power, be they a technology of power like discipline, or a device like sexuality. When it comes to the scale of resisting disciplinary power, which we all do resist in some way since we all encounter it, it is possible to find common cause with almost anyone else in society in the name of this resistance.

People are undoubtedly frustrated by Foucault's failure – indeed, his pointed refusal – to identify his position in conventional political terms. For example, in relation to the prison, the obvious question with which Foucault's position is confronted in conventional political discourse is 'What would you do instead if you are so opposed to the prison?' Now, there is an existing movement, prison abolitionism, which simply says we should abolish the prison without replacing it with anything. Foucault's stance obviously tends in this direction, but he certainly does not take this stance. The most concrete stance he takes is demanding, concretely, the abolition of the death penalty, a mainstream political stance. Why does Foucault not demand the abolition of the prison? It is clear that from his point of view the prison has a kind of overall negative effect. The reason I would suggest is the following: Foucault will never advocate an alternative, because this would amount to affirming a strategy of power that we do not yet appreciate, like Bentham's panopticon did; Bentham designed the Panopticon without knowing what it would be like in practice, and in so doing produced multifarious and inherently unpredictable effects of power. Foucault also, however, refuses to advocate the simple negation of something, because in fact negation is never simple. If one abolishes something, something new will rise in its place. Abolitionism risks being utopian in imagining how things will be in a determinate way once the targeted nuisance is abolished, when in fact we know for certain only that unforeseen and multifarious effects of power will ensue. This does not mean that one should not act, that one should not resist. It does, however, mean that one should not imagine that we can 'simply' do away with any aspect of our society, even things that we do resist. Resistance does not equate to a demand for any particular alternative, and it does not even amount to a demand for the abolition, or reform, of the thing resisted. It is merely resistance. Resistance resists, and in resisting it points beyond the thing it resists, to some change or negation, but this does not determine in itself the type of change or negation it will occasion. To pretend it does, as is routinely done alongside resistance, is an illusion. We may say we are fighting for abolition and merely achieve reform – or indeed vice versa. The Provisional IRA fighting for decades for a united Ireland achieved a power-sharing agreement within the United Kingdom. Revolutionary upsurges can, by contrast, begin with modest demands, or with none. This was the case of the Events of May 1968, which began in demands for changed conditions for university students, but quickly grew to threaten the French Republic.

Rights

Foucault's relation to state power straddles an interesting line. On the one side, he shows no compunction in demanding certain actions of the French state, particularly after the election of a left-wing government in 1981. On the other, he refused to associate himself with that government, and to offer any opinion on electoral contests (DE1 73).

Foucault's demands towards government were always in relation to specific causes. He denounced the death penalty already in the 1970s, for example, both in France during an intense period leading up to its abolition (DE1 52), and internationally. In 1975, he travelled with a group of French intellectuals to Madrid to denounce the Franco regime's execution of political prisoners. This resulted in the protestors' prompt arrest and deportation, but seems to have immediately provoked the French government into condemning the executions in turn (DE1 65). The question would be whether their action, or specifically Foucault's participation in it, was aimed at changing government policy. I think generously one could say that it was about changing the policy of governments in general, Spanish as well as French.

In the 1980s, there were two issues on which he was particularly vocal. One was the plight of Vietnamese 'boat people', refugees fleeing the Communist regime in Vietnam. The other was the declaration of martial law in Poland in 1981, shortly after the change of government in France. Having lived in Poland himself, Foucault had reason to be particularly concerned about this issue. The issue in respect of the French government was its failure to decry the military takeover in Poland. More generally, in relation to both issues, Foucault felt it necessary himself to decry them, not as a person of influence, but simply as a person. In a collective statement penned by Foucault for an 'International Committee against Piracy' (the 'piracy' in question being that of those who interdicted boat people), he put forward the idea that people around the world had a certain right not to accept the actions of governments, even those of governments in other parts of the world (EW3 457). Quite what this means in material terms is rather moot.

Now, 'rights' are an essentially legal concept (in French, as in German, the word for 'right' and 'law' are the same). As such, one could expect Foucault to have no time for talk of rights, representing as it does either legal realities (rights guaranteed under existing laws) or alternatively reference to a supposed universal law (as in the discourse of abstract 'human rights' where these are not legislated). Yet Foucault uses the rhetoric of rights in a number of places. He repeatedly demands a right of citizens of the world to object to the actions of governments (EW3 474–5). However, this is essentially like his 'moralism': he is not demanding this right be legislated, but rather is speaking essentially rhetorically, suggesting that anyone can authorise themselves to speak against power. It is also worth noting that Foucault is here not writing on his own account, but making a statement on behalf of a group in which he is involved, as he often did, and thus his use of the vocabulary of rights can be taken as a matter of his assuming a more popular discursive register. As early as 1974, for example, Foucault was one of the joint authors of a statement by a group called the Association de défense des droits des détenus (Association for the defence of the rights of the detained; DE1 61). Such an invocation of rights, and indeed their actual defence, should not be interpreted as a philosophical endorsement of the concept of rights. Jessica Whyte (2012) has pointed out the closeness of Foucault to those who were paving the way for more recent notions of a 'right to protect', a right of states to intervene in the affairs of other states in the name of protecting the people of those other countries. But Foucault does not voice support for any such thing himself.

Resistance does not have to be on one's own account in the strictest sense. It can, in a sense, be on someone else's behalf: we may intercede between the abused and the abuser as an act of resistance to the abuser. What Foucault steers away from is action where the oppressed have no active role to play, and others replace them entirely, with the oppressed being only a pretext for the exercise of power. To be sure, one is dealing here with something like a continuum, on which it is possible to stray from resistance into oppression. The prophylactic that Foucault prescribes is surely the analysis of power relations, which should allow us to see at which point resistance has become power. Foucault never advocates any direct action by the French state against the Polish or Vietnamese states, only humanitarian aid and verbal denunciation.

Note

1. This English word appears as a translation of a much vaguer French term of Foucault's, but captures perfectly Foucault's meaning (cf. Foucault 1976b, 122).

6

Sex and Life

This chapter deals with the two themes from the first volume of *The History of Sexuality*: the politics of sex and the politics of life.

Sex

Foucault's explicit primary concern in the first volume of his *History of Sexuality* was not power, of course, but sexuality. Foucault's thesis concerning sexuality is that, whereas sexuality has been widely thought of in the twentieth century as a natural human need that has been 'repressed', it is in fact an invention of a recent date. This is of course a signature move of Foucault's with a number of topics. While Foucault allows that there has been, in the nineteenth century in particular, a repression directed at human sexual behaviour in Western societies, this has been specifically directed at a limited category of overt sexual exhibitionism, while society has overall become more and more preoccupied with sex, talking about sex more than ever, albeit in roundabout, scientificised ways. The idea that human beings have a certain, inherent 'sexuality', peculiar to each individual, is for Foucault a completely new invention of our period. The very object 'sex' is new by his lights. No prior period had an equivalent concept.

This object 'sex' can be thought of as combining several dimensions into a single new category. Most obviously it includes 'sex' in the sense of 'having sex' or 'sexual intercourse'. But this is of course not where the concept originates. Its original meaning is the difference between male and female, something that is increasingly not called sex any more in the English language, but rather 'gender', though this sense of 'sex' certainly still persists. 'Sexual intercourse' literally just means an exchange or interaction between men and women – but it has come, initially as a euphemism for coitus, to mean sensual physical activities of a certain type, such that they can occur between people of the same sex. Hence, one now has a distinction between 'homosexual' and 'heterosexual' – what is called a 'sexuality'. But if one seeks to define objectively what constitutes sexual as opposed to nonsexual activity, it is less than clear what now defines it. One might perhaps say the involvement of the genitals, and this would certainly seem to be implied in French, the language in which Foucault was writing, since the French word *sexe* has a sense, not found in the English cognate, of reference to the genitalia as one's 'sex', even if in English we do refer to 'sexual organs'. So, until recently, there simply was no word or idea in any European language that grouped together these things – the difference between men and women, coition, sensual touching and genitals – into a single category. Both sex and sexuality for Foucault are correlative inventions, with 'sex' being the concept around which the historical apparatus of 'sexuality' forms itself (HS1 157; see Kelly 2013b, pp. 115–16, for a discussion of this distinction).

The stakes of this study are profoundly political. Firstly, the position that Foucault is concerned to debunk, what he calls 'the repressive hypothesis', is characterised by Foucault as broadly Marxist in complexion. It amounts to the position that the repression of sexuality is of a piece with the general repressiveness of capitalism. Specifically, it casts sexuality as something threatening to the capitalist order, a potential disturbance to the order that people are supposed to follow to be good workers and consumers. Foucault rightly explodes such ideas, pointing out how they depend on an exclusively negative conception of power that can see it only as repressing, and ignoring power's productive capacity, that is, its operation not by denying people things but precisely through encouraging people to have new desires. Sexuality for Foucault is not merely made up of such desires, but rather is itself a kind of desideratum on his account, something that is itself desired, indeed something that is itself a focus, a sexual excitement in its own right. The very idea of sex is sexy.

There is a problem here of identifying exactly who is supposed to be propounding this repressive hypothesis. Foucault speaks as if it is what 'everyone' believes, but it is hard to identify any named individual who actually subscribes to it. Still, one can take the point that there is a widespread notion of sexual repression, which logically gives rise to notions of sexual 'liberation' and even sexual revolution. It is a commonplace to see the 1960s today identified as the locus of a sexual revolution, by which sexual behaviour and social attitudes more broadly changed fundamentally in Western societies. For Foucault, this misses the rather greater continuity: people are today, as they were already in the nineteenth century, obsessed with sex.

Foucault (2011a, 388) proposes to free us from our liberation, that is, to liberate us from sex and sexuality, effectively completing what has thus far been a partial liberation at best, freeing us only from certain narrow strictures regarding what can be said and done in relation to the constant figure of sex.

For most people, Foucault argues, sex and sexuality have been an imposition. This imposition began in the nineteenth century in the medicalised bourgeois family, where a great suspicion of sexuality as a corrupting influence arose, and the resources of nascent medicine were mobilised to hunt it out, to prevent a rot taking root that would imperil the biological health of the bourgeoisie. Foucault associates the emergence of psychoanalysis, which was originally developed as a cure for the sexual disturbances of Sigmund Freud's bourgeois Viennese patients, mostly women and children, with this movement. Thus, within the bourgeois family, women and children were the first targets; sexuality was first an attempt to buttress the waning power of the paterfamilias. Foucault reads the prominent place given to the parents in the psychoanalytic view of the mind, particularly its central notion of the Oedipal complex, as an attempt to reinstall the power of the parent at a psychological level, to compensate for the denigration of that power in practice.

From this start, sexuality was imposed on the lower orders. This sequence, for Foucault, shows the inadequacy of a Marxist approach. While Foucault is perfectly happy to use the same class categories as Marxists, any Marxist account of sexuality, whether it sees sexuality as something repressed in capitalist society or agrees with Foucault to the extent of seeing it as a tool for repression, cannot explain why it is first both applied and repressed (for it must be applied in order to be repressed, since it does not by Foucault's lights previously, naturally exist) amongst the bourgeoisie itself. Sexual morality is only later, at the end of the nineteenth century, imposed on the working classes, once the bourgeoisie discover that the working classes were living in ways that appear to them as shockingly immoral: in irregular kinship groups rather than neat nuclear families, copulating and reproducing out of wedlock. Even though the top-down imposition of sexuality on the lower orders might seem to follow the pattern we expect of bourgeois society, by which the rich can impose their will on others, sexuality was applied for reasons that are not primarily economic. It is not something necessary to ensure that workers do what is necessary for capitalism to keep running, or to ensure that they reproduce enough to produce a continuing supply of labour, or that they themselves continue to turn up at the factory door, because these things were already happening. The motivation for the bourgeoisie in enforcing sexuality on the working class for Foucault was rather closer to home. It was, namely, the worry that the working class would infect the bourgeoisie with degenerate sexual maladies. There was ample scope for this given the extent to which wealthy men consorted with prostitutes of the lower class, yet this was not merely the worry we might have today about sexually transmitted infections, but about a broader, moral degeneracy that could spread through a population.

For Foucault, the bourgeoisie were preoccupied in a way no previous dominant class had been with their biological health, and this spilled over into a generalised concern with the biological health of the population at large. Foucault believes that the previous ruling class, the aristocracy, had drawn their status from their 'blood', that is, the relationships of kinship. But with the rise of capitalism, kinship no longer mattered so much: the new ascendant class, the bourgeoisie, were concerned with money, not with their blood. However, they are also paranoiacally concerned with health, theirs and that of their family. They had a new, scientific attitude towards breeding. Rather than seeking to unite bloodlines to make effective alliances, their focus was on breeding so as to produce a physically more robust specimen, while also of course keeping an eye on making matches that would increase their influence. It is this concern that leads them to sexuality. Or rather, it is the combination of this eugenicist concern with the older concern about connections of alliance that leads to sexuality: sexuality is what is produced when one combines a deep concern about family and marriage that forbids incest and wanton sexual behaviour with a new sensibility that wants to maximise breeding outcomes and also seeks to maximise pleasure. Sexuality in our society is still constrained within a much older framework of familial relations, precisely because, as we've seen, it was introduced as a device originally within the family and indeed in order to strengthen certain aspects of family life, namely parental authority.

These then are the specifics of sexuality: what one can discern when one analyses power relations in tandem with discourses, rather than trying to impose a predetermined schematic view of history on to the evidence, as Marxism may be accused of doing. They link up to much broader trends in power, including both discipline and what Foucault calls 'biopolitics', which we will deal with later in this chapter.

THE GAY SCIENTIST

When it comes to sexuality, Foucault's personal life, his scholarship and his activism form a triangle that holds together slightly uneasily. A generation of queer scholar-activists have followed Foucault in establishing 'queer theory', an area that is a form at once of scholarship and of activism, aimed at the defiance of sexual categories. One could see Foucault in a similar vein, but even though there is a clear agenda of opposing sex (that is, opposing the concept of sex, not the activity called sex), Foucault's activism rarely extended to sexual matters. One might say that this is precisely because militant homosexuality plays into the strategies of power by appropriating the label of the 'homosexual'. One might mention in this regard a remark of Foucault's that he found the gay movement less interesting than the movement for women's liberation (PK 220). This is because he found the homosexual movement to be essentially concerned with the demand to be treated the same way as heterosexuals are treated, whereas it is feminists who tend to call our conceptions of sexuality and gender into question. The demand for homosexual rights may be said to be 'caught at the level' of sex from Foucault's perspective, because all it can ever do is demand the identity of a certain sexuality. One might mention in this regard the extent to which the struggle for gay rights today has become focused on marriage equality, which is nothing if not a right for gays to be just like everyone else within the normative framework supplied by our society, though of course there is a significant radical queer strand that refuses the marriage issue, not least under the influence of Foucault's ideas. To the extent that homosexuality has become acceptable then, we can say that it is because it is or has become a normalising category: it is held to be OK to be gay, as long as one adheres to the stereotype of gay perfection – attractive, fashionable, clean – by which lights gayness has come to be a variably desirable commodity.

Foucault is clear in the first volume of the *History of Sexuality* that he approves of the manoeuvre of demanding equal rights for gays initially, when it took a label, 'homosexual' – which had been applied to people as a psychiatric diagnosis of their abnormality, under which people suffered, which saw them imprisoned as deviants – and made it into a positive thing. However, it is equally clear that Foucault thought that this strategy had been played out and was beginning to simply provide a hook for power. With every success of the struggle to recognise homosexual rights, homosexuality becomes ever more a mould one is expected to slot into, ever less a radical stance. This may be one reason that Foucault almost never identified himself as gay in his public statements, though he did do so on occasion (e.g. EW1 163–73) and was certainly a gay man in the sense of being physically attracted primarily to other men.

This fact of his same-sex attractedness can hardly be accidental to Foucault's political trajectory. He grew up in a society that was anything but accepting of homosexuality. Not only bourgeois society but its ostensible alternative, the PCF, was homophobic. It would seem that persecution played a role in Foucault's depression while a *normalien* in Paris (Eribon 1991, 26–7), and in his desire to leave France thereafter (Eribon 1991, 29). Foucault was forced to leave his job in Poland because of the discovery of a homosexual liaison of his, following an earlier, less grave, but none the less embarrassing incident (Macey 1993, 86–7). Foucault was beaten up in Tunis in connection with his homosexuality – although Macey (1993, 205) clearly implies that Foucault was set up for this beating by the Tunisian authorities because of his political activities. And while Foucault was living proof that a discreet homosexual could have great success in French public life, even in a French educational system from which homosexuals were officially barred (see Macey 1993, 30), according to Eribon (1990, 133) Foucault's homosexuality did stymie a bid for high office in the French Ministry of Education.

One could certainly say then that Foucault's homosexuality meant that, for all his success in his academic career, it also made him an outsider, and gave him a reason to side with other outsiders, such as student rebels, or prisoners, or later immigrants. It is surely impossible to avoid connecting his homosexuality to his decision to write a historical study of sexuality itself, which he claimed he had contemplated writing as early as 1961 (PK 184). His categorisation as a homosexual is not readily separable from the psychiatric attention he received as a student that led him to his critical studies of the history of madness. As Jana Sawicki (2005, 393) notes, homosexuality can be seen as the 'linchpin' of Foucault's genealogical studies.

There are specifics of Foucault's philosophy which are obviously autobiographically tied to his sexuality; certainly his problematisation of fixed identities and of sexuality itself are. On the other hand, one might argue that his hostility to fixed identities is itself rooted in his flight from the fact of his homosexuality. Some, notably Sawicki (2005, 394), have argued that Foucault did not refuse fixed identities, however. A perennial problem of English-language discussion of Foucault's thought, particularly perhaps in queer theory, is the use of the term 'identity', a term Foucault almost never used and never problematised. 'Identity' is thus a problematic foreign to Foucault's thought. What is clear is that he wanted us to try to move away from, to resist, the categories of sex and sexuality in general. But this does not imply though that Foucault's position should be interpreted as demanding that people absolutely refuse any kind of sexual identity, however, or that all sexuality dissolve into something polymorphous. Indeed, he is willing to embrace homosexual identity to an extent, saying that 'I think the concept "gay" contributes to a positive (rather than a purely negative) appreciation of the type of consciousness in which affection, love, desire, sexual rapport with people have a positive significance' (EW1 142) and that it is 'necessary to struggle to establish homosexual lifestyles' (EW1 157).

RESISTING SEX

This brings us to Foucault's most prominent practical advice for resistance anywhere in his corpus, a single sentence, in which he says that we need to use 'bodies and pleasures' to attack sexuality rather than 'sex-desire' (HS1 157). Owing, I think, to the paucity of such practical advice in Foucault, this has been seized on to an extraordinary degree. An entire book, Ladelle McWhorter's *Bodies and Pleasures*, has been written detailing one woman's attempts to think through this advice in her own life. The amount of attention given to this phrase is also a mark of how deceptively tricky it is. There are a number of different possible interpretations, as McWhorter's work attests to, but I think the interpretation of this passage can be broadly taken in two directions. One, an interpretation associated with perhaps Foucault's most influential interpreter, Judith Butler (1989), is to say that 'bodies and pleasures' here refers ineluctably to the cultural-historical concepts we have of bodies and pleasures, as well as to some material substrate of the body beneath our conceptualisations. Thus, Foucault is seen as recommending particular concepts to us against other concepts that he associates with the device of sexuality, desire and sex – as well as also making a reference to the materiality of bodies and pleasures in themselves. Butler (1989) rightly points to Foucault's definition in 'Nietzsche, Genealogy, History' that genealogy's 'task is to expose a body totally imprinted by history and the process of history's destruction of the body' (EW2 376). The body here is seen as a material substrate that is not just covered over conceptually but materially altered by a form of historical constitution. An example of this materiality of this effect of power on the body is seen in disciplinary power, where the body is trained and indeed changed as a result of its enmeshment in power relations. However, Foucault more generally claims that *all* power ultimately finds its 'point of application' in the body (PP 14).

The question is whether Foucault is referring to the thing that exists, that continues to exist, albeit transformed and overcoded, or whether he means us to also think about the various connotations that the word 'body' implies. I take it Butler's answer is the latter. I favour the former, however. That is, I think Foucault is simply talking about bodies and pleasures, the actual things, even if obviously there is a conceptual mediation here inasmuch as Foucault is appealing to us through the use of language: although Foucault uses the words 'bodies' and 'pleasures' to point us to our own bodies and pleasures, for Foucault bodies and pleasures are relatively unproblematic things, given to us in immediate experience, and not artificially historically constituted in the way that, say, sex is. This, indeed, is his basic point about sex and desire. Sex, on the one hand, is for Foucault simply an artificial category. It includes body parts ('sexual organs', sometimes simply called *sexes* in French), actions ('sex' in the sense of 'sexual intercourse') and the distinction between men and women ('sex' in the sense of gender). There is nothing objective uniting these things: they are a contingent, historically constructed assemblage. Desire, for its part, though Foucault does not explain his opposition to it in detail, of course has a specific content that is related to our conceptual framework: we have no desires that are not framed in terms of our culture. Consequently, under the regime of sex, we have desires that are sexual in a strong sense, being inseparable from the category of sex.

Now, one problem with this interpretation is that it seems to have Foucault saying that we need to get back to a natural state, currently distorted by the concept of sex and by our desires. This indeed has seen Foucault accused of himself repeating the general form of the repressive hypothesis he attacks: while he criticises others for wanting us to get to our true sexuality, our true desires, he appears to want us to get back to our true bodies and pleasures. I think this is a misreading, however. Foucault talks about bodies and pleasures as being a *point d'appui*, which his English translator renders as 'rallying point', taking it plausibly to be a military metaphor. *Point d'appui* however literally means a 'point of support'. The implication is that bodies and pleasures are not somewhere we need to get back to, but rather something we need to lean on, to jump off, not the destination but an aid to our move.

It seems to me that the problem with Foucault's position here is not that he proposes to return to bodies and pleasure, but that pleasure is not a particularly good point to lean on. It's true that, unlike desire, pleasure is not inherently conceptual. The problem is that it is nevertheless cognitively dependent. If one imagines a pleasurable sensation, say the tracing of fingertips over skin, this is in fact not so much inherently pleasurable as pleasurable depending on context. If the fingers belong to someone we are sexually attracted to, we are more likely, perhaps, to enjoy the sensation than if we are repelled by that person. And here the contingent categories of sexuality come into play: our pleasure is not separate from whether we deem the touch 'sexual', for example.

Now, Foucault's advice is perhaps that we can precisely try to focus on the pure sensation, without regard to the cognitive associations. But, by that token, we could say that we could try to focus on forming desires that are outside of the circuits of sex.

One may here link Foucault's position to his own sexual practices, since he himself does talk about these. He developed an interest in the late 1970s in the gay sex scene of the San Francisco Bay Area, where he had begun to spend time visiting scholars at the University of California, Berkeley. This scene involved sado-masochistic fetishism and anonymous sex in bath houses. Regarding the former, Foucault recognises a radically decentred form of pleasure involving all parts of the body (PPC 299). This presumably can be said to be desexualised pleasure, inasmuch as it does not focus on the sexual organ. Foucault speaks of the peculiar appeal of the latter, as indeed being a form of 'desubjectivising' practice, due to the anonymity involved. Bodies and pleasures, indeed. This then ought to provide the kind of pivot-experience necessary to do what Foucault thought was necessary: to construct some new form of subjectivity. He describes 'laboratories of sexual experimentation' emerging in San Francisco and New York (PPC 298). His contraction of HIV-AIDS is a grim epitaph to this experimentation, though it need not have been – safe sex does not preclude experimentation with bodies and pleasures and the main reason that it was not practised in this context was that no one knew of the looming danger of this then undiagnosed disease.

Such practices have clear merits as ways of resisting sex. They clearly defy conventional understandings of what sex is. Moreover, they oppose sex as a concept without trying to repress it qua act. Foucault is not calling for a new prurience: opposing sexual activity as a means of opposing sex would in fact merely be another way of obsessing about sex, one found today in religious conservative viewpoints, and formerly widespread in our society.

However, I think it should be noted that it is far from clear that the novel forms of sex being produced in this scene actually defied sexuality per se, even if they tend to push the envelope, so to speak, of sex. Indeed, they would seem if anything to still be under the sign of sexuality, still a form of obsession with sex. If sado-masochism is not centred on the sexual organ (and this 'if' is quite active – it is by no means clear that this is the case), is it not instead a sexualisation of other parts of the body? That is, rather than opposing the body to sex, isn't it just sexualising other parts of the body and other pleasures? I think one may be suspicious even of the extent to which these activities may be pleasurable precisely because they are sexual, involving that familiar frisson of transgression while in fact playing a sexual game.

'Bodies and pleasures' are analogous to the contact with experience in order to produce criticism that Foucault talks about in his prefaces to *Birth of the Clinic* and *The Order of Things*. In this much, Foucault is right: we can only hope to produce a new order to replace sexuality by revisiting bodies and pleasures. While not wishing to begrudge Foucault his bodily pleasures, however, I think he goes in for something of a romanticisation of those practices he enjoyed, even if he also recognises their negative aspects (see Foucault 2011a, 401).

I was once asked by a student in a class reading the first volume of *The History of Sexuality* why Foucault wanted to resist sex. The student didn't like Foucault's stance at all – it seemed to her to be a matter of opposing fun. Indeed, Foucault himself points out that we today derive sexual pleasure precisely from our attachment to sexuality. Why then indeed would we want to get rid of it?

The answer that occurred to me was rather bald, but I think does cut to the core of this question. Sexuality means precisely being labelled 'heterosexual' or 'homosexual' or indeed 'bisexual' or 'polysexual' or whatever other label might be invented. Foucault gives in the first volume of *The History of Sexuality* a veritable menagerie of categories of sexual 'perversions' which were invented by nineteenth-century sexology to categorise people, of which homosexuality was one (HS1 43). Basically, it seems to me that these labels do not exist apart from a pernicious play of power that serves to divide people and target them in particular ways. The heterosexual/homosexual distinction in particular has historically existed with the clear effect of stigmatising anyone categorised as homosexual. If this is indeed now ceasing to be the case, it becomes radically unclear why we need to insist on maintaining this distinction. What is our interest in doing so? There are many obvious possible answers. One might say that one does it simply to facilitate one's sexual life: if we know who is gay and who is straight, we know who is a potential sexual partner for us and who is not. But of course things are never that simple: knowing sexual orientation does not answer this question, because there are so many other variables. Something similar may be said of the distinction male/female. Foucault indeed makes clear in his introduction to the *Herculine Barbin: Being the Recently Discovered Memoirs of a Nineteenth-century French Hermaphrodite* (the title of which accurately explains the contents of the book; their discoverer was Foucault) that his critique of 'sex' does also mean to target sex in the sense of the male/female distinction.

Now, this claim may seem looks rather odd. Things have changed rather since the time Foucault was writing, a twentieth century in which any child born with indistinct sexual characteristics would be *immediately* assigned a sex by the attending physician. This stretches back to the nineteenth century in the West, whence the story of Herculine Barbin, an intersex person made to live in the opposite sex to that with which she identified, who ultimately committed suicide. Foucault's historical researches indicate that, in other times and places, these things were rather more malleable. These days, indeed, intersex children are much more likely to be allowed to come to their own conclusion regarding their sex.

So, we can allow that, at least until very recently, modern Western culture demanded conformity to a sexual binary to an extraordinary degree. But surely other historical cultures have been deeply given to machismo, have treated women with a contempt apparently relatively absent from recent Western society. Here, we must refer to something else that Foucault thinks has happened in power in recent times, a move from power based on the law to power based on the *norm* (HS1 144). The best way to grasp this change I think is by thinking of it as one from a society governed primarily by negative rules, telling us what not to do, to a society in which we are given detailed models of how we *should* behave, which we are expected to live up to. Of course, rules and laws continue to exist, but the norm eclipses them. Thus, we can say that, where gender is concerned, we have moved from rules to norms (everyone is expected to display a full and appropriate range of emotions). The most obvious example of gender normalisation is the pressure women feel under today to conform to an impossible model of perfection in their physical appearance. While beauty has long been seen as a quintessential female virtue, things have changed in this regard in many ways. For one thing, where once older women were no longer expected to be beautiful, today femininity is associated so essentially with attractiveness that even older women are expected to conform. For another, beauty was not previously defined in the way it is today, notoriously by the images presented in magazines. That is, there was not a norm of beauty operating in the past, at least not in the same way or to the same extent. We can encapsulate the difference by saying that to be beautiful was not identified with being *normal*. Indeed, the entire concept of being normal is, Foucault shows, a nine-teenth-century invention. Today, everyone worries that they are not normal, because of their inability to live up to an impossibly perfect vision of what they should be.

This example is instructive. It's quite clear that the distinction between men and women has a currency in all known cultures, and throughout history. What then can Foucault possibly mean by castigating this distinction? Foucault's claim is that the male/female distinction in our society has become absolutised and stereotyped to an unparalleled degree. We may understand him to be saying something similar in relation to the homosexual/heterosexual distinction. Certainly, we may suppose that there have for a long time been those who preferred to consort with members of their own sex. This does not imply that there existed something equivalent to today's essentialising gay/straight dichotomy. As Foucault shows in the second and third volumes of his *History of Sexuality*, which deal with ancient Greece and Rome, there was nothing equivalent to the concept of the 'homosexual' there. While we might popularly think of ancient Greece as rife with homosexuality, it was not homosexual-ity in the sense we might understand it, as implying consensual rela-tions between two adults of the same sex. Rather, in Antiquity such a union would have been considered most inappropriate. In ancient Greece, adult males were expected to be sexually dominant. That meant they could have sex with slaves and women, who had a much lower status than adults in Greek society – and also with boys, who had a lower status with adults. Since the boys were aspiring to be men, however, it was expected that the boys would not consent easily to being in a sexually subordinate position. Acts we would consider paedophilia as well as acts we would consider rape were more acceptable in Antiquity than our idea of homosexuality as an equal relationship between adult men. This is not to say, of course, that homosexual relationships as we conceive of them, that is between consenting same-sex adults, did not occur in Antiquity. The point is simply that the Greeks did not have a concept corresponding to our concept of the 'homosexual', which emerged in the nineteenth and twentieth century in the West as a category of criminal perversion, and has more recently been reclaimed as a positive lifestyle. It is very common to see people in historical dramas portrayed these days anachronistically as covert, or even overt, homosexuals, with all the traits we expect of that today, but it is less than clear that such stereotypes existed in the past. The same, of course, can be said of our portrayals of heterosexuality in historical fiction, and indeed all the cultural detail of historical fiction.

The resistance to sex must be seen moreover in the context of bio-power, the topic of the second half of this chapter.

POLICY

Foucault also engaged in a rather different form of practice, less personal and more public, in his struggle against sexuality. This one bore on public policy. His position, though never explicitly formulated as such, would seem to be that the categories of sex and sexuality should be struck from the law and state policy. Foucault was active during this period in a campaign for the abolition of age of consent laws. The significance of this issue is doubtless in part that age of consent laws had been used particularly to persecute homosexuals, but it is clear that Foucault had some disdain for the emerging problematic of 'paedophilia'. The rapid rise in public panic around paedophilia in the last few decades gives an extraordinary example of sexuality. It is a pity Foucault did not live to comment on it. It is clear that paedophilia has transformed in the last forty years from being a marginal and largely ignored phenomenon to being one of the primary moral evils posited by our society, fear of which haunts relationships between adults and children. This is of course only the latest turn in a long history that Foucault details of the treatment of childhood sexuality since the nineteenth century. Childhood sexuality is a paradoxical object. On the one hand, there is ample evidence that children do behave in ways that are classifiable as 'sexual'. On the other, it is seen as absolutely unnatural and scandalous.

At the centre of the first volume of the *History of Sexuality* is a case study of a French peasant who is institutionalised for life after having been accused of engaging in sexual activity with an underage girl. Foucault gives more details of this case in *Abnormal*. What fascinates Foucault is how unprecedented this nineteenth-century case is. On the one hand it is a moral scandal that garnered substantial public interest, such that the medical case notes were published as a book. On the other hand, Foucault notes, this can hardly have been an unusual case – indeed, these kinds of sexual relationships between young girls and simple men must have existed many times in the rural France of the period.

Foucault's public policy stance is in effect to try to strip everything specifically sexual out of such questions. When it comes to determining criminality, the important thing to stress is consent, and, in the absence of consent, what one is left with ought to simply be assault, a non-consensual action on the body of another. This effectively means the abolition of any special juridical category of rape, qua specifically sexual assault.

Foucault adopts this stance in the context of a public, broadcast discussion with multiple participants. His argument is quickly rounded upon by the two female co-discussants. The issue is one of the specificity of the trauma occasioned by sexual vis-à-vis common assault. Foucault seems rather at a loss in this face of this criticism. It seems to me, however, that he might have availed himself of the following defence of his position: if someone is physically assaulted non-sexually, but in a way that penetrated their body, involved being held down and harmed over a period for the enjoyment of a tormentor, this too would have been traumatic, and lastingly so. That is, this discussion tends to underestimate how traumatic non-sexual assault is, and that the very serious trauma that can follow from non-consensual assault may be on a par with rape. Moreover, to the extent that there is a peculiar trauma experienced only in cases of sexual assault, one can certainly argue that this is because sex is for us so important, for reasons that Foucault presents. One might thus make the argument that the reduction of sexual categories is actually something that will contribute to lessening the specific trauma of rape, because it will lessen the stigma and emphasis attached to the experience.

Still, the problem remains of dealing with a society in which the category of sex is central, and in which therefore acts categorised as sexual are experienced very differently from acts not so categorised.

This naturally, as it were, leads to demands for the special treatment of sexual crimes.

Foucault's project of resisting sex was the site of an unprecedented crossover of his research with the formulation of public policy: he was contemporaneously consulted by the French government about their reform of sexual laws. With other intellectuals, when it came to it, he proposed that the age of consent be lowered to 'the thirteen to fifteen age range' (Foucault 2011a, 402), within which range indeed the French law, in common with law of most European countries, now sits.

FEMINISM

Episodes like this give some indication of why Foucault is a controversial figure among feminists. Foucault's work on sexuality has actually been enormously influential for feminism in the last thirty years. The idea that the sex distinction itself is historically constructed and malleable is at the heart of this and is seminal to the so called 'third wave' of feminism in the United States.

While Foucault did acknowledge the laudable radicalness of the women's movement, as mentioned above, he generally had almost no engagement with feminism. At the risk of making excuses, this might partly be due to the relatively undeveloped state of feminism as a movement in France in Foucault's day. It also probably has something to do with the fact that the most famous French feminist of Foucault's lifetime, Simone de Beauvoir, was an ideological enemy of Foucault's, aligned with her partner Sartre in Marxist opposition to Foucault from an early stage.

It is sometimes alleged that Foucault ignored the problems of women, though this seems to me to be false when one considers the prominence of women's sexuality as a problematic in the first volume of the *History of Sexuality*, though this is doubtless a relative question, and there are many who find the fact that Foucault's archaeological works are focused exclusively on the writings of men highly objectionable, even if there are methodological justifications that could be made in terms of the historical (and largely continuing) dominance of the relevant fields by men. It seems perhaps fair to say that Foucault was himself no feminist.

So, Foucault stands accused of ignoring women, and of being somewhat misogynistic in his relations with women. His views on rape seem to some to confirm at least a breathtaking insensitivity to women's concerns. It would not be inappropriate either to point out Foucault's position as a member of a canon of mostly male 'great thinkers' of his generation. Indeed, I perhaps ought to note qua male my awareness of my own pitiful allocation of such a small section of this book specifically to women's concerns.

Still, significant women thinkers have emerged in the wake of Foucault who are profoundly influenced in their feminism by his attack on fixed identities, most prominent of these perhaps being Judith Butler, though it is perhaps worth underlining how much of her framework and that of other recent feminist thinkers is *not* drawn from Foucault: notions of identity and performativity (of identities) are not found in Foucault's thought as such in particular. The more important influence on Butler's thought, I would argue, is actually not Foucault but Derrida. When it comes to the philosophical issues of most interest to feminists, the two thinkers are not incompatible. Despite the differences between their respective perspectives, Derrida and Foucault's thought had a similar and complementary influence on feminist thought, by challenging the male–female binary, pointing towards a fluidity and ambiguity between these terms, in an effort that built on the somewhat equivocal legacy of psychoanalysis in this regard.

This is not to say that there is no biological fact of male and female sex in most cases. It rather points to the pernicious component of normativisation that insists people live up to an ideal of what it is supposed to mean to be a man or a woman.

A notable feminist critique of Foucault on sex that proceeds from a factual – albeit autobiographical – basis is that of Sandra Lee Bartky (2002). Bartky in effect defends the repressive hypothesis against Foucault, pointing out how she was actively repressed sexually as a youngster and how liberation from this was important for her, trying to retain sexual liberation as a feminist cause. This seems to me to be a fairly straightforward misunderstanding: Bartky believes that Foucault's position is that there never was any sexual repression, but in fact Foucault clearly does allow that sexual repression is real. He only denies its primacy and the efficacy of the attempt to liberate ourselves from it by talking or by using the concept of sex. More generally, Foucault does not deny that power can be repressive, only that today repressive forms of power are less prominent than productive forms. As we will see, they certainly still exist. To this extent, Bartky's critique of the first volume of the *History of Sexuality* resembles Alford's critique of *Discipline and*

Punish: both critics take it that Foucault thinks older forms of power have simply vanished without a trace in the face of new ones, when in fact he never makes such strong claims. Indeed, such straw person attacks on him resemble the misreadings of *The Order of Things* as a totalising and monolithic account, when his intention is to produce just the opposite, that is, to bring to light new insights, connections and ruptures that challenge the received view of things.

Biopolitics

Where *Discipline and Punish* has two main theses, one relatively specific, about the prison system, and the other more general, about discipline, the first volume of the *History of Sexuality* manages to fit three into much less than half the number of pages. The most general thesis of these three is of course about power, the most specific about sexuality itself, but in between these two lies a thesis about the form of power which exists in our society, which incorporates the technology of discipline with a new formation Foucault calls 'biopolitics', to produce a new unity, 'biopower'. The terms 'biopolitics' and 'biopower' have been the foci of profligate confusion. Several factors come into play in producing this confusion. One is the fact that Foucault uses two terms that are so apparently similar to mean two subtly different things in the *History of Sexuality*, but elsewhere, notably in *Society Must Be Defended*, uses them apparently interchangeably (SD 243). One might think that the division between 'biopolitics' and 'biopower' maps to a more basic distinction between politics and power, but Foucault does not make any such basic distinction in a consistent way, nor, when he does make such a distinction, does it map to the distinction he makes between biopower and biopolitics.

Not only are the 'power' and 'politics' parts of these terms thus apt to confuse but so too is the 'bio-' prefix itself. This prefix comes from the Greek *bios*, meaning life (specifically human life). These terms therefore imply, prima facie, the existence of a politics of and power of life itself. But this is so vague it could mean almost anything. Indeed, it is not immediately clear it means anything in particular at all: where is the politics or the power that does not involve life?

This confusion has been propagated by later appropriations of these two terms by other thinkers. Giorgio Agamben (1998) takes the 'life' reference at face value, and, since power and politics are actually always about life, Agamben ends up concluding that biopolitics is synonymous with politics per se, seeing it as a phenomenon that stretches back to the dawn of history. Agamben does at least acknowledge his divergence from Foucault, though he also speaks in terms of trying to correct lacunae in Foucault's thought. He in any case significantly muddies the waters in terms of wider perceptions of what these terms might mean. Worse than Agamben in this respect are Michael Hardt and Antonio Negri in their joint work (2000), where they take up the terms directly from Foucault, citing him without signalling that they are using the concepts in ways that have almost nothing in common with Foucault's use of them. Adding to the general confusion, their usage of these terms goes in more or less the opposite direction to Agamben's. Where Agamben focuses on the 'bio' of biopower, expanding the concept to mean more or less the same thing as power itself, Hardt and Negri focus on the 'power' and 'politics' distinction. Where Foucault used the two words to mean subtly different things, 'biopower' being the broader phenomenon of which 'biopolitics' is a component, in Hardt and Negri the two become absolute opposites. For them 'biopower' and 'biopolitics' are simply the most recent instantiation of an ancient antinomy between the constituted power of states and the constitutive power of the people respectively.

It is worth noting, incidentally, that the terms 'biopower' and 'biopolitics' do also have multiple older usages, and indeed multiple contemporary usages, that have nothing demonstrably to do with Foucault's use of the terms. These uses have been mapped by Thomas Lemke (2011b) in an excellent study.

The upshot of all this however is that the use of the terms in the theoretical humanities outside Foucault studies is, I fear, forever confused. Attempts to clarify things, such as Roberto Esposito's (2008), inevitably only add further definitions which confuse things more. What we can hope to do here is only to clarify what Foucault intended by his use of these terms.

Foucault's derives the terms from a contraction of 'biological politics' and 'biological power'.[1] It is a matter then for him not of how life itself has been invested by politics or power but of how the specific scientific discourse of biology came to ground politics and power. Such a concept is a natural outcome of his long researches into the history and interaction of biological discourses and power. Really, then, biopolitics is not so much about life itself coming together with power (something Foucault in an aside in the first volume of the *History of Sexuality* terms 'bio-history' – HS1 143), but about biological science coming together with the control of human beings (STP 1). What this combination of life sciences and power produces, according to Foucault, is essentially the constitution of a new object: the *population*.

Disciplinary power had constituted the individual as a single unit of political control. Biology was implicated in this constitution via the advent of modern medicine. But medicine found itself faced with problems that went well beyond the individual. Disease outbreaks, for example, had an existence qua epidemic above the level of any individual, and individuals themselves come into existence only through reproduction, which of course necessarily involves multiple persons and is variable according to wider social dynamics. Biopolitics arose when institutional power sought to try to control the spread of disease, the reproduction of people and the general health of the population. While such efforts, as with discipline, have their origins in attempts to control plague in the Middle Ages, it is only with modernity that the practice emerges of trying to intervene at the level not of the local outbreak but of the whole population as such. This biopolitics of the population seeks not simply to control outbreaks of disease but to prevent them from occurring in the first place, to intervene in the constitution of the population to make it healthier. Where previously it was appreciated that one needed to have people in the land, and that it was perhaps beneficial for disease to be absent, the attempt to think of the people of the land as a unified 'population', to regulate this population as such, was new at this point. This indeed produced the population as such, as a real entity, for the first time, by producing the systems of control that organised it as a whole. This is not to say that they do not have much deeper roots too in Western culture for Foucault, in what he calls 'pastoral power', which will be explored in the next chapter.

Now, one might say that biopolitical control is fundamentally benign. Indeed, more than benign, it aimed precisely at maximising the life of the people, keeping them healthy, and often trying to increase our numbers. Biopolitics is thus fundamentally a logic of protection and enhancement. Many caveats have to be added, however. Firstly, it fundamentally remains a system of control. It is founded on the basis of discipline. Discipline provides the microscopic interventions into individual lives, provides the individuals themselves, that become the basis of the larger-scale control measures of the entire population. You must, in effect, control individuals if you are to control the population as such. Biopolitics is not merely about herding people as a mass – this could already be done by sovereign power hundreds of years before, but is a crude method, capable only of the most general effects, not a meticulous control of everyone. This new form of power, combining both biopolitics and the 'anatomo-politics' of discipline (HS1 139), Foucault calls 'bio-power' in the *History of Sexuality*.

Furthermore, this biopower has not actually abolished the pre-existing sovereign power. It has rather only displaced it as a tool for the control of masses of people. That sovereign power which marked and destroyed bodies as a spectacle of its own authority, as we have already seen, was displaced by a disciplinary power which trained bodies and made them docile. However, this replacement occurred only in particular domains, and then only up to a point. For a long time (and still today in many jurisdictions), at the extreme end of the practice of carceral punishment, execution still lurked as the ultimate sanction. Moreover, the use of physical, corporal force has always been required as a resort in cases where bodies prove less than docile, where prisons, or people more generally, break out in rioting, for example. It is moreover frequently used beyond, and sometimes behind, the borders of society, in wars.

For Foucault, the coexistence of biopower with older forms of violent power necessitate a distinction between their respective areas of operation. One way of distinguishing them is the division between criminal and law-abiding citizen, with the former marked out as vulnerable to the application of violent measures – though of course prisoners typically retain a right to care by the state, and are generally exposed to violence only when being apprehended, and then only within strict limits. Racism is for Foucault another, rather typical, way in which the distinction has been made. The geographical border of the state is a more tangible way in which this distinction is marked, with those outside deserving no care of the state whose border they lie outside, and potentially being exposed to its use of violence in the case of military adventures. This distinction is in fact not purely geographical, but rather depends on multiple factors: there are rights of citizenship by which the state will try to protect its citizens wherever in the world they might be, and conversely by which non-citizens may find themselves unprotected biopolitically by the state whose national borders they are within (especially if they do not have permission to be there). In this context, William Walters (2002) has coined the concept of the 'biopolitical border', which allows a considerable variability in relation to different people and places, overflowing and underflowing conventional national boundaries.

For Foucault, there is, moreover, a fundamental reversibility of biopolitics itself: 'Since the population is nothing more than what the state takes care of for its own sake, of course, the state is entitled to slaughter it, if necessary. So the reverse of biopolitics is thanatopolitics' (EW3 416). The most extreme example of this reversibility, given by Foucault, is Nazi Germany: Hitler was willing to wager the very existence of the German people on the war, and when they lost was willing to commit national suicide, ordering the effective destruction of the nation in the face of advancing foreign armies (an order which was not carried out, however – SD 260). While this is the extreme case, it exemplifies a more widespread tendency, a paradox that Foucault notes by which wars got bloodier just as life was being maximised biopolitically. The world wars of the twentieth century in particular saw slaughter on an unprecedented scale. While this has much to do with the invention of unprecedentedly terrible weapons of war, it also owed much to the political technology of biopolitics. The invention of the population made armies larger than ever before – indeed, this was one of the initial purposes of biopolitics, to produce a regular supply of soldiers for national armies. The national solidarity brought about by the cohesion of populations around biopolitics made possible conscription: where previously soldiering had been left to the professionals, either aristocrats or freebooters, who fought for their own interests or for money, the nation's wars were now seen to be in every person's interests, since the national state took care of everyone. This magnified killing in two directions: it meant a new savagery towards the nation's enemies, since they threatened not merely the king's prestige but the life of the nation itself, and allowed a new scale of death among the nation's own soldiers to be tolerated, since they died for the good of the population.

Thus biopolitics is inherently problematic, dangerous, though Foucault sees no obvious way out of it. The most he seems to allow us to hope for is to excise the racism from the biopolitical-thanatopolitical coupling (SD 263). That is, it is neither desirable nor possible for a population to negate the care of its state, and there is no obvious way to have a state without the use of force, but we can try to ensure that its care and its violence are not administered on a racial basis. Foucault's invocation of 'racism' here implies something rather broader than we might ordinarily understand the term to mean. In its narrowest sense, 'racism' refers to distinction on the basis of a

biological 'race' (a category that has no basis in contemporary biological knowledge, but was widely posited as a category in the racial
pseudo-science of the late nineteenth and early twentieth centuries,
which indeed saw racial purity as an aspect of the biological vitality
of the population). Today, 'race' is usually thought of in terms of
skin colour. Foucault's *Society Must Be Defended* however offers a
genealogy of racism which shows that it has rather deeper roots in
a much wider way of thinking that Foucault designates 'the great
discourse of race war' (SD 63). Foucault has nothing against this
greater discourse, which includes Marxism, and indeed which he
sees himself as part of. Specifically, he sees himself as partaking in
the form of analysis that sees society as made up of contesting forces,
which is one strand of 'race war' discourse. Any discourse of class
struggle Foucault sees as one manifestation of the great discourse,
with racism in the narrower sense being another, right-wing way of
dividing people up into groups, and Marxism is clearly a form of
analysis in terms of struggle – but it has also always been guilty, like
other forms of left-wing thought of the nineteenth century, of being
racist in a more pejorative sense (SD 261). While it has not always
been *ethnically* racist, it has nevertheless for Foucault engaged in a
'social-racism', by which it castigates its enemies as parasites and has
vilified them absolutely (SD 261). This played out in extraordinarily
vicious and bloody ways in the twentieth century. It is in this context
that Foucault's desire to abnegate racism must be understood: not
only to get away from racial discrimination in the strict sense but to
get rid of the systematic exclusion of political dissidents, the mentally
ill, criminals, foreigners, etcetera. His criticism of socialism would
seem to be that it aimed at getting rid of the state, but in so doing
produced a racist state which victimised those who seemed to stand
in the way of its project.

We must remember that Foucault classifies biopolitics, thanatopolitics and anatomo-politics as 'technologies' of power (DP 30, SD
243, DE3 392), and this implies that, like any technologies, they can
be turned to a variety of purposes (though that is not to say that
the purposes one develops are indifferent to the technologies at our
disposal).

DELEUZE AND CONTROL

The reason Hardt and Negri are able to use the terms biopolitics
and biopower with explicit reference to Foucault, but with almost

total diversion from him, is that they have got them not directly from Foucault but from a much more important influence on their thinking, Gilles Deleuze; specifically, from a short piece by Deleuze about Foucault's biopower called 'Postscript on Societies of Control'. In this piece, Deleuze agrees with Foucault's understanding of societies as having a framework of sovereign power, biopolitics and discipline, but argues that things have crucially changed since Foucault was writing in the 1970s. Deleuze believed that a new technology of power, which he labelled 'control', was replacing discipline. This 'control' corresponds to what is often called 'post-Fordist' production, which is a touchstone of Negri's broad project of updating Marxism. Post-Fordist production has moved beyond the mass-production, assembly-line factory discipline previously practised, in the direction of much more variable, intellectual, creative, individualised, 'affective' work. Hardt and Negri take things a step further by associating 'biopower' and 'biopolitics' only with the 'society of control', while also mangling the terminology beyond recognition.

I disagree with Deleuze that such developments represent a departure from discipline on Foucault's conception. It seems to me that whatever has changed in our society since the 1970s continues to conform to the broad pattern of discipline as portrayed by Foucault. Indeed, I think we can say that the changes we've seen recently are precisely in line with a kind of logical development of discipline indicated in Foucault's studies, from initially relatively crass attempts to control masses of bodies, which are honed through increasing psychologisation and individualisation to the point where individuals control themselves. It is worth noting that Foucault uses the word 'control' precisely when talking about the emergence of disciplinary power and the prison in particular, saying of it, 'This is the age of social control' (EW3 57), of 'control of the population, continuous control of the behaviour of individuals' (EW3 59): control is for Foucault precisely the unifying feature of the technologies of discipline and biopower.

Note

1. This is not made absolutely explicit by Foucault, but can be seen in many places (e.g. HS1 139, SD 250). Foucault's first use of the notion of biopolitics comes in explicit relation to the biological, though at this point he does not differentiate anatomopolitics from biopolitics (EW3 137).

7

Government and Governmentality

In 1976, Foucault delivered the lectures entitled *Society Must Be Defended*, and then finished and published the first volume of his *History of Sexuality*. The following year, 1977, for the only time after his appointment there, he took a year's sabbatical from the Collège de France. He returned to lecturing duties in 1978 with a series entitled *Security, Territory, Population*. That title signals little change; indeed, it would have been an apt alternative title for *Society Must Be Defended*. The problematic of population is clearly a continuing concern. The first sentence of his first lecture moreover announces an intention to continue to study biopower. He follows with a run-through of his views on power, largely repeating what he had said previously on the topic. He soon moves on to unfamiliar ground, however. Despite his stated intention, the terms 'biopower' and 'biopolitics' appear only a few more times in the course of the lectures. It is another term that rather appears at the fore as the lectures progress, namely 'government', and the related concept, invented by Foucault himself in the lectures, of 'governmentality', which he identifies as the key concept of the series. These remain the signature concepts for the following year's lecture series, *The Birth of Biopolitics*. It too has a title which clearly points to the conceptual problematic of the earlier lectures, specifically to 'biopolitics', but in fact, excluding the title, this concept is mentioned even less often than in *Security, Territory, Population*. This is again despite Foucault explicitly stating an intention in the lectures to deal with this topic again there (BB 78, 185). These two lecture series may thus be grouped together as 'the governmentality lectures' – indeed, the German translations of the two series have been marketed as volumes I and II of the *Geschichte der Gouvernementalität* (History of governmentality).

Now, it seems quite logical that a concern with biopolitics should lead to questions about government: it is hard to imagine how the population could have been constituted without government. However, to be concerned with government actually indicates quite a profound shift in Foucault's attitude, given the extent to which his previous work on power had been concerned to correct what he characterised as an exaggeration of the role of the state within contemporary political thought. His focus has thus turned towards the state, though this does not in itself contradict his previous claims that others were overestimating its importance. He never claimed that the state was politically unimportant – and indeed that would surely be a mistaken view – but rather only that it was less politically central than others seemed to imagine. He still however pointedly refuses to provide a 'theory of the state' (BB 77). As usual, we must understand this refusal by contrast with Marxism, specifically the Marxist theory of the state. In orthodox Marxism, the state is seen as the expression of a 'class dictatorship', reflecting the class domination of society (see Lenin 1992). For Foucault, by contrast, there is no general formula for understanding the state as such. Moreover, he does not proceed by simply analysing the state itself – he refuses also to do anything like a 'genealogy of the state itself' (STP 276) – but characteristically by analysing discourses of and about the state, with the aim of explaining how the state had come to be such a central political preoccupation. He will now argue that the state can be understood only as a phenomenon produced within a larger history of what he will call government (BB 6).

I think one can see Foucault's position on the state in the early 1970s as analogous to his position in relation to politics more generally in the late 1960s, which is to say, as essentially agnostic, instead pursuing a form of analysis that leaves an apparently all-pervasive element to one side. In both cases, Foucault comes later to see his agnosticism as inadequate. But, as with his novel conceptual approach to politics through the lens of power, an obvious but somehow underexplored concept, he now performs a similar gesture in relation to the state with the concept of government.

Concepts and Context

Understanding Foucault's talk of 'government' is fraught with difficulty, primarily because his usage of this term fluctuates considerably, from a narrow usage of the word that is close to its conventional sense of 'statecraft' to a much broader notion of governing that seems to encompass all power, including the control people exercise over themselves, with 'government' replacing war as the exemplary model of the operation of power (EW3 341). This variation in usage occurs both within and between texts: he uses the term in different ways even within *Security, Territory, Population*, but then uses it in different ways again in later texts. This lack of conceptual precision is, I think, connected to the fact that Foucault uses the term during a period of his thought without major publications, thus with an unusual lack of impetus for him to pin down his concepts (an imperative he in any case was never particularly strict about obeying). When he came to produce two books at the end of his eight-year publishing hiatus between the first volume of the *History of Sexuality* in 1976 and the second and third volumes in 1984, he does use the vocabulary of 'governing' in a way that is consistent with the trajectory of his thinking in the interim, but he does not thematise the notion, using it only in an incidental way unlikely to attract any particular notice from readers.

THE PERIOD

Foucault's work of the late 1970s is in this respect a period like no other in his oeuvre: conceptually distinctive, but without major contemporaneous publications. It is significant, and I think should be emphasised, because it is so easily forgotten, that the lectures of this time were not a body of work with which Foucault felt sufficiently satisfied to publish. While much of his work from the early 1970s and early 1980s found its way into books he was writing, almost none of the final two lecture series of the 1970s did. It is thus known to us rather almost entirely from the publication of the Collège de France lectures only in the last decade, close to thirty years after they were originally given. The very important exception is the single lecture of *Security, Territory, Population* he allowed to be published contemporaneously, under the title of 'Governmentality', in an Italian journal. Despite this relatively obscure beginning to its dissemination, it was soon translated into English, and thus came to have a considerable impact on English-language scholarship, grounding a whole 'governmentality school' in sociology, long before the full series was widely available.

The remit for Collège de France lectures was specifically to give an account of work in progress, and Foucault had to give them regardless of the state of the material he had to hand. He tried to limit the audience for the lectures, moreover, though mainly because there was simply an overwhelming demand and he wished to engage in collaborative group work, rather than because he wished to limit access to his ideas, but nevertheless this indicates his preference for presenting unfinished work not suitable for a wide audience. Perhaps most significantly, he forbade any posthumous publication of his works. Though it has rightly been said that this was probably mainly directed at preventing the publication of personal correspondence and the like, and hence has been interpreted by those who control his estate not to be a barrier to publication of the lectures, Foucault certainly did not imagine that so much of this material would be published.

Foucault explicitly couched the lectures as a matter of 'trying out' the concept of governmentality (BB 186), and one might conclude from the absence of publications on the topic that he didn't regard it as an unmitigated success. In two lectures given in North America after the governmentality lecture series at the Collège de France, 'Omnes et Singulatim' in late 1979 and 'The Political Technology of Individuals' in 1982, he talks about governmentality without using the name – that is, he abandoned the term, or at least considered it unsuited to an Anglophone audience, preferring instead to use the less outlandish phrases 'political rationality', 'state rationality' and 'the art of government'.

Now, there are motives other than a lack of things to say for Foucault's lack of book publications between 1976 and 1984, by far the longest such silence he maintained during his career, namely a decision not to write any books during a five-year period in which he remained under an exclusive contract with Gallimard (DE1 68). However, this explains only his silence up until 1981, whereas he in fact published no books till 1984. If he had wished to publish his reflections on governmentality as a book, would he not have thus done so at that point? I think we can say rather that, having decided not to publish during these years, he was free to explore material he didn't want to publish – to think aloud, as it were.

Foucault during this period was intermittently trying to write the second volume of the *History of Sexuality*, intended then as a kind of prequel to the first volume, dealing with the medieval period preceding the modern period dealt with in the first volume (DE1 73, 77). It is perhaps indicative of the difficulties he had in this effort that, unlike with that first volume and *Discipline and Punish*, little material obviously pertaining to this book project appears in the contemporaneous lecture series, though his attention to premodern roots of contemporary subjectivity in *Security, Territory, Population* certainly does point in the direction that he will follow more concertedly in the 1980s to produce those final volumes.

So, the status of the two lecture series dealing with governmentality is somewhat experimental and I would speculate that it is to this status that they owe their conceptual messiness. This messiness is the central difficulty in dealing with them, inasmuch as the meaning of the core concepts is unclear.

DEFINING THE CONCEPTS

This lack of clarity unavoidably leads to dissension in the secondary literature. In the case of 'governmentality', the scholarly literature disagrees even about its etymology. According to Colin Gordon (1991, 1), it is a portmanteau contraction of 'governmental rationality'. According to Michel Senellart (STP 399 note), certain German scholars have claimed that it is a portmanteau rather of 'government' and 'mentality'; to which Senellart prefers the prosaic etymology that it is simply derived from the adjective 'governmental' (i.e. it means governmentalness). Senellart is I think right here about the relatively banal nature of the word-concept itself, and this makes 'governmentality' and 'government' close to synonymous. However, the variability of Foucault's use of both these terms remains as the big difficulty.

Already in *Security, Territory, Population*, Foucault specifies 'three things' he means to connote by the use of the former term:

> [Firstly,] I mean by 'governmentality' the ensemble formed by the institutions, procedures, analyses and reflections, the calculations and tactics that allow the exercise of this very specific, albeit complex form of power which has population as its target, political economy as its principal form of knowledge, and apparatuses of security as its essential technical instrument. Secondly, I refer to the tendency which, over a long period and throughout the West, has steadily led towards the pre-eminence of this type of power which one may call 'government' over all other forms of power (sovereignty, discipline, etc.) resulting, on the one hand, in the development of a whole series of specific governmental apparatuses, and, on the other, in the development of a whole series of knowledges. Lastly, by 'governmentality' I think we must understand the process, or rather the result of the process, through which the judicial state of the Middle Ages turned into the administrative state during the fifteenth and sixteenth centuries, gradually becoming 'governmentalised'.[1]

These are thus three rather distinct senses of 'governmentality', with varying degrees of historical specificity.

By the first definition in this list, governmentality is a combination of knowledges, institutions and actions that arose in a particular

141

historical situation. Its focus on the population means it was biopolitical, but the fact that it was tied to the discourse of political
economy locates it, on the most stringent reading, in a particular
historical period, namely that before the emergence of the contemporary discipline of economics, which displaced political economy as a
form of knowledge (this transformation, from political economy to
economics, is a major object of study in Foucault's *Order of Things*).
As Foucault points out himself, the term 'political economy' was
initially, during the period 1750–1820, ambiguous: it could mean
reflection of an economic nature, or of a political nature or any combination of the two (BB 13); the term thus points to an absence of any
distinction between economics and politics as intellectual disciplines
at this time. Foucault in fact seems to use 'governmentality' both in
a sense which restricts it to this period and to mean any reflection
which centrally involves reflection on either politics or economics or
both – that is, even the first sense he lists above splits into two uses.
The latter, somewhat broader sense makes it essentially coextensive
with biopolitics, though the emphasis on political and/or economic
reflection differentiates the two notions. Governmentality is, in
effect, the form of managerial thinking proper to biopolitics.

The first listed sense of 'governmentality' itself invokes a term
which here for the first time becomes a special term in Foucault's
vocabulary: the eponymous concept of 'security'. He speaks now in
terms of three 'mechanisms': the law, the disciplinary mechanism
that enforces it and a third mechanism, security, which involves
calculations of a statistical nature about risk and reward in law and
its enforcement (STP 7). Security here seems to replace biopolitics
in the listing of historically accumulating technologies (just as
government itself does elsewhere). We can none the less distinguish
biopolitics from security as from government: biopolitics is the
specific technology that appears when power begins to utilise biology;
security is what happens when power incorporates the calculation of
risk; government(ality) (in the narrow sense) is what happens when
biopolitics combines with political economy and security. These
things may never occur without one another historically, but they
may none the less be seen as distinct concepts.

This first sense of 'governmentality' is the concern of the bulk of
Security, Territory, Population, its first four and its last four lectures,
which deal with the history of political and economic thought from
the sixteenth to the eighteenth century. In the middle four lectures
of the course, however – that is in the fifth to eighth of its twelve

lectures – he deals with the development and crisis of what he calls 'pastoral power' from Antiquity through the Christian period. He thus situates governmentality in its narrower sense as the most recent instance of something he confusingly also calls 'governmentality' which stretches back to Antiquity, which is the second sense outlined in the above-quoted extract. The third sense he introduces in the above-quoted extract is historically intermediate between the other two senses: it refers to a shift in Western governmentality (in the second, broad sense) since the sixteenth century that has, since the eighteenth century, led to governmentality in the first, narrower sense. While Foucault in this extract delineates three distinct senses of 'governmentality', his use of it in the last two lecture series of the 1970s seems on occasion to encompass all points in between.

The History of Government

Having thus mapped the conceptual confusion in Foucault's first explorations of government, we may move on to the actual history he set out for us. We will reconstruct this chronologically, rather than in the order it is presented in Foucault's texts.

PASTORAL POWER

Foucault's second sense of 'governmentality' points further back in history than any of his genealogies and archaeologies have thus far (notwithstanding reflection on Greek literature in lectures in the early 1970s). Foucault posits what he calls 'pastoral power', which for him leads from ancient Israel via Christianity to modern biopolitics (STP 123ff.). Pastoral power may be understood as a particular model of government (in the loosest sense) based on a metaphor of a shepherd caring for his flock. This for Foucault is the deep precursor to the caring biopolitics of modernity, and constitutes the basis of its emergence in the West.

I think one should be cautious about accepting at least this most antique part of the genealogy of government, in which Foucault (STP 130) asserts that the ancient Greeks could not accept being seen as sheep in a flock in the way that Semitic peoples did. Perhaps tellingly, this claim is challenged in between lectures by an auditor (STP 136). Foucault responds in the following lecture by considering the evidence in detail. He maintains his position, but to do so has to dismiss the Pythagoreans, Greek philosophers who do cleave to the model of the shepherd. Indeed, by some lights, the Pythagoreans are the quintessential Greek philosophers. Foucault has recourse to two arguments to dismiss the significance of their model. His first is to say that 'this Pythagorean tradition is, if not marginal, at least limited' (STP 137). This is to say that, while the Pythagorean tradition is central to Greek intellectual life, the Pythagoreans do not make up its mainstay, and perhaps that their contribution to ancient political theory in particular is relatively minor, at least as compared to what Foucault deems 'the classical political vocabulary', which is largely without references to shepherds (STP 138). Foucault's second argument is to cite the nineteenth-century German philologist R. F. Gruppe to say that the Pythagoreans themselves got their model of the shepherd from Eastern, non-Greek sources (STP 138). This is a common claim about the Pythagoreans, but it is contested. Foucault goes on to allow that the Pythagoreans may have formed a social basis for the spread of pastoral ideas with the advent of Christianity (STP 147), but he is left with the fact that the model of the shepherd was none the less present in ancient Greek political thought.

Furthermore, Mika Ojakangas (2012) has argued that there are many apparently biopolitical concerns, including extensive control and monitoring of the populace, found in classical, non-Pythagorean ancient Greek and Roman thought. So it seems that the claim that biopolitics and governmentality are peculiarly traceable to Middle Eastern and not European roots is dubious.

Clearly, Foucault's sudden extension of his genealogical purview, from at most a few hundred years to one that takes in two-and-a-half or even three thousand years of history, is fraught with problems. Not only does the tracing of lineages become more speculative and dubious, but its relevance is also diminished. While the genealogy of the prison system in *Discipline and Punish* shows us much of the essentials of the regime of punishment we continue to have today, the tracing of our social form back to wandering tribespeople in the Near East, in a time from which the surviving accounts are mythological in character, clearly does not inform us so directly about present realities. It seems to be a departure from Foucault's 'history of the present' to a form of history conducted more for its own sake. We will consider the stakes of ancient history for the present in greater detail in the next chapter, which deals with Foucault's increasing emphasis on ancient sources in the last years of his life.

Less dubious is Foucault's characterisation of pastoral power in medieval Christian Europe. He argues that the model of the shepherd, applied directly to God by the Hebrews, is now applied mediately, to the Church and to the priest. It is now the churchman who has a flock to watch over. This leads to a new form of power, not seen either in Semitic or Greek politics. In Christianity, one must be humble and self-effacing, even when one holds power, and must genuinely care for the people one has power over. This new power had to be imposed forcibly on the people of Europe in a process of Christianisation. This implies a resistance, which shaped pastoral power as it was applied in Europe. Once established, it was moreover resisted from within, most spectacularly in the Protestant Reformation. This saw a full-scale revolt against temporal pastoral power, bypassing the Church in favour of a direct relationship of believer to God. But this does not restore, it would seem, the pre-Christian pastoral model, with God as pastor, as it threatens too. Rather, the radical Protestants are crushed, and the version of Protestantism that wins out is the render-unto-Caesar version propagated by Martin Luther. This sees the Church displaced from the governing role, leaving temporal power now in the hands of 'the state'. Where previously temporal rulers in Europe had been concerned primarily with their own selfish and petty power games, simply taking from the common people and leaving the Church to care for them, the state itself now takes on the pastoral position.

THE STATE AND REASON

Foucault traces the prehistory of governmentality in its narrow, recent sense to the emergence in the sixteenth century of government as a problematic of looking after oneself and one's family. This 'flourishing' of reflection of government in the sixteenth century is itself, like so much in this time period, based on the revival of ancient Greek and Roman modes of thought, hence is indicative of a much older tradition of reflection on the government of oneself and others that will become the major object of Foucault's studies in the 1980s. Concerns we would today identify as 'governmental' represent only an extreme end of a spectrum of this governmental reflection (STP 88). This is the reason for Foucault's variable usage of the term 'government', namely that the term has itself changed in the scope of its meaning. Hence, Foucault uses it to refer to different things depending on what it meant in the relevant historical context.

This genealogical line from Antiquity through the sixteenth century to the present can be seen in the etymology of the word 'economy', which derives from the Greek *oikos*, meaning household – hence 'economy' originally meant government of the family specifically (STP 94). 'Political economy' thus originally meant applying the practice of household government to the state (STP 95). It is for Foucault the entry of the notion of population that frees the art of government from this old model that simply sees the state and family as different scales of the same practice (STP 104).

He details two main phases in the development of governmentality in its narrow sense out of these very general reflections. The first is what he identifies as *raison d'État*, literally 'reason of state'. The invocation of 'reason' in relation to the state is part of the general valorisation of reason during the European Enlightenment as the privileged way of understanding the world (STP 285–6). *Raison d'État* represents an attempt to regulate society to the fullest extent possible, what was contemporaneously called 'police', a monumental effort to expand the state's control over the population in the late eighteenth and early nineteenth century.

This represents a considerable shift in the horizons of political thought. According to Foucault, *raison d'État* is the first form of thought to focus purely and specifically on the state, rather than considering it only in relation to some natural or supernatural logic outside itself (STP 257). *Raison d'État* indeed places the state at the centre, subordinating all other considerations to the service of the state, including the law (STP 263). Foucault describes *raison d'État* as 'complete governmentality' or 'governmentality with a tendency to be unlimited' (BB 37), which found its limits in a law (as well, to a much lesser extent, in the continuing hegemony of Christian values) that constrained its operation (BB 7). The law was a holdover from the old order that retained great importance, even if it lost some of its status in the face of the emergence of the modern state (BB 8). By the same token, *raison d'État* is not truly concerned with the population; rather, the state itself is its primary object, with the population as an implicit calculation, rather than an explicit theme (STP 277–8); specifically, the crude idea that the sheer size of population gives strength to the state, an old idea, is the main way in which the population enters into governmental calculations at this time (STP 323).

The state allows the nation, rather than the monarchical dynasty, to appear as a political unit for the first time (STP 294). The strength of the state and its increase replaces the acquisition of territory as the main concern of rulers (STP 295–6). There thus emerges the possibility of 'balancing' power between states (STP 297). This viewpoint is associated by Foucault historically with the 1648 Treaty of Westphalia (STP 291). Standing armies are introduced; territories, previously fragmented, are consolidated into contiguous unities.

This leads to a new 'precarious and fragile eschatology' of universal peace through a balance of strengths (STP 300). This stands in contrast to the more dramatic eschatological outlook of earlier political perspectives. During the medieval period, says Foucault, any art of government was seen as essentially temporary: the period understood itself as temporary, partly because of the coming Apocalypse and partly because it saw itself as an aberration from a more natural order represented by the Roman Empire. This meant that, in practical terms, the politics of this period was bounded by the real power of the Church on the one hand and by the spectral image of the Empire on the other, both of which offered forms of transcendent universality (STP 291). By contrast, with *raison d'État*, the current state of things is grasped as an eternal reality: while events may happen, and indeed things may be made better to some extent, the essentials of politics are already established once and for all (STP 260). The eschatological horizon now becomes one of the perfecting of the existing state system.

LIBERALISM

Raison d'État originates in economic problems, and the attempt to think about ways in which government can solve these, hence the centrality of political economy to it, and the indistinction at this time between politics, economics and government. The initial attempts of government to regulate the state were disciplinary, which is to say an attempt to control closely how things should occur by micro-regulation. In this early phase of economic thinking, which later came to be characterised as 'mercantilist' economics, the state engaged in simple direct interventions in the economy. This was not very effective. For example, people were found to be hoarding foodstuffs in order to sell them during times of shortage at high prices, which in fact led to starvation when people couldn't afford these prices. The direct intervention to deal with this problem was the imposition of price controls. This solved the problem of high prices, but, because it eliminated the hoarding of foodstuffs, it led to the absence of any grain stored against hard times, leading to acute shortages and starvation. This failure led to the next big economic movement, the physiocrats, who first introduced the notion of 'laissez-faire' economics, of allowing things to find a natural level without direct government interference, using regulation to guide things gently. By examining this transition in *Security, Territory, Population*, Foucault effectively correlates his survey of the development of economic thought from *The Order of Things* to his newer interest in (bio)politics.

Raison d'État had dispensed with the notion of nature which had been central to previous forms of reflection about politics and economy. It now returns, with society itself being understood now 'as a specific field of naturalness peculiar to man ... which will be called civil society' (STP 349). So, rather than nature previously being something extrinsic to human society with which it had to strive to accord, society itself is now conceived of for the first time as natural and thus a domain of natural scientific inquiry. The naturalness of society is now counterposed to the artificiality of the state. The political correlate of laissez-faire is liberalism, which reacts against the failures of governmental regulation with the idea that society should be left to regulate itself naturally, with the power of police applied only negatively in extremis. Here, the specific logic of security is operative, a more subtle concern with ensuring outcomes rather than trying to control things directly. From this point, there is a split between the regulation of the population and economy, on one side, and 'police in the modern sense of the term', which is to say the use of force to maintain order, on the other (STP 354). This for Foucault is broadly the governmentality that has lasted to this day. The emergence of liberalism is the object of study of the last lectures of *Security, Territory, Population*, and of *The Birth of Biopolitics*, which focuses on the most recent permutation of liberalism, what is called 'neo-liberalism'.

If laissez-faire economics derives from the economic problems of mercantilism (i.e. that government expansion into the economy threatened the efficiency of the economy that was necessary to generate the wealth that supported government), political liberalism emerged from an impetus to limit government for legal reasons (i.e. for the reason that a rule of law was itself required as the scaffold of government, hence superseded government). In both cases, there is a need to incorporate certain considerations, legal and economic, into 'governmental reason' itself.

The emergence of liberalism was gradual and faltering, theoretically articulated from the eighteenth century, but widely practised only from the nineteenth. The legal limitation of government is for

Foucault the move made by revolutionaries (particularly the French Revolution) at the end of the eighteenth century and during the nineteenth century in response to the unlimited *raison d'État* (BB 40). Another, more pragmatic limitation of government is found in 'English radicalism', which asks what the point of government is and when limitation benefits its purposes (BB 40); this approach is basically economic (BB 41).

The two circumscriptions, legal and economic, are not mutually opposed, but represent for Foucault two 'ways of doing things' that are both characteristic of what we may call liberalism, and which coexist strategically (BB 42). Foucault pointedly rejects 'dialectical' logic here, by which these 'contradictory' tendencies are reconciled in a new 'unity': for Foucault, the two aren't truly contradictory, but nor are they united. For Foucault, the more economic logic has grown stronger at the expense of the legal-revolutionary one over the years (BB 43). Foucault designates this combined-but-uneven situation as 'liberal governmentality' (BB 78).

Limitations are both internal to and external to liberal governmentality: they are conditions of its possibility, while appearing to be constraints upon its scope. They thus constitute a specific historical stage of governmentality's development: up to a certain point in time, governmentality was simply expansive, growing in a world in which there was initially relatively little government, but eventually coming up against a limit and a backlash by the end of the eighteenth century that saw governmentality circumscribed. Foucault now understands the change in punishment according to this shift, with the power of *raison d'État*, which was concerned with individuals and things (in this case the criminal's body), being replaced by a more subtle calculus of interests that tried to achieve results for various stakeholders (BB 46).

Liberalism is a brake on governmentality in one sense, and a distinct type of governmentality in another. In liberalism, freedom becomes an essential marker of effective government (STP 353). Foucault is keen to point out that this does not mean that liberalism actually brings greater freedom, however: indeed, for Foucault, it is impossible to quantify something like freedom, to say whether we have more or less (BB 63). It requires only that certain key freedoms exist (those necessary for the market to operate, specifically). The fundamental commitment of liberal governmentality for Foucault is indeed not to liberalism per se (which would imply a commitment to freedom) but to naturalism, the understanding of how things work

(BB 61). It was not afraid to extend the state and mechanisms of control in practice, albeit precisely in the name of 'freedom'. This works via the logic of security: we are encouraged to accept control as necessary to protect us (BB 65 – we might add that these are often couched these days in terms of protecting our freedom itself). Thus, freedom of the individual and regulation of the population subtly intertwine.

NEO-LIBERALISM

For Foucault this leads to a tension between political liberalism and the state apparatus. This has led to crises of liberalism, in which liberalism rebels against the overbearing state power with which it has come to be combined. One example of this combination might be the contemporary situation in the United States, where 'liberalism' has come to be almost synonymous with the advocacy of the public sector – even when, from a more technical academic point of view, almost all mainstream politics in the USA is liberal. The United States is also a privileged site of the rebellion of liberal values against the compromises of liberal governmentality, though confusingly the 'liberal' label in the United States is so closely tied to state-centred policy that those who invoke liberal values against the state define themselves as 'libertarian' or even just as 'conservative'.

This brings us to the primary target of *The Birth of Biopolitics*, *neo*-liberalism – occupying him for the middle seven of the twelve lectures – which comes out of precisely such a crisis. Foucault first details neo-liberalism's German origins, before moving on to more recent American outgrowths of it.

Foucault's attention to neo-liberalism seems rather prescient. While neo-liberalism was certainly fashionable as a doctrine at the time of the lectures – hence Foucault's interest in it – it was not yet as clear as it has come to be since that neo-liberalism is the hegemonic ideology of our time. Foucault's historical account of neo-liberalism challenges a popular conception of it as an Anglo-Saxon disease of privatisation, pointing out that in fact English-speakers came to it late, initially immunised against it by Keynesianism, while France and Germany became neo-liberal. The reason neo-liberalism seems distinctively Anglospheric is perhaps that we Anglophones have carried it to a much greater extreme.

What differentiates all neo-liberalism from classical liberalism is a much deeper fixation on freedom and the market. Where liberals had classically simply sought to limit the state only to the extent that it led to effective government, the neo-liberals were concerned with freedom in a more fundamental way, seeking to limit government itself, not only in practice to the extent it will harm itself if not limited, but as something that is essentially bad or dangerous.

German neo-liberalism arose initially as a reaction to Nazism. The neo-liberals seminally came to see Nazism as the inevitable outcome of the tendential growth of the state (BB 111). They thus believed that the state must be much more strongly contained than it had been in order to prevent such a thing from happening again.

What differentiates these German 'ordoliberals' both from classical liberals and from later neo-liberals is that they acknowledged that the market was artificial. Like the state it is an artificial institution, but unlike the state they regard it as being inherently on the side of freedom, such that they advocated subordinating the state firmly to the market. However, they also recognised that the market had negative effects that had to be ameliorated in the way it was set up and regulated (BB 243).

American neo-liberalism effectively combined this 'state-phobic' view of the German neo-liberalism with a classical naturalism about the market. This meant believing that the logic of the market pervaded nature (BB 243). This leads to the now-familiar conception of the human subject as essentially a rational utility-maximiser, already found in classical liberalism but now carried to a greater extreme, and following this selfish nature as essentially virtuous.

Liberalism is in all its forms essentially an attempt to combine government with rationality. It shares this characteristic with *raison d'État*, meaning that governmentality (but only in its historically narrow sense) for Foucault is indeed a matter of 'governmental rationality' (BB 311), even if the term is not a contraction of that phrase. The difference, as he puts it, is that in the former case it is the sovereign that is held to be rational, whereas in the latter case it is the people who are (BB 312). This fidelity to rationality is also characteristic of political discourses opposing the status quo such as Marxism (BB 313).

OUTSIDE GOVERNMENTALITY

The relationship of discourses such as Marxism to governmentality is vexed. Marxism is not, Foucault is at pains to stress, a governmentality in its own right. Foucault seems to identify only two modern governmentalities, *raison d'État* and liberalism, although in the latter case he distinguishes several varieties. He believes that socialism has functioned primarily within these governmentalities, rather than as an alternative to them (BB 92).

Significantly, Foucault ends *Security, Territory, Population* by cataloguing what he thinks are three forms of 'counter-conducts' that have responded to modern governmentality (STP 356–7). The first of these is what he calls the 'revolutionary eschatology' that seeks to finally get rid of the state and have only civil society responsible for itself, rejecting the basic logic inherited from *raison d'État* that the state is inevitable (STP 356). Such a position is clearly characteristic of anarchism and communism, though Foucault points origins for it as early as the sixteenth century, which I take it to be an allusion to the eschatological movements of the early Protestant Reformation, which hoped to bring about a Kingdom of Heaven on earth in a prompt fashion, but which were defeated by the determination of pastoral power as the province of the state. The second counter-conduct he lists is an insurrectionary one, consisting in 'the absolute right to revolt' (STP 356). Foucault identifies this too as eschatological. Anarchism again, in its more individualist and spontaneist guises, corresponds to this, though this counter-conduct would not seem to need to name itself as an ideology at all. Rather, in this kind of immanent resistance lies a potential for a mass revolt that has no definite political aim, but simply refuses something and desires absolutely to overthrow it, regardless of whether this is a realistic prospect. Lastly, he names the idea that the nation itself, rather than the state, is entitled to become the subject of *raison d'État* (STP 357). The distinction of the first counter-conduct from the third is somewhat subtle, but it may be taken to differentiate anarchism and communism from a state-oriented socialism. The third counter-conduct here might be taken to correspond to the thought of Jean-Jacques Rousseau, to the French Revolution and other nationalist revolutions, and indeed to some extent to fascism, to social democracy and even to Communist government, in practice if not in principle (since Marxists always aimed in theory at the 'withering away of the state' rather than just its nationalisation, while never accomplishing this maximal goal in reality). Foucault neatly characterises these three counter-conducts as (1) civil society against the state; (2) the population against the state; and (3) the nation against the state; but points out that all three of these things – civil society, population and nation – are in effect creatures and components of the modern state (STP 357). The point of course is that the very things constituted within modern governmentality also constitute the basis of opposition to it (STP 357).

Now, neo-liberalism does oppose to the state as such, but it is not eschatological inasmuch as it does not actually seek finally to abolish the state. It is indeed for this reason that neo-liberalism is a governmentality rather than a counter-conduct; though, by the same token, these counter-conducts are incapable of actually establishing a new order. Like neo-liberalism, these counter-conducts may be seen as misguidedly subscribing to what Foucault deems 'state-phobia'. For Foucault, hyperbolic attention to the state may be either positive, thinking that the state is the be-all-and-end-all of politics, capable of solving all problems that can be solved, or negative, focusing on the state qua 'cold monster' and ignoring the much wider and more variable problem of power that Foucault seeks to bring to light.

One failing of state phobia for Foucault is its failure to accurately characterise the specificity of totalitarian governmentality. While neo-liberals, anarchists and communists all in their distinct ways regard welfare-state social democracy as fundamentally similar to fascism (the neo-liberals because of the power of the state, the anarchists and communists because of the specifically capitalist character of that state power), Foucault thinks that totalitarianism is not, as it might appear to be, an extreme form of police state. Rather, he argues that it is actually less state-focused than *raison d'État*, because its real apparatus is not the state but the party, hence constitutes its own unique party-centred governmentality (BB 191). This would be true of the role of the Nazi Party in Germany or of the Communist Party in the Soviet Union, notwithstanding the significant differences in the political organisation of these two states.

Thus, while the Soviet Union was not simply a return to an old form of police power, it still did not represent a distinctively Marxist form of governmentality. For Foucault, socialism's essential problem is to invent a new, socialist governmentality (BB 94).

A Governmental Turn?

One major treatment of the late 1970s lectures, Thomas Lemke's (the main expression of which, the monograph *Kritik der politischen Vernunft* (Critique of political reason), dates from before the full publication of the lecture series, and remains untranslated from the original German), sees them as representing an extraordinary change in Foucault's thought. More recent scholarship has also followed this pattern, be it Eric Paras's (2006) provocative work emphasising apparent discontinuities in Foucault's perspective, or Paul Patton's (2010) more recent attempt to reconcile Foucault's thought from the late 1970s with liberalism.

I sit resolutely on the other side of a fence here, seeing Foucault's work on government as continuous with his earlier work. It is indeed the fulfilment of his intentions of the early 1970s to study power's strategies. Foucault remarked in a letter in 1974, on the occasion of completing the manuscript of *Discipline and Punish*, that its subject matter – *marginaux* (that is, marginal people or things) – was all too familiar, and that he intended to move on from studying marginalisation to study 'political economy, strategy, and politics' (DE1 61). But his next book, the first volume of the *History of Sexuality*, remains within the horizon of the history of marginal people and practices, although its explicit thematisation of power goes beyond this. It is only in *Society Must Be Defended*, however, that political economy and politics come to the fore, albeit of course in the form of the study of political discourses, since his methodology remains firmly rooted in the excavation of archival materials. He signals this break at the beginning of the second lecture of the series, saying 'Until now, or for roughly the last five years, it has been disciplines; for the next five years, it will be war, struggle, the army' (SD 24). This, as I have already discussed at some length, was not entirely accurate: the military inflection that Foucault commits to here was indeed already on the way out by 1976, not that it ever disappears entirely from his thought. Foucault's intention immediately on finishing the first volume of the *History of Sexuality* in August 1976 was to embark on a study of the relation of scientific institutions to politics in the USA and Soviet Union (DE1 67), a more concrete study than what he went on to do.

Despite his stated intentions to continue his studies of power and biopolitics, however, it might seem that references to 'government' actually *replace* those to biopolitics, and to some extent even those to power, for example in a passage in which Foucault speaks of 'a triangle: sovereignty, discipline, and governmental management, which has population as its main target and apparatuses of security as its essential mechanism' (STP 107–8). If one replaces the phrase 'governmental management' with 'biopolitics', this statement could have appeared in *Society Must Be Defended*. However, Foucault does not actually abandon the notion of biopolitics. No term involving 'government' is identical in meaning to 'biopolitics', and (hence)

Foucault never stops using the term biopolitics entirely. The title of his 1979 lectures at the Collège de France, *The Birth of Biopolitics*, is one marker of this, even if it misleads the reader as to its contents, which are scarcely about biopolitics. Indeed, even in 1983, towards the end of his life, Foucault avers that he still has to write 'the genealogy of bio-power' (EW1 256).

Government and governmentality are couched as an additional technology to those already outlined by him, to try to do with the state what he had already done with other objects of study: 'Can we talk of something like a "governmentality" that would be to the state what techniques of segregation were to psychiatry, what techniques of discipline were to the penal system, and what biopolitics was to medical institutions?' (STP 120). Government itself is fundamentally technological for Foucault: 'The idea of a government of men . . . is not an ideology. First of all and above all it is a technology of power' (STP 71).

Furthermore, to the extent that Foucault abandoned the notion of biopolitics, he then did the same thing with 'governmentality': he does not entirely cease to speak of it, but certainly uses it much less in later years after his initial enthusiasm for it had waned. It would seem that his methodology remains genealogy throughout, moreover. He affirms as much in *Security, Territory, Population* (STP 36), reiterating the principles of that methodology (STP 117–18). He is explicit that the *Security, Territory, Population* lectures constitute the movement of the methodology of the analysis of strategies and tactics of power from specific rafts of institutions to the state itself (STP 119–20). He presents the last two lecture series of the 1970s as an experiment designed to show that the analysis of 'micro-power' (which characterises his work of the early 1970s, in particular *Discipline and Punish*, where he talks about the 'micro-physics' of power) leads seamlessly to an analysis of 'macro-power', i.e. governmentality, and that there is no contradiction between these two 'levels' (STP 358).

Here we might invoke the influence of a new political conjuncture on Foucault's thinking and his shift towards questions of government. I don't think it is coincidental that Foucault pays more attention to the state during a period when the French left's hopes shifted from the idea of revolution to the more concrete prospect of an alliance of the PCF and the Socialist Party winning state power. This alliance was inaugurated in 1972, and its candidate, the Socialist François Mitterrand, very nearly won the 1974 French presidential election, losing by only a tiny margin. Mitterrand won the next presidential election which was held in 1981, with the alliance also sweeping legislative elections the same year. This was the best performance of the left since 1956, and the first left-wing president in France since 1954. Thereafter, in the inevitable disappointment of radical hopes that followed this final victory of 1981, Foucault followed others away from politics to the consideration of ethics and subjectivity.

Note

1. My translation of Foucault 2004b, 111–12. Cf. the two published English translations, STP 108–9 and Foucault 1991, 102–3.

8

Ethics and Spirituality

In this chapter I will deal with the last period of Foucault's thought. This may be subdivided into a number of concerns. The overarching concern that characterises this period is a concern with the way people constitute themselves as subjects. Major themes include 'spirituality', invoked both in academic work and in his contemporary journalistic writings about the Iranian Revolution, and, more prominently and influentially, 'ethics', as an example of a broader category of techniques and practices as the self.

Iran and Revolution

The Iranian Revolution

Formerly known in the West as 'Persia', Iran is a large Middle Eastern country, rich in oil, with a distinctive history. For millennia, it was one of the major imperial cultures of the world, like Rome, China or India. It was conquered by Muslim Arabs during the expansion of Islam towards the end of the first millennium CE. Owing to historical contingencies of the beliefs of its rulers, Iran ended up, unlike most Muslim countries, adhering predominantly to the Shia version of Islam, specifically its main, 'Twelver' variant. Shia Islam is highly distinctive, involving a belief in a continuing lineage of supreme imams descended from Islam's prophet Muhammad. Twelver Shiites, who compose the great majority of Shiites worldwide, believe this succession ended with the twelfth imam, who is currently 'occluded' but will one day return.

During the Second World War, in 1941, Iran had been jointly invaded and occupied by Britain (which at that time controlled Iraq, the country to the west of Iran) and the Soviet Union (which bordered Iran to the north), to seize control of its oil. After the war, Iranian independence was restored, but Iran quickly became a strong ally of the West, its ruling class fearing a takeover by Communists. Iran was ruled by a king, the

Shah, who simultaneously brutally repressed dissidents and pursued an agenda of liberal social reforms. In addition to the opposition by Soviet-backed underground Communists, he found himself increasingly at odds with the powerful Shiite hierarchy, who disapproved of his secularising social agenda. One Shiite cleric, the Ayatollah Khomeini, emerged as the fiercest critic of the regime, and a rallying point for opponents. Jailed by the regime in 1963 over his statements, he lived in exile outside Iran from 1964 on.

A cycle of violent protests started at the beginning of 1978, and grew in size and intensity. The Shah attempted to appease protestors by legalising political parties and freeing political prisoners, but this simply created a greater space and more voices for the advocacy of revolution and the Shah's overthrow. The Shah then unleashed more repression. Massive strike action ensued, paralysing the economy. The Shah established a military government in December 1978 in a last-ditch attempt to restore order. Enormous protests then occurred, involving millions of Iranians. The Shah left Iran on 16 January 1979. Khomeini returned from exile on 1 February and quickly assumed supreme authority in the country. Reprisals began against the enforcers of the old regime, armed opponents of Khomeini were suppressed, and in 1980 a crackdown against anyone who questioned the new order followed.

I will begin by writing about Foucault and Iran. By beginning this chapter in this way, I indicate a certain sympathy with Afary and Anderson's (2005, 4–5) line that Foucault's engagement with Iranian politics is seminal to much of Foucault's late work. However, I have little sympathy with the substance of their claims about his writings on Iran, and it must also be said that the interests that Foucault pursues during his last years are actually overdetermined such that it cannot be conclusively stated that any element of them is definitively traceable to Iran.

Foucault's writings on Iran mostly date from late 1978, that is, from the time between the two governmentality lecture series, with some later reflections being published in early 1979, contemporaneously with and shortly after *The Birth of Biopolitics*. But these writings seem to have nothing in particular to do with governmentality, nor does *The Birth of Biopolitics* bear any obvious trace of his Iranian experiences.

Foucault had been approached by the major Italian daily newspaper *Corriere Della Sera* in May 1978 to write for them, owing to the prominence of his ideas on the Italian left (DE1 74). Foucault responded in August by proposing to write about Iran, where a massive protest movement had grown up over the past ten months against the country's American-backed autocratic monarch, the Shah. Foucault went to Iran in September, spurred on by a massacre on 8 September known as 'Black Friday', which is generally thought to have marked the point at which a non-violent end to the revolution became impossible.

Foucault spent about a week in Iran in September. He returned in November for a further, slightly briefer visit. He wrote seven articles about the Iranian Revolution for *Corriere Della Sera*, and one for the French news magazine *Le Nouvel Observateur*. The final one of these journalistic articles, the only one to appear in 1979, was a piece in *Corriere Della Sera* marking the ultimate capture of power by the revolutionaries on 11 February that year.

It is hard to overstate how exceptional Foucault's writings on Iran are. They are very different from his scholarly work: although he does not depart particularly from his general principles, methodologically they are utterly different, journalistic rather than scholarly, concerned with the present directly rather than with the past, dealing with concrete political events rather than in discourses, and based on first-hand experience rather than archival materials.

Foucault's enthusiasm for the revolution he is witnessing comes across unmistakably in these pieces. This enthusiasm wanes markedly after February 1979. His last two publications on Iran are, firstly, an open letter addressed to the prime minister of Iran, published in *Le Nouvel Observateur* in April 1979, appealing to him to observe human rights in light of atrocities committed by the new regime, and finally, in May 1979, a front-page article he wrote for the French daily newspaper of record, *Le Monde*, entitled 'Is It Useless to Revolt?', constituting a meditation on whether the Iranian Revolution had been worthwhile considering that it had resulted in the formation of a new brutally repressive regime.

Foucault was criticised at the time and has been continuously ever since for being sympathetic to a revolution that ended in the creation of the Islamic Republic that exists in Iran to this day, with its intolerance of dissent, and use of capital punishment against opponents and homosexuals, amongst others.

There is a quite simple defence of Foucault here, which is that he sympathised only with the process of revolution itself, not its outcome, and that he could not have predicted the outcome. Others, however, claim that the outcome was predictable and condemn Foucault for being naive in failing to predict it.

Central to the controversy here is Foucault's sympathy for the specifically religious aspect of the Iranian Revolution. Indeed, this would seem to be one reason why Foucault was so interested in Iran. His fascination with what was happening there was certainly to do with the fact that it was a non-Marxist revolution (DE1 76), with Marxists having a less prominent role than in perhaps any other revolution of the twentieth century up to that point.

Marxists have tended to take one of two attitudes towards the Iranian Revolution. On the one hand, there are Marxists who condemn it because it is not Marxist, and a fortiori because it is religious. Such Marxists criticise Foucault for failing to see, as they did, that a revolution that does not follow the correct Marxist schema of conscious class conflict is not a revolution that can have a good result. There are also liberal secularists who condemn the religious component of the revolution a priori. On the other hand, there are Marxists who have taken the religious aspect of the Iranian Revolution to be an unimportant and superficial feature, a kind of ideological packaging of a class-based revolution. Marxists thus either claim that any revolution that doesn't accord with their schema of what a revolution should be is wrong, or simply claim that all revolutions do accord with their schema whatever the participants think. Such attitudes are rejected vehemently by Foucault, who argues that one must study historical events in their specificity, and that the political roles of discourses are context-dependent. It is this attitude that he brought to bear in Iran, describing the peculiar nature of a revolt animated by a particular religious persuasion, Shia Islam. For Foucault, this revolt combined modern tropes, particularly democratic leanings, with a spiritual determination not generally seen in modern Western political movements.

A subtler objection than the Marxist one is that Foucault's opposition to utopianism, including to Marxism, failed to immunise him from the same enthusiasm for revolution that Marxists had had (Afary and Anderson 2005, 5). This seems to me to miss the point, which is that, unlike from a Marxist theoretical perspective, Foucault's enthusiasm for revolution was just that, rather than an enthusiasm for its presumed outcome. That is, he did not have illusions about the outcome of revolution, rather only an appreciation of the process itself qua the opening of various possibilities. Indeed, it must be noted that he did not laud the Iranian Revolution qua 'revolution', but rather qua 'insurrection' and 'revolt' (FIR 222). That is, he supported the negativity of the revolt, the extent to which it amounted to saying 'No!' to existing structures of power. For Foucault, the positive slogans that were raised in Iran in 1978 – 'Islamic government' and the name of Ayatollah Khomeini – were devoid of any particular, determinate content:

> I do not feel comfortable speaking of Islamic government as an 'idea' or even as an 'ideal.' Rather, it impressed me as a form of 'political will.' It impressed me in its effort to politicize structures that are inseparably social and religious in response to current problems. It also impressed me in its attempt to open a spiritual dimension in politics. (FIR 208)

One might ask on what basis one can be enthusiastic about a revolution if one does not expect it to have particular good consequences. But consequentialism is not the sine qua non of politics. There are many things to be enthusiastic about in a revolution other than a belief in a better determinate outcome, such as the liberation immanent to the revolution, and the desired negative consequences, that is the abolition of the tyranny the revolution opposed.

In a sense, there is a grim inevitability about the corruption of any revolution, however pure its complexion may initially appear. The specifics of that corruption cannot, however, be discerned in advance. We can be sure that the corruption of the revolution will involve taking its values and turning them against the revolution, so it was a fair bet for example that some repressive Islamic regime might take shape after the Iranian Revolution, just as a repressive Marxist regime took shape after the Russian Revolution. If we could be sure that the resultant order would be 'just as bad' as or 'worse' than the one it replaces, we would perhaps have a reason to condemn the revolution, but we cannot know this, because the result of the revolution is not knowable in advance, nor is there any clear metric for measuring the relative quality of regimes. Indeed, though many will state that the results of the Iranian Revolution have been disastrous, it is not at all clear that it can be stated that for most Iranians the Revolution is a subject of regret.

Foucault posits an opposition between politics and the will of the people in relation to the Iranian Revolution (FIR 212). Foucault saw the Iranian Revolution as a pure rejection of politics. This pejorative use of 'politics' as such can be found elsewhere in Foucault's work, namely in an injunction in *Security, Territory, Population* never to engage in politics.[1]

Foucault, writing in 1978 while things were still undecided, acknowledges the probability of the restoration of politics after the revolution, but refuses to see it as entirely inevitable: he says that it is not a question of whether the Shah will fall, but rather that

> It is a question of knowing when and how the will of all will give way to politics. It is a question of knowing if this will wants to do so and if it must do so. It is the practical problem of all revolutions and the theoretical problem of all political philosophies. Let us admit that we Westerners would be in a poor position to give advice to the Iranians on this matter. (FIR 213)

Quite simply, Foucault holds that we cannot know what will happen when the dice of insurrection are rolled (it may seem he is suggesting we need to find out what will happen in this quotation, but the questions he refers to are clearly meant to be answered not by inference but by events themselves). This position differentiates Foucault's perspective from all standard political ideologies. Like Marxists and liberals he believes in liberation struggles, but unlike them he does not believe they follow the set patterns. Like political conservatives, he believes that change is dangerous, but unlike them does not conclude that change should be avoided. For Foucault, everything is dangerous, including staticity, not least because change is in any case inevitable, since power relations are never truly stable. His solution, to be sure, is to valorise the moment of resistance, in which political hope lies, against the stultifying moment in which strategies of power form, even though the one is never found without the other in concrete reality.

Now, Foucault realised that a non-Islamic alternative was not going to win out: this much was obvious, that the revolution couldn't lead to secularism, liberalism or communism. His recognition of the specifically Islamic character of the revolution makes his analysis superior to those who dismissed the religious component as relatively insignificant. The essential problem is that what he thought it meant is more or less the opposite of what it turned out to mean in practice. Specifically, Foucault opined that 'By "Islamic government," nobody in Iran means a political regime in which the clerics would have a role of supervision or control', but rather meant vaguely to refer to basic democratic principles, while retaining a spiritual dimension absent from Western democratic politics (FIR 206). In fact, however, this phrase came after the Revolution precisely to refer to clerical supervision and control.

The question is to what extent Foucault should have anticipated this. It is perfectly possible that in 1978 (almost) no one in Iran had this in mind despite it being what occurred afterwards. In particular, the Ayatollah Khomeini, who became the Supreme Leader of Iran after the Revolution, was at that time telling people that both he and other religious leaders were not seeking political power (Hoveyda 2003, 87). Maxime Rodinson points out that Khomeini had argued for clerical control previously (FIR 270), and I think is right to conclude that Foucault was unaware of this crucial fact. However, Khomeini wasn't actually in Iran at the time, having been in exile for years, so Foucault's remark would not have been inaccurate even if he were still cleaving to that line, which he was not. In any case, Foucault explicitly attributed to Khomeini only a figurehead role, a name that was invoked everywhere, but as a rallying point rather than a concrete leader. Foucault attributes the popularity of Khomeini to the fact that Khomeini appeared not to represent any political force or even a potential political force (FIR 222). Of course, as has been demonstrated by events, the use of Khomeini's name as the privileged signifier, along with 'Islam' itself, of the Revolution made it relatively straightforward for Khomeini to take supreme power on his return to Iran. Foucault does indeed seem to have completely missed this possibility, declaring 'there will not be a Khomeini government' (FIR 222). There is here a more general naivety on his part concerning the potential for the Shia religious hierarchy to operate as the basis for a state form. Foucault preferred to think of the Shia hierarchy as essentially flexible, with believers choosing whether or not to follow any particular religious leader. This was perhaps so, but, once the decision had been made to follow Khomeini, the basis was laid for the construction of an inflexible domination. While within the revolution their role was mainly a salutary reference, once given actual power the force of their conservatism came to bear.

This is not to say that this course of events was actually inevitable, however. It is perfectly conceivable that Khomeini would not have used his political capital in this way – or that a different name would have been chosen, that of someone who would not have abused their status. Maxime Rodinson's criticism that Foucault had placed 'excessive hopes in the Iranian Revolution' (FIR 270) fundamentally fails to understand Foucault's position. Foucault did not hope for any particular thing to happen. He believed in the importance of refusal and revolt, even in spite of the inevitability of some negative consequences. This is the meaning of his extraordinary 1979 essay, which effectively capped off his commentary on Iran, 'Is It Useless to Revolt?', in which he of course concludes that it is not useless, though precisely because revolt is not a question of being useful or useless – the value of the revolt is in its refusal of any set logic by which it may be evaluated. This is not to say that any and all revolts are laudable. Foucault said that it was important to wait till the time was ripe. He refused to valorise acts of terrorism by small, isolated groups of dissidents. The point about Iran is that time was utterly ripe, that there was the critical mass. It wasn't without danger, but there was no point in waiting further.

Foucault's argument is something like this: we cannot know ultimately what the result of a revolt will be (whether it will be successful in the sense of defeating what it opposes, or what will arise in the place of what is abolished if it is successful in this first sense), but we do know that if we do nothing, nothing will change, hence at some point a revolt becomes necessary. This perhaps can thus be reduced merely to a descriptive thesis: people will always exceed whatever structures are in place, will always disobey and rebel. In the end it doesn't matter what Foucault said about Iran – he was only describing, both as an intellectual and, unusually, as a journalist, something that was already in train. The question that faced him, simply, was what can be said about the Iranian Revolution? Conventional political theory furnishes us with causal explanations – in terms of economic grievances, political repression, cultural questions, ideologies – and a condemnation of the solution, Islamic government, for its falling back on religious dogmas rather than liberalism and democracy. Foucault's position is that, while he admits the existence of all the standardly cited factors, he thinks none of these can fully explain a political movement. We may find situations where the same factors are present without provoking a revolt, and, conversely, revolts of people who have apparently far lesser problems. He refuses to think revolt in terms of definable causes and solutions. It is precisely the thing that defies logic.

ORIENTALISM

The contemporary relevance of these questions is great, primarily because the combination of Islam and politics has become ever more prominent since the Iranian Revolution. Many on the left and right would have us believe that Islam is inherently reactionary – if not necessarily anti-democratic, then sexist or homophobic. It is indeed hard to find anyone preaching gender equality or homosexual rights in the name of Islam, and the record of the Iranian Islamic state in relation to the rights of homosexuals is particularly horrifying. But we should remember that this was true for Christianity for much of its history. While Muslims might be loath to allow that there are no limits to the interpretations that may be applied to their faith, both the historical evidence and postmodern hermeneutics teach us that we can imagine anything coming to be argued within Islam, just as there are today many who regard democracy, gender equality and the recognition of different sexualities as not only compatible with, but commanded by Christianity. I think the problem with the secular reading of Islam as reactionary is that in fact it buys into the most reactionary self-understanding of Islam available. Foucault's faith in the potentialities of Islam is by contrast laudable.

Orientalism

The word 'Orientalism' in contemporary academic discourse refers to the way Western thinking treats the East as a mysterious repository of exotic behaviours and ideas. This operates subtly to discount the Eastern other, not simply by characterising Easterners as subhuman, as Europeans have tended to characterise most of the 'native' races they have encountered, but by simultaneously romanticising them, while preventing them from being taken seriously. The classic analysis of this phenomenon is found in the book *Orientalism* by the Arab-American academic Edward Said, on which Foucault's archaeological work is a major influence.

The danger of Orientalism constitutes the two sides of a tightrope walk. On one side, one turns the Easterner into something utterly foreign, an absolute other we cannot comprehend, and hence dehumanises them. On the other, one turns the Easterner into a Westerner, overruling the specificity of non-Western cultures. I think Foucault manages to walk this tightrope, acknowledging what is specific about Islamic culture, without endowing it with peculiarly servile qualities that prevent Muslims from innovating or rebelling.

Afary and Anderson (2005), however, argue that Foucault's position in this regard is not only naive but actively Orientalist. They paint a rather odd portrait of Foucault as fascinated by stereotyped fantasies of Eastern cultures. They start by claiming that Foucault sees non-European sexual practices as superior to European sexuality. However, he in fact says almost nothing about Eastern sexuality – but Afary and Anderson (2005, 19–22) then turn this fact itself into an indictment, that he fails to note the importance of East–West interchange to Western sexuality. Yet, Foucault's remarks about Eastern sexuality are actually supposed to indicate that his *History of Sexuality* pertains only to the West, to note what he leaves out in this study. Moreover, when Foucault does talk about 'the East', contextually it is clear that he is talking more about Indian and Chinese cultural zones, but Afary and Anderson (2005, 30–1) take him to be talking about the Middle East, and moreover take him to be asserting that the Middle East is part of a homogeneous and unchanging Eastern culture, when he simply never makes any such claims.

Their general claim is that Foucault denigrates the modern West, valorising both premodernity and the East (Afary and Anderson 2005, 26). This thus casts the Iranian Islamic Revolution, an eruption of premodern and oriental values, as the political fulfilment of Foucault's dreams – although they ignore Foucault's express claims in supporting the Islamic Revolution that it is not a return to the premodern.

Their reading of Foucault can only rest on the premise that, in order to criticise something, one needs to valorise its opposite. Since Foucault criticises Western modernity, they conclude he must be enamoured with the East and premodernity. However, this is a logic Foucault vehemently refuses. Foucault does not often criticise premodernity or the East, but then this would be a largely redundant political gesture for someone concerned with attacking structures of power and domination in his own society. Criticising the way people used to do things is pointless, and criticising the way people do things in other cultures amounts to cultural imperialism – though Foucault indeed did criticise the way governments exercise power in other parts of the world, including Iran's government after the Revolution. Thus when he mentions the East and the premodern in his books it's primarily to create a contrast with the modern and Western phenomena that are the objects of his critique. This is not, as we will go on to explore, to set these things up as specific alternatives, so much as simply to suggest how things might be otherwise.

Afary and Anderson's characterisation of Foucault as valorising premodernity likens him to Heidegger, and his infatuation with the Iranian Revolution is in effect likened to the scandal of Heidegger's sometime allegiance to Nazism. Afary and Anderson cast the Iranian Islamic Revolutionary ideology as a form of fascism and castigate Foucault for failing to notice the similarities between them, namely the nostalgia for an earlier time and the drive to revive spirituality. This is a rather thin resemblance, however. In Iran, one has a movement which is not particularly nostalgic, but intensely religious, indifferent to political questions, more concerned with religious ones. By contrast, European fascism was primarily nostalgic, not particularly religious, and primarily concerned with political questions of the structure of authority. Fascism was fundamentally, foundationally anti-democratic and anti-egalitarian in a way that that the Iranian Revolution never was. As Babak Rahimi (2006) has argued, Afary and Anderson's assimilation of political Islam to European fascism is the real Orientalism at work here.

Afary and Anderson (2005, 9) criticise Foucault for attending to the Iranian Islamic Revolution when he could have studied the less problematic (that is, more Western) phenomenon of the contemporaneous Nicaraguan Revolution, which had its own spiritual movement, Catholic 'liberation theology'. The reasons why Foucault focused on Iran rather than Nicaragua or the many other things happening in the world at that time are of course manifold. One motivation is indeed the specifically non-Western nature of the Iranian Revolution. Coming from a country where Marxism and Catholicism are major ideological forces, examining the combination of these in the Western hemisphere might not have seemed to offer particular illumination. His particular reason for not showing more interest in Nicaragua is that he felt that, compared to Iran, the left already showed an unambiguous sympathy for the Nicaraguan Revolution (FIR 250). Not coincidentally, religion was much less central to the Nicaraguan Revolution.

Iran, by contrast, was a movement neither clearly of the left nor of the right – it fell between the two camps of the Cold War. Something similar was of course said about the Nazis, and was one reason that Heidegger supported them, but we have already said something about the considerable differences between Nazism and the Iranian Islamic Revolution.

For Foucault, what he witnessed in Tehran was 'perhaps the first great insurrection against global systems, the form of revolt that is the most modern and the most insane' (FIR 222). Unlike the more clear-cut liberation struggles against colonial powers earlier in the twentieth century, in Algeria and Vietnam, for example, Iran had not been fully colonised, so its revolt was against the less direct influence of a number of powers that had dominated it during the twentieth century, which included both the United States and the Soviet Union, as well as the British Empire.

Foucault's interest in Iran must also be seen in the context of his earlier experiences in Tunisia, a Muslim country where he had been peripherally involved in a revolt against its autocratic, foreign-backed leader. For Afary and Anderson (2005, 140–1), his Tunisian experience is significant only as indicative of his colonial tourist's attitude towards Islam, and in contributing to a naivety about the profound homophobia of Islam. Their reading of Islam as having a single eternal message is no less naive however, showing a remarkable lack of attentiveness to its extraordinary historical diversity, including a diversity of opinions about the jurisprudential status of homosexuality.

As I have indicated, the claim that Foucault is fascinated with the East is a rather surprising one. While he certainly was interested in things oriental – leading him to spend time in Japan, for example – it's fair to say that his work is more notable for excluding the oriental than for displaying a fascination with its exoticness.

I have suggested this may be explained simply by reference to Foucault's project of providing a history of the present relevant to the context in which he lived. This may be invoked to explain both his Eurocentrism and his Francocentrism – all his books ultimately centre on France, though they also always invoke significant research outside of France. His work is Francocentric, without being parochial. The exception is his late work on Greek and Roman Antiquity. Focusing on ancient Gaul, the ancient country largely coextensive with modern France, would simply not afford enough source material to allow a study of the type he wishes to mount.

The Subject and Truth

From the first words of Foucault's first lecture of his 1980 series at the Collège de France, *Du gouvernement des vivants* (On the government of the living), a change is apparent from the previous years' lectures. Without any particular warning, we are in the midst of Antiquity. This is not a completely new direction for Foucault: there were reflections on Antiquity in *Security, Territory, Population,* and, more prominently, almost a decade before, in the *Lectures on the Will to Know.* There is a clear link to that earlier course inasmuch as Foucault again talks in 1980 about the myth of Oedipus, his major ancient reference during the 1970s.

There is other evidence of continuity, too. Once again, the title seems to look backwards to government and the theme of life. He begins by making reference to the previous year's lectures, and to the concept of governmentality, but does not use it after that first lecture, though the concept of 'government' does linger to an extent. His basic interests remain those that have animated him throughout the 1970s: to examine the relationship of the use of truth to power relations (Foucault 2012, 7). However, he explicitly marks a shift that he thinks has occurred in his thought, in the way he conceives of this relationship. He couches this in terms of a shift 'from the notion of knowledge-power to the notion of government by the truth' (Foucault 2012, 12).

KNOWLEDGE AND POWER REVISITED

There is much that can be said about this brief formulation. One noticeable thing is the phrase 'knowledge-power'. This is surely a reference to what Foucault in his earlier work had called 'power-knowledge'.[2] During the period when he used this notion most, he wrote it invariably with 'power' before 'knowledge'. In the governmentality lectures series, however, he inverts the order of the concepts – though he mentions 'knowledge-power' only once in each lecture series (STP 42; BB 19). It is not clear that this inversion is meant to have any significance at all, but it is perhaps indicative that, even while working with this compound concept, Foucault moves from thinking of power as primary in the relationship to being more concerned to accentuate the role of knowledge. Of course, neither concept is supposed to have priority – the point of the combination is supposed to be precisely that the relationship between the two lacks any priority and cannot be reduced.

Yet, Foucault thinks that this combinatory conception has been superseded. This is a very rare case in his thought of an explicit disavowal, rather than merely the abandonment, of a key concept. Despite the invocation of the concept of 'knowledge-power' in the governmentality lectures, Foucault (2012, 12) now seems to declare retrospectively that the shift had already occurred in those lectures. However, the precise notion of 'government by truth' that Foucault is shifting to emerges only in 1980. The shift for Foucault consists of elaborations in the way he conceives of each of the two components of power-knowledge, that is, of power and of knowledge. He wants to get rid of the notion of power-knowledge, but as a consequence of retaining and elaborating on the notions of power and knowledge. Note there is no implication that there is to be any fundamental change in his conceptions of power or knowledge, only that these are to be developed. The previous two years, the governmentality lectures, have added to his conception of power, whereas this year's lecture is supposed to add to the conception of knowledge.

What Foucault says here, at the beginning of 1980, about knowledge is something that was perhaps not emphasised adequately before: that knowledge has an importance for power that cannot be reduced to anything instrumental. That is, while there are knowledges that are important for power in a direct and instrumental way, as an aid to governing (in the case of knowledge of demographics, for example), governors always make a reference to knowledge which is outside of the directly useful. And this does not mean that they do this simply as a kind of distraction, or a trick to make people think that they are wise, though they assuredly do use knowledge in such ways. Though these may all be considerations, they also refer to knowledge because they believe it is important in and of itself. Indeed, one reason that knowledge does have instrumental force is because of its own peculiar cultural significance.

Foucault (2012, 12–13) situates both his original development of the notion of power-knowledge and his move away from it in relation to a rejection of the (Marxist) notion of 'dominant ideology', which for Foucault implies a simplistic vision of truth and falsehood, of the way power operates and of the way things are represented to people. That is, Marxist theories for Foucault are taken to imply a vision of power as operating to trick people into believing what is untrue. The very notions of knowledge and power for Foucault depose the notion of ideology by insisting on the specificity of these formations. That is, when we think about knowledges in the plural, it means seeing them no longer as things that are simply either true or false but rather as historically variable and contingent structures which determine within them what is considered true and false. Such structures are ignored in conventional accounts of ideology.

Similarly, the invocation of power as a concept allows us to see how it is structured in specific and variable ways, rather than thinking of it automatically and simply as a system of domination by particular interests over the rest of society.

Foucault explicitly connects this to the question of religion, and the Iranian experience is here not far in the background. He points out that if religion may sometimes seem to pacify people politically, it has also been a potent discourse of political revolt. That is, it enables as much as stifles political change for Foucault.[3] Discourses do not have a predetermined political significance: for Foucault, we cannot read the political meaning of discourses from the words they contain.

To this extent, Foucault is not saying anything essentially different from what he had been saying already for a decade in the case of power, or almost two decades in the case of knowledge. He notes that he indeed seems to reject the theory of ideology almost every year in his lectures (Foucault 2012, 73). He sees this constant revisiting of the theory that he rejects as a necessary part of his essentially negative method, that operates by bringing into question received wisdom rather than erecting a system of his own (Foucault 2012, 74). There are two things to note about this. The main point he is trying to make is about the fundamental negativity of his method, which is about bringing into question all existing structures of power. He distinguishes his position on this point from philosophical scepticism, which is a form of systematic doubt about knowledge looking for certainty, because he is not looking for certainty. He also distinguishes his position, on the other hand, from anarchism, which tries to completely destroy power once and for all, since he does not hope to do anything as systematic as that.

Another point we can note is the extent to which Foucault once again here appears tied – albeit negatively – to Marxism. While Marxism is not his immediate negative target, in the sense of being the object of his critical analyses, his methodology itself evolved through a continual revisiting and rejection of the established method of social criticism, Marxism.

How then does he redefine his rejection of ideology in 1980? The distinction of government by truth from power-knowledge is relatively subtle. Indeed it's not clear to me what it means. Clearly, the notion of 'power' is displaced by that of 'government', and that of 'knowledge' by 'truth', though these are not total replacements. In the case of truth and knowledge, Foucault's stated intention is 'to elaborate the notion of knowledge in the direction of the problem of truth'. Truth and knowledge, to be sure, are not separate problems. Government is now invoked in the very general sense it will be used in primarily for the rest of Foucault's life, rather than the narrow, historically exemplary sense that the governmentality lecture series mostly used (Foucault 2012, 13–14).

THE SELF

What is most decisive here, perhaps, is neither government nor truth per se but a focus on a third thing not yet named: the self. Foucault introduces this theme at the beginning of the third lecture (Foucault 2012, 48). The government of people by truth and the theme of the self are connected for Foucault, since he believes that a characteristic form of truth in Western culture in later ages, including ours, is the telling of truth on one's own account, referring back to the self as evidence; in short, witnessing. He finds a very early instance of this in the myth of Oedipus, whereas, by contrast, Foucault thinks formerly people had spoken the truth only by invoking forms of authority external to themselves, such as the gods.

Now, Foucault had already examined one form of this truth-telling in the practice of confession as an interplay of knowledge and power in relation to the constitution of the self in the first volume of the *History of Sexuality*. Foucault's research in 1980 is clearly aimed at tracing back the roots of the confessional impulse. Yet, where he had previously thought confession in terms of 'subjection' (*assujettissement*), our constitution as subjects 'in both senses of the word' (HS1 60), both as active subjects of and as the ones who are subject to power, he now coins a new concept, 'subjectivation' (Foucault 2012, 72). Subjectivation focuses on how the subject forms itself. It is this interest in subjectivation, in relation to the familiar themes of truth and power, that will be Foucault's distinctive preoccupation from this point to his death in 1984. Though the concept of government, and to some extent also that of governmentality, are retained, they are now used to refer to this conjunction of general notions.

In the introduction to the two books that are the output of this process of tracing back the roots of sexuality, the second and third volume of *The History of Sexuality*, Foucault indicates that his turn towards ancient texts was the result of a particular question, namely 'to understand how the modern individual could experience himself as a subject of a "sexuality"' (HS2 5–6). For this, 'it was essential first to determine how, for centuries, Western man had been brought to recognize himself as a subject of desire' (HS2 6). To trace this fully, Foucault explicitly thinks a 'third shift' in his methodology is required, the first having been to study the human sciences after *The History of Madness*, the second to study power and this final one to study the subject (HS2 6). Nevertheless, the change of methodology does not extend to the invention of a new term for his method: Foucault continues readily to define his work as genealogy (EW1 262). The question of *The History of Sexuality* had always been one of subjectivity, but, as the project wore on, the history of sexuality expanded into a broader history of subjectivity. While the main explicit outputs of his thought between 1980 and 1984 were two final volumes of the *History of Sexuality*, one can see from the lectures of the period that sexuality is merely one thread he is following; the main themes are those of subjectivity and of truth. Indeed, sex is hardly mentioned in the lectures of the period. This is not least because, as Foucault discovered, what we today designate as 'sexual' did not have much importance as an area of concern for the Greeks. Indeed, it does not even really make sense, as he readily avers, to talk of sex and sexuality when dealing with ancient discourse, since these concepts were completely foreign to the ancients.

Although this period culminated in two books on sexuality – which are really one book split into two volumes because of its length (DE1 87) – this is the culmination of a project begun ten years or more before. I think one may conclude that the topic of sexuality is a kind of legacy that Foucault has to wrestle with, but is no longer an area of interest; Foucault now even declares sex 'boring' (EW1 253).

So, while, as with the governmentality lecture series, most of the material from the 1980s did not appear in print, in this case this is I think because of a lack of opportunity for this material to come to fruition owing to Foucault's untimely death in 1984. There is evidence that Foucault intended further publications from this material (DE1 85). Certainly, even if he had lived a few more months, a fourth volume of the *History of Sexuality* dealing with the Christian period would have been completed, likely utilising relevant material from the foregoing years' lectures.

As it stands, the last two books are oddities in Foucault's corpus, and we will have little to say about them. While they follow the general pattern of Foucault's books, being historical studies of discourse, they are anomalous in at least two respects. The most obvious is that they deal with a much earlier time period than any of his other books. And they are also extraordinarily dry. The link to the present is not palpable, and the political stakes are almost invisible, making them much more like ordinary histories than any of his other works.

Foucault has changed focus from technologies of power to technologies of the self. This does imply a partial depoliticisation of his thought, corresponding to a move away from politics in the French intellectual scene more generally following the heady post-1968 militancy of the early 1970s. But there are none the less political stakes of Foucault's account of subjectivity, shown in terms of a particular kind of subjectivation involved in politics. And the Iranian Revolution provides a prime example for this. We should remember that Foucault remains politically active for one cause or another throughout this period. The political implications of Foucault's late explorations of subjectivity are largely neglected by Foucault himself, one supposes largely because of the historical context of them, namely ancient Greece and Rome. That said, there none the less emerge pointedly political moments in his exposition. Broadly, we will deal with these under three heads: 'ethics', 'spirituality' and 'parrhesia'.

THE INDIVIDUAL SUBJECT

What then is the status of individual human subjects in Foucault's thought? During his high archaeological phase, the answer was fairly simple: they were simply bracketed from the inquiry. The notion of subjectivity crept into his work as early as *The Archaeology of Knowledge*, however, in the form of the concept of the position of the 'enunciating subject' (AK 92–6), breaking with Foucault's pointed bracketing of any mention of the subject in *The Order of Things* (OT xiv). With genealogy, the concern with the subject becomes prominent, though anti-humanism and anti-subjectivism remain the orders of the day. What we ordinarily think of as natural humanity, our subjectivity and individuality, are treated by Foucault as historical productions, effects of power and discourses. One example of this that we have already seen is his treatment of the soul in *Discipline and Punish*. The notion of docile bodies, however, invites a reading by which this is a recent perversion of an original, natural identity of the body with itself, a kind of natural individual.

Foucault rejects the notion that the individual is natural, however, saying that the individual is rather 'a reality fabricated by this specific technology of power that I have called "discipline"' (DP 194). He clarifies his position on the individual further the following year:

It is . . . a mistake to think of the individual as a sort of elementary nucleus, a primitive atom or some multiple, inert matter to which power is applied, or which is struck by a power that subordinates or destroys individuals. In actual fact, one of the first effects of power is that it allows bodies, gestures, discourses, and desires to be identified and constituted as something individual. The individual is not, in other words, power's opposite number: the individual is one of power's first effects. The individual is in fact a power effect, and at the same time, and to the extent that he is a power-effect, the individual is a relay: power passes through the individuals it has constituted. (SD 29–30)

While the 'body' for Foucault is something like a primitive natural object that simply exists as such whatever we think about it, the constitution of our selves as either a 'subject' or an 'individual' is a contingent historical production on the basis of the body.

Now it might seem that Foucault's thought goes through a substantial shift later with him couching his intellectual project in terms of the self-constitution of subjects, which he does from as early as 1978 (RM 70–1). While he is quite explicit that his focus changes towards the subject, it does not seem to me that his position on the subject vis-à-vis the body goes through any substantial revision, but rather is simply developed by his giving an account of how the individual constitutes itself in relation to power. Clearly, this involves a shift in accent away from the role of power in constituting the subject and towards the subject's own role in constituting itself.

Foucault consistently casts subjectivity as something that is historically contingent and variable (that is, it hasn't always existed, and it hasn't always existed in the same way). He consistently sees it as a matter of a relation of self to self that is produced, and in a certain sense produces itself. That is, the self that relates to itself is produced in the process of the construction of this very relation of self to self. There is no self without a relation to itself. Now, this paradoxically seems to cast the self as a *causa sui*, something which causes itself to exist, which seems impossible. I have argued that this is not in fact a problem because Foucault defines the subject as a 'form' rather than a 'substance' (EW1 290; see Kelly 2013, 514). The substance here is, namely, the body: the body is the material basis for the production of the immaterial reality of the soul or subject, on Foucault's account. The body does not produce itself.

For Foucault, the core meaning of subjectivity would seem to be the articulation, and creation, of something that is me that is not my body (HS 54–5). While it might seem obvious that there is such a thing, the way this non-corporeal element has been thought of has varied greatly, from a substantial soul capable of existing independently of the body to simple 'consciousness'. It is indeed not necessary to assert the existence of anything non-corporeal in the human being to make this distinction, as contemporary philosophy of mind demonstrates. What distinguishes Foucault's position from standard physicalist views of the mind is the extent to which he considers the self to be historically constituted, whereas conventional views of mind identify the self with consciousness and see it as something that simply exists naturally in humans, without any work being required to produce it, and without historical variation.

Foucault traces the textual evidence of subjectivity qua the positing of a distinction between self and body back to ancient Greece, though he never engages in any deliberate attempt actually to locate the origin of subjectivity, hence we can assume it may be much earlier (Foucault 1996, 472). This kind of distinction indeed seems germane to human culture in general – Foucault indicates that at the very least all human cultures have what he calls 'techniques of the self' (EW1 277), which are all used for constituting one's self in different ways.

Thus subjectivity is not merely cognitive, but rather, for Foucault, it is a matter of practices we engage in; subjectivity thus varies according to what we do:

> You do not have the same type of relationship to yourself when you constitute yourself as a political subject who goes to vote or speaks at a meeting and when you are seeking to fulfill your desires in a sexual relationship. Undoubtedly there are relationships and interferences between these different forms of the subject; but we are not dealing with the same type of subject. In each case, one plays, one establishes a different type of relationship to oneself. (EW1, 290)

This question of self-constitutive practices is primarily thought by Foucault in terms of ethics.

Ethics

Ethics is perhaps the signature concept of Foucault's late work, more so even than subjectivity. The idea of an 'ethical turn' seems to take Foucault away from politics. But 'ethics' for Foucault means something highly specific, and quite different from the sense in which it is normally used today. Foucault reserves the term 'ethics' for a highly distinctive set of ancient practices which according to him no longer exist. He distinguishes this from 'morality', which is the adherence to a code of behaviour found in all kinds of societies (HS2 25). Foucault links our contemporary subjection (*assujettisse-ment*) to this code.[4]

Ethics for Foucault was the way in which the ancients fashioned their subjectivity as a deliberate practice. This is what the Greek root of our word 'ethics', *ethike*, refers to, namely the cultivation of *character*. This ancient practice was reserved exclusively for the small elite of free men in Greek society (EW1 254). This self-cultivation was, according to Foucault, a matter of *epimeleia heautou*, which is usually translated into English as 'the care of the self', though *epimeleia* can be translated more equivocally as 'concern' or attention'. Ethics, in essence, is simply a matter of attending to your self, cultivating and constituting your self deliberately to produce certain effects, namely ones that were aesthetic, aimed at producing a beautiful life (EW1 254). This is not necessarily a selfish concern per se, because it may involve trying to make oneself more altruistic, for example (EW1 287), although Foucault sees ancient ethics as having changed from being initially civic-minded to being more egocentric by Roman late Antiquity (EW1 260). This egocentric ethics then collided with the growth of Christianity in the late Roman Empire, which effectively led to the end of ancient ethics. Christianity preached self-effacement and self-abnegation (HS 250), submission before God and a focus on salvation rather than this life (EW1 284), and thus had no time for the careful construction of a beautiful life. While there was some kind of revival of ethics during the Renaissance, Foucault thinks that this has disappeared and that more recent attempts to recreate an ethics have failed (HS 251). Foucault thus 'suspects' that it is today impossible to constitute an ethics of the self (HS 251).

This conclusion of Foucault's is often ignored by his readers. There is a substantial literature referencing his work on ethics which advocates the restoration of an ethics of the self in diverse areas of modern life, disregarding Foucault's estimation that this is quite likely to prove insuperably difficult. People seem to imagine that the constitution of an ethics is as easy as enjoining people to care for themselves. But in fact, ancient ethics was a substantial accretion of techniques of the self, a cultural formation that cannot be resurrected to order.

The essential problem Foucault thinks exists for us today in reconstituting an ethics is not just that we lack the appropriate techniques, but that our modern attitude towards ourselves precludes ethics. This is, namely, that we see everything as having to pass through the

Truth. When it comes to ourselves, we can do only what is recommended on a scientific basis. That is, we are seeking for the one true, scientifically proven way to live. We eat and live healthily according to medical advice, for example, not to live beautifully. If we ignore that advice, we do it simply out of weakness – or because we believe in an 'alternative' viewpoint on what the correct form of medicine is. Some people in our society eschew vaccines, but they do so on the basis that vaccination is dangerous, not that vaccines are unaesthetic. We no longer view ourselves in an aesthetic way (EW1 261). Of course, many people make a vast effort trying to make themselves *look* beautiful, but this too is a matter of chasing a single ideal of beauty, and not about creating a beautiful *life*.

On the other hand, we must note that Foucault does not feel able to pass judgement conclusively either on the impossibility or on the necessity of creating an ethics today – these remarks about the contemporary relevance of his work on ethics are a barely formulated tangent from his main business of historico-textual research. One could see literature that recommends we recover ethics as a useful and even necessary attempt to contribute to a revival of ethics. Foucault indeed sees his own work on ethics in this way (EW1 300). As with political revolts, we may say that no guarantee of success can be given in advance, and that attempts to live a beautiful life may be worthwhile even if their success is mitigated.

Moreover, Foucault inveighs that we 'may' urgently need an ethics of the self, specifically for political reasons (HS 252). Foucault vacillates about how necessary this is. In an interview in 1983, he suggests that the crucial problem holding back movements resisting power has been their inability to articulate an ethics (EW1 255–6). In a 1984 interview, 'The Ethics of the Concern of the Self as a Practice of Freedom', he moderates this view, opining that ethics is not the only possible point of resistance to power, but none the less maintains that the relationship of the self to itself is an important potential venue for resistance (EW1 299–300). Foucault thus at least holds that, *were* it possible to constitute an ethics (which it probably isn't), this would correct a lot of the problems encountered by contemporary resistance to power. We may suggest this is because of the extent to which not taking a deliberate control of our subjectivation leads us open to subjection, to the construction of ourselves as docile subjects under the influence of disciplinary power. The political stakes of ethics are explicit in the ancient texts: the ancient elite sought to master themselves so as to be able to master others. Foucault thinks that an ethics of self-mastery could be helpful in resisting power too, defining ethics as 'the conscious practice of freedom' (EW1 284). For this reason, he thinks ethics's importance lies not so much in the struggle for liberation as in the situation where we are already free and need to shape our freedom (EW1 284). The danger our lack of an ethics puts us in is one of not knowing what to do with our freedom. One might certainly link this to the kind of dissolution of freedom into authoritarianism that seems to have followed so many revolutions of the last century.

Spirituality

Less prominent in Foucault's 1980s work than ethics is the concept of 'spirituality'. In *The Hermeneutics of the Subject*, Foucault defines spirituality as the way subjects transform themselves in order to gain access to truth (HS 15). He analyses this as consisting of four stages: the subject changes its position, evaluates reality, reflects on itself and lastly experiences the change in itself from knowledge (HS 308). One might notice a certain similarity of this process to Foucault's reflections on his own methodology in the 1960s.

Spirituality is clearly a technique of the self, but one quite distinct from ethics. Where ethics is about beauty, spirituality is about truth. Now, according to Foucault, in ancient Greece the two imperatives, aesthetic and epistemic, coexisted happily for the most part. Indeed, ethics and spirituality were seen as generally complementary (EW1 279). When Christianity suppressed ethics, however, it did so by placing spirituality against it: subjects renounced their concern for their selves in order to access truth.

Christian spirituality itself came under threat, particularly with the Protestant Reformation in the sixteenth century, from the idea that one could have direct access to God without engaging in the spiritual practices prescribed by the Church. This denigration of spirituality was followed by the emergence of scientific modes of thought that banished spirituality entirely (or tried to), by asserting that anyone could acquire knowledge through the use of their native rationality, without ever having to use any particular technique of the self. Foucault holds that science nevertheless does employ techniques of the self, and does in fact demand the production of scientific subjects to have access to its truths. What is new about science is that it does not acknowledge the existence of these special practices: the explicit formulation of a spirituality becomes impossible.

Foucault however sees a political need for a new spirituality similar to the need for ethics. With spirituality, the prospects for revival seem better, doubtless because spirituality has never entirely disappeared in the way that he thinks ethics has. Foucault gives two examples of contemporary quasi-spiritual discourses: psychoanalysis and Marxism (HS 29). While not spiritualities as such, psychoanalysis and Marxism both make demands for subjects to transform themselves in order to access truth. In Marxism, which is the example that most concerns us as it is the more directly political, it is its demand for people to achieve 'class consciousness' that approaches spiritual status. There is in Marxism a conversion experience in which people feel they have accessed the real truth of society. Of course, the problem for both these discourses from this point of view is that they think of themselves as scientific, rather than spiritual. Marxism in particular has tended to think of access to the truth as essentially requiring no transformation of the subject, beyond the shedding of an artificial 'false consciousness'. Psychoanalysis, particularly Lacanian psychoanalysis, indicates more the direction that would have to be moved in to constitute a fully fledged spirituality. That is, from a Lacanian point of view what is reached through the process of psychoanalysis is not so much the definitive truth of a situation, as a narrative about ourselves that works for us. It thus approaches both spirituality and ethics in its attempt to constitute a knowledge of the self. For Marxism, the more spiritual understanding would be one that admits that Marxism is a kind of fiction, but one that we can adhere to through a form of fidelity. Alain Badiou's form of communism, replacing the science of Marxism with faith in an event, could be said to offer a more spiritual alternative in this regard, though Badiou no more formulates specific spiritual exercises than Marxism does, hence does not propound a spirituality.

When seen in this context, Foucault's fascination with the Iranian Revolution is more comprehensible, because it involved something that was a real political spirituality, undeniable and explicit, a thing apparently absent from the West. This Islamic example is not supposed to constitute a solution for us in the West – Foucault certainly never proposes that we in the West should convert to Islam for political purposes (which wouldn't work, since the conversion would not be genuinely spiritual but would happen only under the imperative of instrumental rationality) – but it does perhaps offer us food for thought. One source of Afary and Anderson's confusion about Foucault's understanding of the Iranian Revolution is the failure to understand what he intends by the notion of 'spirituality'. They cannot be blamed for this, since Foucault's main consideration of the notion is to be found in lectures that have appeared in print only since they wrote their book.

Parrhesia and Enlightenment

This is not to say that for Foucault the only political value of truth is in its relation to subjectivity.

Foucault locates in ancient Greece four distinct forms of truth-telling: prophecy, predicting the future; the literal, technical transmission of knowledge, which may be identified with scientific knowledge; the wisdom of the sage; and parrhesia, the courageous telling of uncomfortable truths to the powerful. While in Greece these were all important, Foucault sees sage wisdom and prophecy as having declined since. In the case of prophecy, Foucault thinks this is a good thing. Indeed, he is strongly committed to the avoidance of prophecy, for the simple reason that we do not actually know what will happen in the future, and that prophecy makes sense only if one posits a metaphysical, mystical or religious basis on which to divine the future. Many intellectuals, particularly, once again, Marxists, continue to engage in prophecy on pseudo-scientific grounds. The form of truth-telling that interests Foucault, already mentioned above, is parrhesia, a courageous pointing out of things that are not allowed to be mentioned. Foucault finds this interesting enough to dedicate what turned out to be his final lectures series to it, giving it the title of *The Courage of Truth*; it is also the subject of a 1983 lecture series he gave in Berkeley, California, published in English as *Fearless Speech*. Parrhesia is perhaps more precisely characterised as 'courageous' than 'fearless': it is a matter of telling truth to the powerful despite one's well-founded fear of the consequences.

Foucault associates this form of truth-telling contemporarily with left-wing political thought, including Marxism, and with his own work, although this is unlike the old form of parrhesia, inasmuch as it generally does not address itself to those in power. Nevertheless, Foucault's aim is to separate parrhesia out again from other forms of truth, such as the prophetic and scientific, with which it is mixed in Marxism.

Foucault's interest in parrhesia is doubtless founded on the fact that he recognises himself in it: it is precisely the kind of practice that he increasingly found himself engaging in. Foucault's efforts of the early 1970s are marked by an ostensible humility: in the Prisons Information Group (GIP), he acted only as a facilitator for other stories to emerge, and then offered up his own analyses as an aid to people in struggle. From the middle of the decade, however, he began to use his increasing fame directly to try to influence events, speaking directly to the powerful, especially to governments, interposing himself in events. This relates perhaps the shift in his estimation of the significance of government in the late 1970s, which we covered in the previous chapter.

One may exaggerate – though Foucault himself does not – his courageousness, inasmuch as he knew that the French state was severely disinclined to persecute intellectuals, even in its relatively repressive phase after 1968. That is not to say there was no courage in these acts. The GIP was no easy commitment: its public activities were frequently targeted for repression, and Foucault was beaten by police (DE1 50), as he was also on other occasions attending demonstrations.

In this effort, Foucault (1984a, 377) in 1983 invokes a concept of philosophical 'ethos', a 'manner of being', to be distinguished from 'ethics' defined as the practice of concern for the self (we should note that Foucault's occasional uses of the term 'ethics' before 1983 are ambiguous and do not conform to this distinction). This ethos is a matter of retaining one's independence from political authority, and hence the ability to criticise it. This is one thing that pointedly differentiates his relation to the Iranian Revolution – he always maintained a separation from the revolutionaries and criticised the revolutionary government once it formed – from Heidegger's relation to Nazism, since Heidegger joined the Nazi Party *after* it had seized power and attempted to integrate his philosophy into its regime. Foucault's general principle here is always to criticise power, which meant moving seamlessly in the Iranian case from criticising the Shah's government to criticising the Islamic Republic that replaced it.

Still, by attempting to differentiate parrhesia from scientific reason, Foucault is following a line found in Heidegger and the Frankfurt School of criticising an instrumental rationality, which seems to have become the sole inheritance of the Enlightenment.

Foucault identifies this critical, parrhesiastic tendency with a certain inheritance of the Enlightenment. By identifying with the Enlightenment, Foucault identifies his work with the mainstream of modern, Western philosophy, and with the thought of Immanuel Kant, but only with a certain aspect of it, namely its criticality. He jettisons its more prescriptive and metaphysical aspects, retaining only what he sees as its critical core. This nevertheless means that Foucault is, by his own lights, not 'postmodern' but simply modern. This casts new light on Foucault's insistence on the historical relativity of truth claims with his ability to diagnose these: he is effectively part of a historical tendency towards the critique of knowledge and power.

While Foucault's invocation of parrhesia is primarily known to English readers from notes on a series of 1983 lectures in the US published in a volume as *Fearless Speech*, and his views on the Enlightenment largely known from a late lecture on Kant entitled 'What Is Enlightenment?', we should note that both themes are treated extensively together in his 1983 Collège de France lecture series, *The Government of the Self and Others*, though his earliest reflections on Kant and the meaning of the Enlightenment date back to a 1978 address, 'What Is Critique?' (Foucault 1997, 23–82).

Foucault's allegiance to the project of the Enlightenment implies a certain progressivism that is rarely explicitly stated in his thought. Kant formulates his understanding of the Enlightenment, in the first line of his own essay entitled 'What Is Enlightenment?' (Foucault 1997, 7–22), as 'man's release from his self-incurred tutelage' (Foucault 1997, 7). This is to say that human beings had hitherto placed themselves under forms of authority in an unnecessary way. We can think of this self-incurred tutelage in several directions, but it amounts to what Cornelius Castoriadis calls 'heteronomy', the formation of a society which sees itself as organised according to an external principle of authority which it cannot determine from within, be this a founding agreement, a god or even the logic of the market. Foucault (Foucault 1997, 35), like Castoriadis, sees the critical movement of thought as allowing us to assume *autonomy* in relation to authority, questioning why we have to obey and eventually coming to the conclusion we do not need to.

How are we to understand the Iranian Revolution in light of this? Foucault was lauding the Enlightenment both before and after that revolution. Did he thus really believe it was a struggle for autonomy? It seems clearly to be heteronomous in Castoriadis's sense, given its reference to religious authority. Here I think we may say several things. Firstly, from Foucault's perspective the be all and end all of resistance is not whether it accords with the strict Enlightenment model, or its outcome as autonomy. While this might be said to set a gold standard for resistance, that does not mean that all other resistance is pointless or pernicious. That said, resistance does never-theless generically constitute a kind of critical movement, by which the status quo is questioned and overthrown. Even if it falls back on existing structures of authority, it does this in a way that makes a radical choice to dispense with other such structures. Thus, we need not say that autonomy is simply a matter of all or nothing, that many revolts have occurred which have fallen short of achieving a kind of full autonomy, but which nevertheless are themselves instances of relative autonomy.

Why the Greeks?

This modernism of Foucault sits awkwardly with his contemporane-ous research on the Greeks. On the one hand, this research seems in a completely opposite direction to valorising modernity. On the other hand, this combination of Enlightenment with a valorisation of the Greeks is not uncommon, but proceeds typically as a dubious manoeuvre which valorises a certain 'European' legacy, including democracy and philosophy, leading from Athens through to the present.

In either case, a retreat to the Greeks seems conservative: it sug-gests either a nostalgic anti-modernism à la Heidegger or a parochial Europeanism. Foucault's proximal reason for his recourse to Greece is the historical sequence of the *History of Sexuality* – but this is not an immediately adequate explanation. Foucault begins in France, but ends up in Greece and Rome. The idea that France is the inheritor of the cultures of Greece and Rome seems to play on imperial con-ceits. However, there is an extent to which this is simply true, and indeed unavoidable. Firstly, contemporary French culture is largely descended from Roman culture, rather than the pre-Roman Celtic culture of ancient Gaul, the culture that existed in the territory now called France. More pragmatically, a serious investigation of the sexual culture of ancient Gaul – or of ancient German tribes who, in the shape of the Franks, also were a seminal contributor to the crea-tion of France – is simply rendered impossible by the lack of suitable source materials. That is, while we have inherited a relative wealth of material from ancient Greece and Rome detailing the concerns of the people in those cultures, we have inherited next to nothing from the other ancient cultures of Europe, and most of what we know of those cultures comes from second-hand Greek and Roman accounts! Where there are textual traces from northern Europe, Foucault does not ignore them, for example mentioning *Beowulf* in *Security, Territory, Population* (STP 137). He is certainly well aware of this cultural history, having associated with the great scholar of prehistorical Indo-European mythologies, Georges Dumézil. We may also exculpate Foucault by saying that he does not claim that he has discovered the entire rootstock of Western civilisation, only that he has analysed certain influences: he does not therefore disallow the legacy of non-Mediterranean pre-Christian Europe, but rather follows the sources as far as he can, which means primarily in the two routes he takes. We can say that there may be work to be done in showing how this alternative legacy has influenced our society, but this must involve a different methodology from Foucault's archivism, most likely following Dumézil's reconstructive researches. The only major cultural influence on the contemporary West that we can study textually not coming from ancient Greece and Rome comes from even further afield, that is, from the ancient Levant. We have already examined Foucault's dubious attempt to trace a lineage of Western politics from this source in the form of pastoral power.

However, harping on about any of these heritages – Roman, Jewish, Germanic – seems to play into different forms of conservatism: classical, Christian, nationalist. Foucault himself points out in *Society Must Be Defended* how appeals to an essentially fictitious German political heritage in the early modern period constituted discourses variously of power and counter-power. While this indicates that such appeals are politically ambivalent, it also highlights the extent to which they are fantasies about the past rather a way in which actual historical research is useful. This is not to say of course that in some ways this ancient heritage is not genuinely important to understand the present, however: for example, the system of law we have is clearly descended in traceable ways from ancient legal codes, Roman in the case of civil law, Germanic in the case of common law.

Foucault (2012, 9) engages with this question of the value of ancient historical research with the observation that, firstly, 'what is residual always has, when we examine it closely enough, its heuristic value' and that, secondly, 'things last longer than we think', pointing out the extent to which practices he notes in ancient Rome can be found essentially to exist as late as the seventeenth century (court astrology in this case). This doesn't make it very clear why Foucault doesn't primarily study the more recent example, though I suppose the point is that it doesn't much matter whether he chooses the example from early modernity or from Antiquity. Later on he notes that, since he is incapable of an all-encompassing 'general ethnology', he lights on one example, namely Oedipus (Foucault 2012, 23–4). This seems slightly disingenuous inasmuch as he seems also to claim that the Oedipus myth has several aspects in relation to truth that are not found in other antique texts. It's very hard to decide to what extent this is arbitrary as a choice, and to which extent any privileging of this text is a kind of inevitable consequence of its arbitrary choice. When it comes to Greek literature and philosophy, indeed, there's an arbitrariness of history in determining even what texts are available to us – we can't really know what is unique in Sophocles, only what is unique in his work in relation to the other cultural artefacts that are extant, because so much ancient culture has been lost to us.

In the end, it's very difficult to claim that Foucault has shown that we have inherited anything very specific from Antiquity, either European or Eastern. Indeed, except in the case of pastoral power, and perhaps in the case of the particular form of truth telling found in Oedipus, it is not clear that he is trying to show that we have. Yes, he seems to think parrhesia has passed down from Antiquity, so too spirituality, but these are defined so generally as to be essentially transhistorical. There is no specific historical practice of either parrhesia or spirituality that has survived, but rather the general area simply continues to exist as a mode of interrelation of subjectivity and truth. Subjectivity itself is defined so broadly by Foucault that it is more or less transhistorical or transcultural, and, though he might seem to be privileging Plato as the inventor of subjectivity, he explicitly tells us he is trying to make no such claim.

The stakes of ancient history from a Foucauldian perspective seem to me largely characterised not by the tracing of what we have today, then, which was the significance of his studies of modernity qua histories of the present, but rather by the contrast with modern conditions. For this reason, the choice of which culture to study is more or less unimportant – it could be any historical or even contemporary culture other than the one we're actually in. Foucault's researches might well have tended towards Eastern *ars erotica* rather than Greek practices after the first volume of *The History of Sexuality* (the choice that Foucault makes here is surely to do with the fact that he finds himself in Europe, already has a basic education in ancient ideas and languages, is surrounded by people with knowledge of these, making ancient Greek texts oddly more accessible to him than more recent non-European texts). Foucault's ancient history is not thus, à la Heidegger, Derrida and Agamben, a matter of showing the resilience of the trace (even if Foucault sometimes indicates ambiguously that he might intend it to), but a matter of showing precisely how hard it is to relate to our own past. The practical point is a matter of showing how things could be otherwise, how in the very space we now inhabit people could come to behave and think in unrecognisably different ways.

This is not to say, as some have claimed (Weberman 2000, 263), that Foucault is trying to undermine subjectivity itself. After all, he is showing us a time before sexuality existed – he never seeks to show how it is possible to get by without subjectivity. He is quite clear that what we should do today is 'to promote new forms of subjectivity' (EW3, 336). The fact that we constitute ourselves as subjects does not imply that we have the facility simply to choose whether or not to do this, only that we have some capacity to determine what specific form our subjectivity takes. Foucault (2011a, 399) does talk about 'desubjectivisation', and indeed clearly advocates it, but this desubjectivisation is temporary, and relative, not a permanent state of affairs. We can link this to Foucault's 'bodies and pleasures' advice, as being a question of engaging in practices which shake us out of our subjectivity, allowing a certain reorientation within it. More concertedly, he talks about 'desubjection' (déassujettissement), but this means getting rid of the specific historical formation of subjection, not subjectivation (Foucault 1990, 39).[5]

Notes

1. This, at least, is what the French version of the lectures says (Foucault 2004b, 6). In the English translation, the word *politique* ('politics') is rendered as 'polemics' (STP 4). I'm inclined to think this is an error, made because he does actually mention polemics in the previous sentence.
2. The phrase 'knowledge-power' does occur in the English translation of the first volume of the *History of Sexuality*, but this is a translation error – the French original has the concepts in the usual order (HS1 143; cf. Foucault 1976b, 188).
3. Foucault (2005, 187) interestingly elsewhere allows that Marx was right to say that 'religion is the opium of the people' – but that this was true only for Christianity during a brief phase in the nineteenth century.
4. EW1 264. It seems in this interview that Foucault's *assujettissement* has been rendered as 'subjectivation', but with the French word retained in

brackets, making it clear Foucault is not here talking about what he in French calls *subjectivation*, that is, the self-constituting of the subject. See Kelly 2009, 87–8.

5. The published English translation of this text translates this word not inaccurately as 'desubjugation' (Foucault 1997, 32).

Conclusion

How can one 'conclude' a book on Foucault and politics? It is possible of course to summarise: Foucault provides us an account of politics in a relation of profound reciprocity to language, knowledge, truth and discourse on the one hand and, latterly, to subjectivity on the other. It is an open account of politics that allows for an infinite possibility founded on unpredictable human resistance, an account that refuses any kind of role in legislating for the future, because that would only be to restrict the openness of our hopes. As such, Foucault's work has been and will continue to be met with varying degrees of hostility by those who think they have the solution to our particular woes, by those who wish to insist on particular norms in this relation. On the other hand, and scarcely less lamentably, Foucault's name will in the openness of its referentiality continue to be appropriated for any and all causes. There is no way to prevent this. One may try, as I have tried to, to fight a rearguard action, insisting on the correct interpretation of Foucault. But such work fits comfortably into a scholarly niche that does not challenge the proliferation of interpretations, though it may have a certain influence with those who happen to have read it. The alternative course, which is surely the one that Foucault would himself recommend, is simply to forge on with new research, ignoring the ignorance of others. The greatest avenue for such research indicated by Foucault, the analysis of power relations, was scarcely begun by him, and enormous work remains to be done in this regard, mapping and unveiling the machinations of power in our societies.

References

Afary, Janet and Kevin B. Anderson (2005). *Foucault and the Iranian Revolution: Gender and the Seductions of Islam.* Chicago: University of Chicago Press.

Agamben, Giorgio (1998). *Homo Sacer: Sovereign Power and Bare Life.* Stanford: Stanford University Press.

Alford, C. Fred (2000). 'What Would It Matter If Everything Foucault Said about Prison Were Wrong? "Discipline and Punish" after Twenty Years', *Theory and Society*, 29:1, 125–46.

Althusser, Louis (1971). 'Ideology and Ideological State Apparatuses', in *Lenin and Philosophy and Other Essays.* London: New Left Books.

Althusser, Louis (2006). *Philosophy of the Encounter.* London: Verso.

Badiou, Alain (2005). 'An Essential Philosophical Thesis: "It Is Right to Rebel against the Reactionaries"', trans. Alberto Toscano, *positions: east asia cultures critique*, 13:3, 669–77.

Baghramian, Maria (2010). 'A Brief History of Relativism', in Michael Krausz (ed.), *Relativism: A Contemporary Anthology.* New York: Columbia University Press.

Bartky, Sandra Lee (2002). '"Catch Me if You Can": Foucault on the Repressive Hypothesis', in *'Sympathy and Solidarity' and Other Essays.* Lanham, MD: Rowman & Littlefield, 47–68.

Berry, David (2004). '"Workers of the World, Embrace!": Daniel Guérin, the Labour Movement and Homosexuality', *Left History*, 9:2, 11–43.

Butler, Judith (1989). 'Foucault and the Paradox of Bodily Inscriptions', *Journal of Philosophy*, 86:11, 601–9.

Defert, Daniel (2004) 'How Michel Foucault Wrote His Lectures' (oral presentation). Michel Foucault (1926–1984): Other questions, new paths. LSE, London. 16 September.

Deleuze, Gilles (1988). *Foucault.* Minneapolis: University of Minnesota Press.

Deleuze, Gilles (1992 [1990]). 'Postscript on the Societies of Control', *October*, 59, 3–7.

Derrida, Jacques (1982). 'White Mythology', in *Margins of Philosophy.* Chicago: University of Chicago Press.

Derrida, Jacques (2001). 'Cogito and the History of Madness', in *Writing and Difference.* London: Routledge.

Dreyfus, Hubert and Paul Rabinow (1983). *Michel Foucault: Beyond Structuralism and Hermeneutics.* Chicago: University of Chicago Press.

Droit, Roger-Pol (2004). *Michel Foucault, entretiens.* Paris: Odile Jacob.

Eribon, Didier (1991). *Michel Foucault.* Cambridge, MA: Harvard University Press.

Esposito, Roberto (2008). *Bíos: Biopolitics and Philosophy.* Minneapolis: University of Minnesota Press.

Fields, A. Belden (1988). *Trotskyism and Maoism in France and the United States.* New York: Autonomedia.

Foucault, Michel (1954). *Maladie mentale et personalité.* Paris: Presses Universitaires de France.

Foucault, Michel (1967). *Madness and Civilization.* London: Tavistock.

Foucault, Michel (1971). *L'ordre du discours.* Paris: Gallimard.

Foucault, Michel (1976a). *Mental Illness and Psychology.* New York: Harper & Row.

Foucault, Michel (1976b). *Histoire de la sexualité I: La volonté de savoir.* Paris: Gallimard.

Foucault, Michel (1980). *Herculine Barbin: Being the Recently Discovered Memoirs of a Nineteenth-century French Hermaphrodite.* New York: Pantheon.

Foucault, Michel (1983). *The Culture of the Self.* Audio recording, University of California Berkeley.

Foucault, Michel (1984a). 'Politics and Ethics: An Interview', in Paul Rabinow (ed.), *The Foucault Reader.* Translated by Catherine Porter. New York: Pantheon, 373–80.

Foucault, Michel (1984b). 'What Is Enlightenment?', in P. Rabinow (ed.), *The Foucault Reader.* Translated by Catherine Porter. New York: Pantheon, 32–50.

Foucault, Michel (1985 [1984]). *The Use of Pleasure: Volume 2 of The History of Sexuality.* New York: Random House.

Foucault, Michel (1985 [1984]). *The Care of the Self: Volume 3 of The History of Sexuality.* New York: Random House.

Foucault, Michel (1988). 'Power, Moral Values and the Intellectual'. *History of the Present*, 4:1–2, 11–13.

Foucault, Michel (1990). 'Qu'est-ce que la critique? [Critique et *Aufklärung*]', *Bulletin de la Société française de Philosophie*, 84, 25–63.

Foucault, Michel (1991). 'Governmentality', in Graham Burchell, Colin Gordon and Peter Miller (eds), *The Foucault Effect: Studies in Governmentality.* Chicago: University of Chicago Press, 87–104.

Foucault, Michel (1996). 'The Return of Morality', in Sylvère Lotringer (ed.), *Foucault Live.* New York: Semiotext(e).

Foucault, Michel (1997). *The Politics of Truth.* New York: Semiotext(e).

Foucault, Michel (1998). 'What Is an Author?', in D. Preziosi (ed.), *The Art of Art History: A Critical Anthology*. New York: Oxford University Press, 299–314.

Foucault, Michel (2001). *Fearless Speech*. Los Angeles: Semiotext(e).

Foucault, Michel (2004a). *Michel Foucault, entretiens*, ed. Roger-Pol Droit. Paris: Odile Jacob.

Foucault, Michel (2004b). *Sécurité, territoire, population: Cours au Collège de France (1977–1978)*. Paris: Seuil.

Foucault, Michel (2005). 'Dialogue between Michel Foucault and Baqir Parham', in Janet Afary and Kevin B. Anderson (eds), *Foucault and the Iranian Revolution: Gender and the Seductions of Islam*. Chicago: University of Chicago Press.

Foucault, Michel (2007). 'The Meshes of Power', trans. Gerald Moore, in Jeremy W. Crampton and Stuart Elden (eds), *Space, Knowledge and Power*. Aldershot: Ashgate.

Foucault, Michel (2011a). 'The Gay Science', trans. Nicolae Morar and Daniel W. Smith, *Critical Inquiry*, 37:3, 385–403.

Foucault, Michel (2011b). *The Courage of Truth*. Trans. Graham Burchell. Basingstoke: Palgrave Macmillan.

Foucault, Michel (2012). *Du gouvernement des vivants*. Paris: Gallimard/ Seuil.

Foucault, Michel (2013). *Lectures on the Will to Know*. Trans. Graham Burchell. Basingstoke: Palgrave Macmillan.

Friedrich, Otto (1981). 'France's Philosopher of Power', *Time*, 16 November, 147–8.

Gordon, Colin (1991). 'Governmental Rationality: An Introduction', in Graham Burchell, Colin Gordon, and Peter Miller (eds), *The Foucault Effect: Studies in Governmentality*. Chicago: University of Chicago Press.

Habermas, Jürgen (1987). *The Philosophical Discourse of Modernity*. Trans. Frederick Lawrence. Cambridge: Polity.

Han, Béatrice (2002 [1998]). *Foucault's Critical Project: Between the Transcendental and the Historical*. Trans. Edward Pile. Stanford: Stanford University Press.

Hardt, Michael and Antonio Negri (2000). *Empire*. Cambridge, MA: Harvard University Press.

Holden, Adam and Stuart Elden (2005), '"It Cannot be a Real Person, a Concrete Individual": Althusser and Foucault on Machiavelli's Political Technique', *borderlands*, 4:2, http://www.borderlands.net.au/ vol4no2_2005/eldenhold_foucault.htm.

Hoveyda, Fereydoun (2003). *The Shah and the Ayatollah: Iranian Mythology and Islamic Revolution*. Westport, CT: Praeger.

Huffer, Lynne (2009). *Mad for Foucault*. New York: Columbia University Press.

Hyppolite, Jean (1969). *Studies on Marx and Hegel*. New York: Basic Books.

Kelly, Mark G. E. (2009). *The Political Philosophy of Michel Foucault*. New York: Routledge.

Kelly, Mark G. E. (2010). 'Michel Foucault', *The Internet Encyclopedia of Philosophy*. http://www.iep.utm.edu/foucault (accessed 10 February 2013)

Kelly, Mark G. E. (2013a). 'Foucault, Subjectivity, and Technologies of the Self', in Christopher Falzon, Timothy O'Leary and Jana Sawicki (eds), *A Companion to Foucault*. Oxford: Blackwell.

Kelly, Mark G. E. (2013b). *Foucault's History of Sexuality Volume I: The Will to Knowledge*. Edinburgh: Edinburgh University Press.

Kelly, Mark G. E. (2014). 'Against Prophecy and Utopia: Foucault and the Future', *Thesis Eleven*, 117.

Lemke, Thomas (1997). *Eine Kritik der Politischen Vernunft: Foucaults Analyse der modernen Gouvernementalität*. Hamburg: Argument.

Lemke, Thomas (2011a). 'Critique and Experience in Foucault', *Theory, Culture & Society*, 28:4, 26–48.

Lemke, Thomas (2011b). *Biopolitics: An Advanced Introduction*. New York: New York University Press.

Lenin, Vladimir (1992 [1918]). *The State and Revolution*. London: Penguin.

Macey, David (1993). *The Lives of Michel Foucault*. London: Hutchinson.

May, Todd (1994). *The Political Philosophy of Poststructuralist Anarchism*. University Park, PA: Pennsylvania State University Press.

McWhorter, Ladelle (1999). *Bodies and Pleasures*. Bloomington: Indiana University Press.

Merleau-Ponty, Maurice (1964 [1960]). *Signs*. T. Richard C. McCleary. Chicago: Northwestern University Press.

Merleau-Ponty, Maurice (1968 [1964]). *The Visible and the Invisible*. Ttrans. Alphonso Lingis. Chicago: Northwestern University Press.

Miller, James (1993). *The Passion of Michel Foucault*. Cambridge, MA: Harvard University Press.

Nietzsche, Friedrich (1968 [1906]). *The Will to Power*. Trans. Walter Kaufmann. New York: Vintage.

Nietzsche, Friedrich (2006). *Thus Spoke Zarathustra*. Trans. Adrian Del Caro. Cambridge: Cambridge University Press.

Nietzsche, Friedrich (2007). *On the Genealogy of Morality*. Trans. Carol Diethe. Cambridge: Cambridge University Press.

Ojakangas, Mika (2012). 'Michel Foucault and the Enigmatic Origins of Bio-politics and Governmentality', *History of the Human Sciences*, 25:1, 1–14.

Paras, Eric (2006). *Foucault 2.0: Beyond Power and Knowledge*. New York: Other Press.

Patton, Paul (2010). 'Foucault and Normative Political Philosophy: Liberal and Neo-liberal Governmentality and Public Reason', in Timothy O'Leary and Christopher Falzon (eds), *Foucault and Philosophy*. Oxford: Wiley.

Pickett, Brent (2005). *On the Use and Abuse of Foucault for Politics.* Oxford: Lexington.

Rahimi, Babak (2006). 'Review of Afary, Janet; Anderson, Kevin B., *Foucault and the Iranian Revolution: Gender and the Seductions of Islamism'. H-Net Reviews*, http://www.h-net.org/reviews/showpdf.php?id=12437 (accessed 10 January 2014).

Said, Edward (1978). *Orientalism.* London: Routledge & Kegan Paul.

Sartre, Jean-Paul (1946). *L'existentialisme est un humanisme.* Paris: Nagel.

Sartre, Jean-Paul (1948). *Existentialism & Humanism.* London: Methuen.

Saussure, Ferdinand de (1983). *Course in General Linguistics.* La Salle, IL: Open Court.

Sawicki, Jana (2005). 'Queering Foucault and the Subject of Feminism', in Gary Gutting (ed.), *The Cambridge Companion to Michel Foucault.* Cambridge: Cambridge University Press.

Taylor, Charles (1984). 'Foucault on Freedom and Truth', *Political Theory*, 12:3, 152–83.

Times Higher Education (2007). 'Most Cited Authors of Books in the Humanities, 2007', *Times Higher Education*, http://www.timeshigher-education.co.uk/story.asp?storyCode=405956 (accessed October 2012).

Wall, Irwin (1977). 'The French Communists and the Algerian War', *Journal of Contemporary History*, 12:3, 521–43.

Walters, William (2002). 'Mapping Schengenland: Denaturalizing the Border', *Environment and Planning D: Society and Space*, 20, 561–80.

Weberman, David (2000). 'Are Freedom and Anti-humanism Compatible? The Case of Foucault and Butler', *constellations*, 7:2, 255–71.

Whyte, Jessica (2012). 'Is Revolution Desirable?: Michel Foucault on Revolution, Neoliberalism and Rights', in Ben Golder (ed.), *Re-reading Foucault: On Law, Power and Rights.* Abingdon: Routledge.

Wilson, Frank L. (1981). 'The French Left in the Fifth Republic', in William George Andrews and Stanley Hoffman (eds), *The Fifth Republic at Twenty.* Albany: SUNY Press.

Index